CW00927385

A FAMILY STORY

The Greenings and some of their relatives

Michael Greening

A FAMILY STORY

The Greenings and some of their relatives
(including the Elgars)

Copyright © 2006 Mike Greening

The moral right of the author has been asserted.

Apart from any fair dealing for the purposes of research or private study,
or criticism or review, as permitted under the Copyright, Designs and Patents
Act 1988, this publication may only be reproduced, stored or transmitted, in
any form or by any means, with the prior permission in writing of the
publishers, or in the case of reprographic reproduction in accordance with
the terms of licences issued by the Copyright Licensing Agency. Enquiries concerning
reproduction outside those terms should be sent to the publishers.

Matador
9 De Montfort Mews
Leicester LE1 7FW, UK
Tel: (+44) 116 255 9311 / 9312
Email: books@troubador.co.uk
Web: www.troubador.co.uk/matador

ISBN 1 905237 45 6

Cover design: Troubador

Typeset in 11pt Stempel Garamond by Troubador Publishing Ltd, Leicester, UK

Matador is an imprint of Troubador Publishing Ltd

This book is dedicated to our ancestors, yours and mine. We are their product and their lives have shaped ours, more possibly than the sum total of every outside influence that has moulded us from the moment of our birth.Their lives were very different to ours. With each preceding generation they inhabited increasingly foreign worlds of which we can only gain the fleetest glimpse. Yet perhaps some of their fears and hopes, their periods of sorrow and their moments of happiness – and their loves were similar to ours. Learning only a little more about them may help us to celebrate their existence, give them our respect and perhaps understand ourselves a little better.

AWRE
by John Greening

'One of the places where the surname was first noted'

It is a hopeful name to be born to.
It promises Spring; it sings of pickings
from a lost family orchard, an Eden

on Severn banks, a fruit that is ripe
yet always green. Hold it to your cheek
for the faint enigma. Lick it, your tongue

buds an estuary. Cast, it will bob
the equinox deep into English
etymologies: grig and girn and groin…

Watch it running on a playing field
with others of the inner city, picked on,
nicknamed, yellowed to a cartoon brat.

Or beneath the hundred thousand crosses
left by men who could never spell
themselves, imagine it grinning from their skulls

or groaning in the pelvic bones of women
who bore it, a surge from this serpent bend
of the river into every green corner.

John Greening

CONTENTS

ACKNOWLEDGEMENTS

As a very amateur historian I hope I may be excused for not giving a bibliography. It would require a book, almost as long as this one, to list the hundreds of sources from which the facts that follow have been obtained. However, I would like to thank my many correspondents who have given me information and assistance.

I am especially grateful to Chuck Greening, in California, for letting me have transcriptions of his grandfather's Civil War diary and letters – also his great-grandfather's Journal, with permission to publish it. John Greening, who was Sir Edward Elgar's uncle, wrote a most atmospheric account of his journey from Liverpool to Wisconsin in 1847. It forms the final chapter of the book. I am indebted to Pat Morris for deciphering and transcribing many of the early records, especially the 16th, 17th and 18th Century wills. In addition to the seven or eight mentioned in this book, I hold over two-dozen others. All of them make fascinating reading. I thank Jane and Michael Woodall, in New South Wales, for telling me their family 'secret' (the main mystery story in the book) – also Bill Brand in Victoria and Ted Greening in New Zealand for helping me with the antipodean connections. Peter Pascoe helped me sort out some of the many 'Elmore' Greenings, and I am most grateful to him.

Finally, a thank you to my daughter Jane, for drawing the map, and to my daughter Marie-Ann and son-in-law Gerard for reading the many earlier drafts of all the chapters and giving me advice.

PREFACE

In 2002 I published as small book titled *GREENING – an English surname over 500 years*. One of the principal reasons for doing this was to tidy up some of the information, which I had accumulated over a large number of years of rather haphazard family history research. It was the best way of clearing out those files, both the ones held physically and those in my head, knowing that the facts were together – before my demise scattered them again to the four winds.

There was another reason. After forty-two years together my wife Laura had died two years previously and, by writing about many other people whose lives had run their course, I was able to derive some comfort and put in perspective Laura's life and my own. My wife was not quite sixty-four and died the day before I qualified for my British state pension. Like many couples of our age we had expected to grow old together. I know that, for however many years I may continue, I will never fully adjust without her but have found that researching my ancestors has helped me to cope with death. I can recommend this area of study to anyone who has been bereaved.

As I knew it would only be of interest to a small number of people, my first Greening book was not intended as a commercial venture. I certainly had no thoughts of writing and publishing a sequel. However not only was I pleasantly surprised to sell enough copies to cover the cost of its production, but it generated much correspondence with new information and unearthed many fascinating leads which required following up. I therefore felt compelled to do more research and put together this rather more comprehensive version. This book is not a sequel but it does contain some of the information that was in the first book. If you have read the first book and now read this one, you will understand why I had no option other than to put pen to paper again.

Tracing our surname line back many generations will not teach us much about ourselves. Of our four grandparents only one was born with our surname. The most likely candidate for my eight times 'surname' great-grandfather was Nathaniel Greening, who was born at Moreton Valence in Gloucestershire in 1679. However he would have just been one out of 512 'eight-times' great-grandparents. Nathaniel, in turn, was most possibly descended from a John Greeninge who lived about eight generations before him. John, the earliest Gloucestershire Greening mentioned in my first book, was shown in Manorial Court records as farming in the village of Awre in 1493. If I am a direct line descendant of John there can be very little of him in me. I have another 131,071 forebears of his same generation. It is quite likely that my surname is duplicated on one or more of those lines.

If some of your ancestors are in this book I'm sure you will find it of interest. If they are not here, perhaps it may encourage you to try and find out a little more about them.

Mike Greening
January 2006

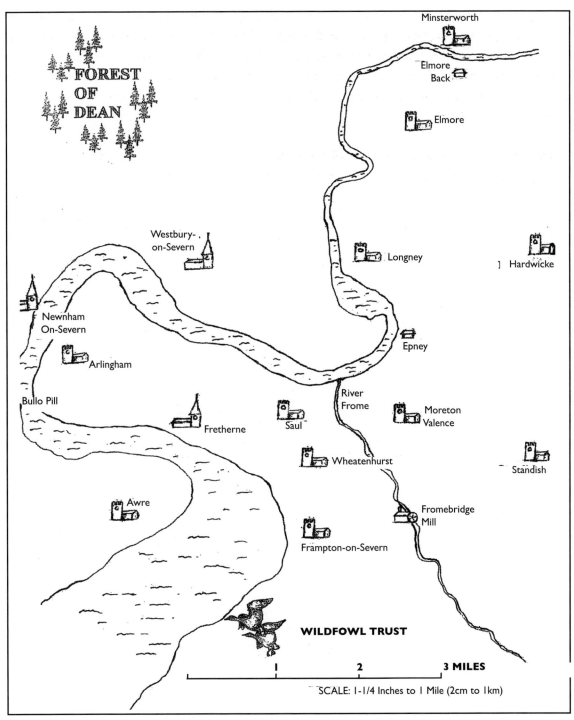

The River Severn south-west of Gloucester City

CHAPTER ONE

✛

The estuary of the Severn, Britain's longest river, dominates the southwestern quarter of England and Wales. The outer area, with the land of Wales to the north and the 'West Country' counties of England to the south, is termed the Bristol Channel – after the historic city and one-time distinguished port a little inland on the English side. From the area dominated by that city the estuary bends northwest and now takes its name from the river. Today two magnificent road bridges, joining Bristol and the English motorway system to the expanding city of Newport and Cardiff the Capital of Wales, span the entrance to the upper reaches of the estuary. The river itself is fairly quiet, commercial traffic is almost non-existent and although there are some pleasure craft this is not ideal yachting water. Except at high tide and in times of flood the upper estuary is notoriously shallow and at low tide this part of the estuary is filled with wide sandbanks. It is and always has been a dangerous place for amateur sailors.

The Severn is tidal up to and beyond the famous cathedral city of Gloucester forty miles to the north. For three quarters of the way it remains between one and three miles wide then, eight miles south of Gloucester, rather suddenly it contracts and twists into a large S-bend. After this it narrows again so rapidly that the tide often turns into a bore. This is a tidal wave that is generally higher around the time of the Spring and Autumn equinoxes but which also requires a number of other complementary factors, like the strength of the wind and its direction, to be particularly impressive. Although a number of other tidal rivers have this phenomenon, the Severn Bore is the second most spectacular surge of water in the world (the most powerful is in China) with its water wall occasionally reaching a height of nearly ten feet. It is one of Britain's most fascinating natural wonders.

Three hundred years ago the scene in the estuary would have been completely different. The river would have been teeming with mercantile craft. This was before the days of canals and railways or very usable roads and the Severn was one of Britain's most important trading arteries. Trows and Frigates, sailing barges with very shallow drafts, loaded with a wide variety of commodities would be sailing from Bristol to Gloucester and back throughout the year. During winter months, when water levels were higher, these craft would be sailed and hauled – by teams of muscular men more often than horses – much further up country to the inland ports of Worcester and Shrewsbury. Some will have stopped at the World's first industrial area at Coalbrookdale or travelled even as far as Welshpool in mid-Wales. The twin Welsh cities at the mouth of the river did not then exist. Newport was a small market town and Cardiff a tiny fishing port, which one hundred years later was still only home to one thousand souls.

Of particular interest to us is the area of land near the 'S' bend where the river joins its estuary. This had been Gloucestershire Greening homeland since before 1500. The county stretches down both banks of the river and on the western side, in the promontory of land in the lower horseshoe of the S, we have the village of Awre – one of two places in the county where the surname was first noted. Directly opposite, at the base of the larger upper horseshoe on the east bank, we have a cluster of small villages, Frethern, Saul, Wheatenhurst and Moreton Valence with the rather larger village of Frampton-on-Severn a mile or so to the south. All of these villages appear in our story. They were mostly agricultural communities but, as some of them were right on the river and had jetties or small harbours, a number of their inhabitants were sailors or involved in some way in the river trade.

The River Frome, one of the Severn's many tributaries, flows through three of these parishes; Saul – where it joins the big river, Wheatenhurst – where it is crossed by a bridge and Moreton Valence – a little further inland. Wheatenhurst was only a small hamlet in the 18th century but today is part of a larger village renamed Whitminster. It was near here, in the hamlet of Epney, that Nathaniel Greening owned a farm in 1722. Nathaniel was a successful yeoman with freehold land in both the parishes of Moreton Valence and Saul. He was a widower with five sons and, realising that he was unlikely to survive for much longer in this world *being sick & weake in body but of sound & perfect mind & memory* was keen to protect their interests and leave his affairs in order.

Nathaniel was only 43 years old and we do not know why he was failing in his prime. He may have contracted a terminal illness or been badly injured in an accident but his will, made on the 16th day of April that year, has the appearance of being hurriedly thought out. It seems highly likely that its rather unspecific bequests would have created problems for its beneficiaries. Nathaniel does not mention his wife Martha in the will, which would indicate that she had pre-deceased him and he only gives the name of one son – his first-born also Nathaniel. As the eldest son was likely to have been named after his grandfather, the Nathaniel making the will was almost certainly Nathaniel, baptised at Moreton Valence on the 26th March 1679, the son of (an earlier) Nathaniel.

Here we must digress for a paragraph, before proceeding with this family history. In a surname saga like this we will soon get baffled with first names. The Greenings, like many families – especially in the 17th, 18th and 19th centuries, tended to use the same group of Christian names for generation after generation. Sometimes a name was dropped or a new name added but many were used so many times that, not only will you certainly be unable to follow who I am writing about but I will also get confused putting this together. I will therefore use a device to help us both. Unless it is obvious from the text which particular Greening I am indicating, I will follow the first name with, where known, the year of birth or baptism (in brackets).

A transcription of the will of Nathaniel (1679) is printed as appendix 1 at the end of this book. You will read that he left all his freehold lands, premises, tenements and *hereditaments* to his three brothers (Samuel, Thomas and William) for a period of five years after his death. His brothers were his executors and he gave them the task of managing his assets, so that the income could be used to support and educate his sons until they were a little older. This was his way of trying to protect the interests of his younger sons. The youngest, Daniel, would have been eleven in 1722 and so sixteen after five years. At this juncture the property assets were to be equally divided between the sons – *only my eldest son Nathaniel to have ye first choice*. His other goods and chattels were left to pay his debts and funeral expenses with the surplus divided among the children when they reached the age of 21.

We do not know how this all worked out but it reads like a recipe for discord between five young men and their three uncles. As well as provoking family divisions, the will may also have had the effect of splitting up a substantial yeoman's holdings into financially unviable portions.

Nathaniel (1679) probably died shortly after making his last Will and Testament and appraisers made an inventory of his *Goods, Cattles and Chattels* on the 27th April (copy at appendix 1A). The inventory shows that Nathaniel was a wealthy man, living in a reasonably large farmhouse with chambers above both the parlour and the kitchen. He was not a large spender on the house and its contents, he was an entrepreneur whose main interests and holdings were in his farm stock and crops; 34 acres of corn, an ox-plough team of eight working bullocks, five horses with their harnesses, nineteen cows and a bull, nineteen sheep, thirteen lambs and six pigs. The inventory doesn't give us a record of his land holdings but this is likely to have been over fifty acres. Although we cannot make a direct comparison with the value of a small farm today, Nathaniel's assets were certainly on a par with a smallholding of our time worth between a quarter and half a million pounds.

The inventory gives us the location of Nathaniel's farm. In the hamlet of Epney, which is right on the River Severn and not far from St Andrew's church at Wheatenhurst, where he and Martha baptised their five sons. The eldest, Nathaniel, was christened on 5th May 1702, William in February 1703, Benjamin in March 1706, Joseph on 11th March 1708 and Daniel in February 1711. Although baptisms were not always held a few days after birth, it is interesting to note that it seems likely that the four younger sons had their birthdays within a few weeks of each other

Nathaniel (1679) is a particularly interesting person in this narrative as, although it is possible to trace back four generations before him – with some certainty, he is at the head of the family tree for most of the Greenings in this book. He is not only my likely ancestor, but he is also the ancestor of around one hundred people living today whom I have met or spoken to or with whom I have had correspondence! His eldest son Nathaniel (1702) was the grandfather of 'Old' Ben, the main character in my earlier book and whose story I retell in this. His fourth son Joseph (1708) was the grandfather of a later Joseph who, in turn, was the grandfather of Sir Edward Elgar, who will also put in an appearance later in this chronicle.

The father of Nathaniel (1679) and his three brothers was fairly definitely the Nathaniel mentioned in the list of Gloucester Diocese Marriage Allegations for 1677. An allegation was a sworn statement, usually made by the groom, that he and his intended wife were not already married and that there was no other impediment why the wedding should not proceed. By doing this, the ceremony could take place at short notice without the requirement of banns being read in each of the couple's parish churches. Allegation records, although not proving that the marriage actually took place, are interesting because they usually give us much more information than the actual wedding entry in a parish register. This often only gave the names of the bride and groom.

The allegation of 31st March 1677 informs us of the proposed marriage between *Nathaniel Greening 30, yeoman of Saule, and Elizabeth Collins 24 of Harefield*. Under this is written *'His wife brought to bed on midsomer eve'* . I would guess this means that Elizabeth was heavily pregnant and that this was the reason for the haste. I have found no record of the ceremony, which we can presume took place at the village of Haresfield – a couple of miles from Moreton Valence. Midsummer Eve was the twenty-third of June and baby Samuel was baptised at Moreton Valence eleven days later on 4th July 1677. As well as second son Nathaniel (1679), baptisms are also recorded for William (March 1684) and Mary (February 1687) and like Nathaniel these are in the Saul parish register. I have found no christening records for Nathaniel and Elizabeth's fourth son Thomas or their other daughter Elizabeth, but we know of their existence because they are both mentioned in wills. Samuel died on 3rd January 1743 aged 67 and was described as a *Yeoman of Saul*. This information is recorded on his tombstone in Moreton Valence churchyard. William, who made a will like his brother Nathaniel – and only two years later in 1724, describes himself as a *Clothier of Saul*. He would have been forty and his will does not mention any living wife or children. He left the bulk of his estate to be divided equally between his brother Samuel and sisters Mary and Elizabeth. We can therefore assume that Thomas had also died during the intervening two years. An extract from William's will is also included in Appendix 1 – showing his sisters' married names. Elizabeth had been married at Frethern on 21st April 1720 to John Blanch of Eastington.

From his given age in the Marriage Allegation, we can deduce that Nathaniel senior was born in or around 1647. Few records have survived for that year. Although most children may have been baptised, the country was in turmoil because of the civil war and few parish register entries were either made or have survived for posterity. The archives also hold no will for Nathaniel (1647) but there is a will left by the man who was almost certainly his father, the four brother's grandfather. He was yet another Nathaniel, I think the first with that name (excepting an older brother who died in infancy) and his will is a fascinating social history document. It was made on the 6th of October 1680, when his same name grandson would have been eighteen months old. Mostly updated into current English, the main body of the will reads as follows:

> 'In the name of God Amen, I Nathaniel Greening of Saul in the County of Gloucester yeoman being sick in body, but of sound mind and of good and perfect memory, laud and praise be given unto Almighty God, do make and ordain this my present testament concerning my last Will in manner and form following. First I commend my soul unto Almighty God my maker and redeemer, and my body to the earth to be buried (at the discretion of my Executrix herein after named) in steadfast hope (through the merits of my blessed Lord and Saviour Jesus Christ, my Redeemer) to rise again at the last day to be made partaker of Eternal life. And as for that portion of worldly goods, which God in his mercy hath blessed me withal; I do dispose of as follows –
>
> *Imprimis*, I give and bequeath unto my son Nathaniel; the Bedstead over the kitchen and my pear-tree cupboard, and the cupboard which is over the buttery, the Settle in the hall, the two window leaves belonging to the hall windows, my Cider mill and all the appurtenances belonging to the same, and also my *Ricke Stadle and all the tallet polls*.
>
> *Item*. I give and bequeath unto my two sons-in-law, William Hammon and Richard Nayle, Twenty Shillings apiece, as a remembrance of my love unto them. As for the residue of my goods and chattels not already bequeathed I do give and bequeath unto my Daughter Abigail whom I do make my sole Executrix of this my last Will. And I also do give and bequeath unto

her the said Abigail, all the Close or pasture ground lying in the parish of Morton Valence in the county aforesaid, known by the name of the Green-moors with the appurtenances belonging to the same together with all my Deeds and Evidences that I have in, and to the Farm, to have and to hold all the said Close of pasture ground with all and every appurtenances unto the said Abigail her heirs and assigns for ever etc..'

One of the three witnesses to this Nathaniel's will was Jeremiah Greening, yeoman of Epney, who may have been the benefactor's brother.

In documents of this period the term 'sons-in-law' sometimes refers to stepsons. This might explain why the will does not mention their wives who, if Nathaniel's daughters, might have been expected to receive at least token legacies. Nathaniel appears to have survived his own wife as he leaves the bulk of his estate, his farm (presumably at Saul) and pasture land at Moreton Valence, to his unmarried daughter Abigail who will have stayed at home to look after her father. Son Nathaniel had no doubt already established himself elsewhere, probably with his father's help. The Bishop of Gloucester's Transcripts record the wedding of Abigail to *Richard Gofre* (Godfrey?) at Frethern on 10th February 1695. In today's dates this was 1696, as we were still then in the days of the Julien Calendar with the year ending on 24th March – the Quarter Day. It was 1752 before Britain followed European Catholic countries and changed over to our present Gregorian arrangement, with the year starting on the first of January.

Many farmhouses at this time were 'Hall Houses' in which the hall was the main room. Screens divided it from a passageway with doors at the front and the back. This was a basic medieval plan, which had continued with variations. By the 17th century the medieval hall usually had an inserted upper floor with a fireplace and chimney on one end wall, often replacing the wooden screen. There would be a stair on one side of the fire and a door on the other. Nathaniel's house would have been of this general form. The hall was the main room and had two windows of glass, which were not permanently fixed, probably in addition to wooden shutters. The hall contained a settle, the cupboard of pear wood and probably a table and other furniture left to Abigail. The buttery stored the cider butts and other wet goods of that sort and both the buttery and pantry had upper floors, in which the bedstead and cupboard left to son Nathaniel had been standing.

This will was written during the 'Restoration' reign of Charles II, within a year or two of the publication of John Bunyan's *Pilgrim's Progress*. It was an age of comparative peace and a gentle rise in prosperity. Much of Nathaniel's life had taken place in troubled times, when he was a younger man Gloucestershire had suffered particularly badly in the Civil War. In the early spring of 1643 Sir William Waller, who was the leading Parliamentary commander in southern England during the first three years of the conflict, captured the City of Gloucester and then took his army through Moreton Valence and Saul before crossing the Severn at Framilode on a fleet of boats that had been brought all the way from London for that purpose. Sir William went on to capture Monmouth and Chepstow, on the other side of the river, before being defeated by a Royalist army near Tewkesbury in April. A few months later, in the summer of that year, the Royalists tried to retake Gloucester. The largest field army ever assembled in the Civil War, said to number about 35,000 men, sat outside the city and tried to bring it to its knees. There were only about fifteen hundred Parliamentary defenders inside the walls, but they managed to hold out for the whole of the month of August until the Cavalier besiegers were dispersed by the arrival of a new Roundhead army in early September. These battles and sieges would have impacted on nearby villages like Saul and Moreton Valence. If not a soldier himself, some of Nathaniel's male relatives would certainly have been conscripted. We do not know which side had Nathaniel's sympathies. Another difficult period not long after the war saw England ravaged by the Bubonic Plague, although this mostly affected London, its tentacles reached many rural areas including Gloucestershire.

This 'first' Nathaniel Greening was a yeoman. He was an owner-occupier, with orchards large enough to be worth the ownership of a cider mill. Green-moors pasture suggests grazing land and a *rick staddle* possibly a grain rick, which was raised off the ground to reduce the numbers of invading rats and allow the air to circulate beneath. A *tallet* was a loft, the space under the roof, so this was probably a wooden open barn. A Nathaniel married Mary Humphries (*Mary Vmfres*) at Moreton Valence on 17th May 1636. It is possible that he was not the Nathaniel whose birth is mentioned in the next paragraph. However, as there would appear to be only one Greening of this name around at this time, it seems likely that they were the same man.

As we go further back in time, fewer records were made and there are greater possibilities of these being destroyed or lost. Conversely, as we also have fewer Greenings and – if some of the ones we are trying to trace had more unusual first names (not Thomas, William or John) – there is more chance of us finding likely candidates for earlier branches of our tree. There was a Nathaniel baptised at Stone on 26th December 1618 who would be about the right age. The parish register gives his father's name as Richard. The village of Stone, not far from Berkeley Castle – where England's King Edward the Second was murdered with a red-hot poker in 1327, is eleven miles south of Moreton Valence. Although this was a fair distance at that time there is strong circumstantial evidence to link the families in the two locations (explained in the next chapter), which makes it reasonable to conclude that this Nathaniel was the man who made the will in 1680.

A very fascinating document, that tells us some more about the 'Stone' Nathaniel has survived. This is a very early 'Indenture' or what we today would call a property conveyance. Dated 18th October 1656, this deed relates to the sale – by Richard and his son Nathaniel – of what in present terminology would be a commercial investment holding. It gives us some interesting information about business transactions at that time and takes us back a further generation to Richard's father, Guy Greening. Having been involved in quite a number of property conveyances in my life, it is amazing to me how little of the legalese has changed in three hundred and fifty years.

All land in England originally belonged to the Crown and this early deed details its change in ownership from King Edward the Sixth (Henry the Eighth's son who died age 16 in 1553) to the Greenings and then on to their purchaser.

> ...all part of the possessions of the late dissolved Chauntery of the Blessed Mary in the Church of Stone aforesaid and were heretofore purchased among other things by Sir John Thynne knight and Lawrence Hyde gent deceased from the late King Edward the Sixth and by them .. conveyed to Anthony Throkmorton deceased late citizen and mercer of London and his heires by the name of Anthony Throgmorton merchant .. and by him lately conveyed onto John Bowser the elder late of Totworth clothier and heretofore purchased of Thomas Bowser of Stone aforesaid gent brother and heir of Anthony Bowser the younger deseased sonne and heir of the said John Bowser the elder deseased by the aforesaid Guy Greening and afterwards settled by him on the said Richard Greening, his heirs .. (who agree) to deliver to Samuell Mallett before the feast of Jesus Christ next ensuing ...

The conveyance is a fairly long document as it lists (and describes) eight separate small plots of land. I will not reproduce it in full here but to give you some idea the first parcel is defined as follows – *All that one meassuage and tenement in which the said Richard Greening then dwelled with a curtillage adjoining And all houses buildings barnes stables and outhouses with a backside and garden to the said messuage belonging sett lyeing and being in Stone aforesaid.*

The Indenture was between *Richard Greening of Stone in the county of Gloucester yeoman Sonne of Guy Greening of Rockington otherwise Rockhampton in the said County yeoman deseased and Nathaniel Greening of Rockhampton aforesaid yeoman Sonne and heir apparent of the said Richard Greening and Judith now wife of the said Nathaniel and daughter of Katherine Linck widow late deceased, of one parte and Samuell Mallett of Newton ..yeoman of the other parte ..*

Although the sale was to Samuel Mallett, the property and land had been leased four days earlier to John Taylor. Mr Mallett was making the purchase for the rental income. Unfortunately the document does not mention the annual rent Taylor was paying so we cannot work out Mallett's return on capital. The consideration the Greening father and son received was *threescore and fifteen pounds* (seventy-five pounds). The conveyance gives Nathaniel's wife's name as Judith Linck not Mary Humphries but, as this is twenty years later than the Moreton Valence wedding, it is possible that Judith was the same Nathaniel's second wife.

Guy Greening and his wife Elizabeth, the earliest ancestors of the family lines followed in this book – with a reasonable degree of certainty, would have been born between 1550 and 1570. Although most of Guy's adult life would have been lived during the golden age of the first Queen Elizabeth, his childhood probably took place during a particularly turbulent eleven-year period in English History. Henry the Eighth had died in 1547 and the crown had passed to his sickly son, nine year-old Edward. When he succumbed to tuberculosis six years later, some members of the nobility tried to install Lady Jane Grey as sovereign. This very intelligent but unlucky sixteen year-old only lasted nine days before being imprisoned in the Tower of London. Here she was beheaded on the orders of her successor, Henry's eldest daughter Mary. Protestant historians usually precede this Queen's name with the adjective 'bloody', because of her determination to execute all her prominent subjects opposed to the 'old religion'. The country would have returned to Romanism but Mary herself died within five years, allowing the long reign of her half sister – one of England's greatest monarchs – to commence.

Guy, who was a contemporary of Sir Francis Drake, Sir Walter Raleigh and William Shakespeare, made his will on the 20th March 1612 and died just over a year later. There is a little confusion about his status or occupation. In his will he is described as a husbandman whereas the property conveyance states that he was a yeoman, which must be so as it details land and buildings conveyed to him from Thomas Bowser of Stone. Possibly, as he was living at a leasehold farm in Newton at the time his will was made, he was then regarded as a husbandman. In any event Guy appears to have been materially very successful as he left three separate properties. He left two of his houses with adjoining orchards, gardens and land to Richard. *I give and bequeath unto Richard Greeninge my sonne and his heyres for ever lawfully begotten of his owne bodye **my house situate in Stone** within the p(ar)ish of Barkley, with an orchard a garden and ten acres of meadow, errable, and pasture land be itt more or lesse thereunto belonginge and appertaineinge, butt if itt shall happen that Richard my sonne shall dye without any heyre as aforesaid then it shall remaine unto Thomas Greeninge my sonne and to his heyres for ever. It(em) I give and bequeathe unto Richard Greeninge my sonne and to his heyres for ever lawfully begotten by his owne bodye **my house in Woodford** within the aforesaid p(ar)ish of Barkley with an orchard a garden and one close of pasture by estimation an acre be itt more or lesse belonginge and in any* *wise appertaineinge butt if it shall happen that the said Richard my sonne shall have no heyre as above sayd that then it shall remaine unto Thomas my sonne and to his heyres for ever.* Guy left his share of his third and largest property, his leasehold home, to his widow Elizabeth. *All my parte of the lease of **my house in Newton** within the p(ar)ish of Rockhampton, with the Barnes, Stable, orchard, garden and one yardland thereunto belonginge and appertaineinge. One yardland,* an Old Saxon land measurement that varied from place to place, was probably about forty acres. He also left ten shillings to his granddaughter Mary, Thomas' daughter, and ten shillings to the poor of the parish of Rockhampton and Stone. Guy had a daughter, Jane, who was baptised at Rockhampton in February 1606. As she does not appear in his will we must presume that she had died. At first glance the will seems extremely unfair on Guy's son Thomas. When we read into it, however, we can see that he was the eldest son and had already become an established farmer. He would have been the other shareholder of the lease on his father's main forty-acre farmstead at Newton (a hamlet adjoining Rockhampton), which they would have farmed together. After the death of his father he would have lived here with his wife, his daughter and his widowed mother. Thomas is definitely the *husbandman of Rockhampton,* included in the Gloucestershire 'military census' of September 1608, which recorded *all able and sufficient men in body fitt for his Majestie's service in the warrs.* In this survey Thomas is listed as a man in his thirties and of middle stature – so suitable to be a musketeer. At the time of the *Review* he had one servant who is also on the list. Richard's name does not appear, so we must conclude that he was very much younger than his brother and still regarded as a child in 1608.

It is interesting to note that one of the two executors of Guy's will was Thomas Mallett of Newton. He was no doubt a neighbour, friend and probably the father or grandfather of the land purchaser of 1656. Another interesting record has come to light, which gives us more information about the social status and level of education of the Rockhampton Greening family. In about 1620, a few years after Guy's death, his eldest son Thomas must have had a son who was also named Thomas. I have not discovered a record of his christening, but he is listed in the Alumni of Cambridge University. Thomas, son of Thomas Greening, Yeoman of Newton, Gloucestershire, entered Sidney College on the first of April 1637 at the age of seventeen. He obtained his BA degree in the 1640/41 academic year and was ordained a Deacon at Lincoln Cathedral on the 5th of June 1642.

At the time of Guy's death, his youngest son Richard was still single. However, on 19th February the following year, he married Alice March at St Mary's church in the small town of Thornbury a few miles south of Stone and Rockhampton. St Mary's has a baptismal record in September the same year for a Nathaniel Greening and, although no parents' names are recorded in the church register, this must have been Alice and Richard's son. These two 1614 entries are the only ones recording the surname in that parish. I'm pretty sure that this Nathaniel was the very first in the family with that name, but he must have died as an infant. The Nathaniel baptised at Stone four years later was a 'replacement' son. To put 1614 in historical context, it was the year the very first shipment of *Nicotiaiia tabacum* arrived in England from Virginia.

CHAPTER TWO

✢

It is not possible to say when or how the surname originated. It is likely that it first appeared in England in the thirteenth or fourteenth century and may be a derivation from the word, name or colour green. However it is equally feasible that it evolved from a completely different word – Grin, Gren, Grig or something else. In some early spellings the surname is written Grining and Griging. In my earlier little book I speculated that the answer might be found in heraldry, as the 'listed' Greening shield is obviously an early one – a simple red crusaders cross with wavy (engrailed) lines on a silver background – "Argent a Cross engrailed Gules".

As a fourteenth century knight, Sir Richard Dalin(grigge) held the same 'Engrailed Cross' coat of arms, I thought there might be some connection. Sir Richard fought in France during the Hundred Years War for one of the mercenary 'free companies' and, in 1385 was ordered by King Richard II to build Bodiam Castle in Sussex as an invasion from France was threatened. Bodiam is a romantic picture-book castle and well worth a visit if you have not seen it. The coat of arms is engraved in the stonework over the main entrance. Sir Richard was Lord Mayor of London in 1392 and appointed Keeper of the Tower by the king in 1395. A fiery character he once threw down his gauntlet challenging a dual with John of Gaunt, the father of King Richard's usurper and successor Henry IV.

Because of the shield connection I contacted the College of Arms in London and commissioned one of the Heralds – Rouge Dragon Pursuivant – to do some research on the Greening arms. The Herald sent me a very full report but it was disappointing. The College of Arms was founded in 1484 and they have had to approve all arms from then. The college have also documented many coats of arms in use before that date but there are few records of their source. The early 'knights' just adopted whatever design caught their eye and before 1484 some families would have chosen the same design as others. Rouge Dragon states that there is *no trace of this coat of arms ever having been officially granted or confirmed to anyone of the name of Greening and he thought it unlikely that Greening* had any connection with Dalyngrigge. He writes that the Greening ascription to *Argent a Cross engrailed Gules* first appears in Joseph Edmundson's 'System of Heraldry' published in 1780. He was not able to find where Mr Edmundson obtained his information, as it is not attributed in any earlier records. In the sixteenth and early seventeenth century these arms, or similar ones, do appear in the 'quarterings' of some other more complex shields. These have associations with the surname Gourney or Gurney. Later the engrailed cross shows up in arms tied with the names Dalegrigs, Delalind, Green, Grene and Greene. So this line of enquiry, in my search for the surname's early history, has not really helped at all.

I estimate that there are probably between nine and ten thousand people with the surname Greening in the world today. Almost all of these live in English speaking countries, possibly about half in the United States, two thousand or so in the British Isles and most of the balance in Canada, Australia and New Zealand. A substantial minority in the States, perhaps as high as twenty percent of the total there, have no connection with the Greenings in this book. These are people descended from Prussian or German emigrants, who originally had family names like Grunnig, but then anglicised their name after their arrival in the US. It is however possible that some of the German's ancestors came from Britain; there were some early Greenings in Russia! A few Greenings in England have written to me, relating a family legend that they also came from continental Europe and changed their name after arrival here. One of the American Prussian Greenings sent me an email – *You are barking up the wrong tree, we are from Prussia.* I am not up a wrong tree just a different one. From my research I can categorically state that the majority of Greenings in the world today, plus millions of other people with other surnames who are descended from Greening trees, come from English stock. Although a substantial portion of these are descended from one or two families which were first recorded in Dorset in the sixteenth century, the majority have their roots in Gloucestershire – where they are first mentioned in late fourteenth century documents. I suspect but am not sure if the Gloucestershire Greenings had any family ties with the Dorset ones, but they certainly did with some who appeared in Dorset's adjoining county Devon in the seventeenth century. Near the porch of Bideford Church, there is a memorial with the inscription *Underneath and near this stone are deposited the mortal remains of the Ancient Greening Family late of Gloucester. They came to reside at Bideford in 1666, a time of great persecution.*

From 1509 to 1547 England was ruled by, if not its most famous, certainly its most colourful king – Henry the Eighth. His reign was one of the most crucial in the country's history and many of the vast changes that occurred in England, were designed and enacted by Henry's two henchmen who, in turn, ran the affairs of state on his behalf. Both men were of humble origin, the first the son of a butcher the second the son of a blacksmith, and they were in consequence hated by the established nobility. However both were of the highest intellect and are today regarded as two among the greatest statesmen in English history. The first was Thomas Wolsey, who rose rapidly through the church to become Archbishop of York, a Cardinal and then Henry's Chancellor. When he fell into disfavour and died in 1530 his place, as the king's chief advisor and administrator, fell to his lawyer secretary Thomas Cromwell. The second Thomas barely lasted ten years before losing his head, as the result of a plot by his enemies in the nobility, but among the many ordinances passed during his time in power historians are grateful for the one without which family history research (prior to Civil Registration in 1837) would be practicably impossible. In 1538 Thomas Cromwell ordered the priest in every parish in the realm to keep a register of all baptisms, marriages and burials taking place in that parish. Although many of the early records have been lost, luckily a considerable number have survived – including many of those for the Gloucestershire parishes in which we are interested.

There is a connection between Thomas and his even more famous namesake Oliver, who came on the scene a century later. Thomas had a sister Katherine who married a Welshman, Morgan Williams. It was their son who adopted the more illustrious surname Cromwell in honour of his maternal uncle. Oliver was his great-grandson. So the true ancestral name of the Lord Protector of the Commonwealth of England, Scotland and Ireland in 1653 was Oliver Williams – which does not quite have the right ring to it!

Manorial Court records predate Parish Church registers and, in those of the Manor of Awre, John *Grenyng* is documented as having paid six shillings and ten pence rent for land in that village in 1493. This is not the earliest mention of a Greening in Gloucestershire that I have found. However as the thickest concentration of families with the surname – in the sixteenth and seventeenth century – are to be found within a ten-mile radius of Awre (mostly on the other side of the river), I have started my story here. At the time, seven shillings was a fairly sizeable amount of rent so we can assume that John was a farmer of some stature. He would have been a husbandman (tenant farmer), as almost certainly all land in the village at that time would have been held by the manor on behalf of the king. Although the entry does not give his age or anything more about him, John was living in England during the reign of the first Tudor king, Henry VII, and on the eve of the age of exploration. In 1493 'historic' Europeans had not yet discovered America. Christopher Columbus had just returned from his first voyage west. He thought he had journeyed to islands in Asia, but he had been to the Bahamas, Cuba and Haiti. Before the turn of the century, seven years later, Columbus had returned twice more to the West Indies, Amerigo Vespucci had sighted mainland America, Vasco de Gama had navigated round the Cape of Good Hope to India and from Bristol – thirty miles south of Awre – John Cabot had sailed to Newfoundland, the first piece of 'foreign' soil that would later be called the British Empire.

John Greening, or possibly his son of the same name, next appears in the Awre Manorial Court Roll of 1507. This informs us that: *John of Awre surrendered one messuage, 6 acres of land and appurtenances called mydways in base tenure to the use of John Greening and Christian his wife Henry Greening her son. Mariana Greening married Christopher Browne, gent, wife's part.*

The lord of the manor would grant tenancies, through his steward, for generally no more than three lives. Usually each incoming tenant would surrender it in order to receive it back again in his name and in the names of two further generations, who he wished to succeed him. Base tenure was a form of tenure in use in this part of Gloucestershire where the descent was to the youngest son or, if a son did not exist, to the youngest daughter. It may be that older sons were assumed to have made their separate way in the world and if there were only daughters, the elder ones were more likely to be married.

John and Christian were therefore the tenants of Mydways Farmstead, with Henry named as principal heir to the smallholding. We do not know why he is described as 'her' son. This could have been a clerk's error, but a possible explanation is that Christian was the daughter of John of Awre and that John Greening had other children by a previous wife. John of Awre may have been protecting the right of succession for his grandson? Mariana was probably John and Christian's daughter. There is still a dispute on how the name of the village should be pronounced, some people say "Or" and some say "Ar". In the Doomsday Book it was spelt Ow and in later chronicles Owr. John of Awre may have been descended from Gilbert de Ow who was made Lord of the Manor after the Norman Conquest of 1066. As surnames did not evolve until much later it is not possible to trace the early descent of the family who take their name from the village. What is truly remarkable is that the Awre family are still farming in Awre today (2004). By a further twist of fate, not only have the Greenings returned to Awre but also quite recently both families became united in marriage. Today there are children growing up in the village who are of mixed Greening and Awre ancestry.

Awre, on its promontory in the River Severn, exists because of the river and has always been dominated by it. The river itself provided livelihoods for some villagers in trading and fishing and for others the land, especially near the river where the annual floods made it particularly fertile, provided their income. The village has always been noted for its abundant crops and productive orchards. In the sixteenth century Awre and its adjoining villages on the west bank of the Severn were all small ports with quays, where timber from the nearby Forrest of Dean would be loaded and shipped downriver to the shipbuilding yards of Bristol. Both Francis Drake and Walter Raleigh are said to have come here when selecting timber for their ships. Commercial fishing is still carried on today, some of it in much the same way as it was in Tudor times and before. Eels and lampreys are caught in nets and even sturgeon are sometimes landed, but the main fish in the Severn are salmon that are trapped in banks of 'putchers' – hand made funnels, like large bottomless wicker baskets, which are made from withy especially grown in Awre for that purpose. The river has also brought much sadness to the village. Over the centuries it has claimed the lives of countless hundreds, from complete boat crews to young children, as the church burial records testify.

Henry Greneynge is shown in Gloucester Diocesan Records as being a churchwarden at St. Andrews parish church in Awre in 1551. We also have his will dated 26th April 1552. It is one of the earliest Greening wills to survive. This is definitely the same Henry, named in the 1507 court entry, as he mentions his mother who was still alive at the time the will was made. She was likely near death as the will states …*and then my mother christian grynnynge maye have a honest* (unreadable) *at the cost and charge of my executors* …. The unreadable word is probably burial.

Henry's will does not mention any sons, only his wife Als (Alice), his eldest daughter Margerye and his other daughter Marian. The lack of a male heir may have caused a later dispute with the Browne family, which I explained in my earlier book. However as there is no mention of Mydways in the will, Henry is likely to have had a son who had already taken over the farm tenancy.

Generally speaking wills only appear from 1541, when the 1540 Statute of Wills became law. This statute gave people the right to bequeath their interests in real property (by will) and leave their personal possessions (by testament) to whomever they wished. Before 1541, interests in property and possessions were inherited according to a strict formula that would vary in different parts of the country. Wills are not only fascinating documents – some, especially those of our ancestors, can be particularly moving. A transcribed copy of Henry's will can be found at the end of this book – Appendix 2.

Unfortunately there is a large gap in the Court Rolls of Awre for much of the sixteenth century. When they resume in the late 1580s the Greening name crops up frequently, sometimes recording an appointment as an official of the Manor, sometimes recording a rent for land and – on a number of occasions – for either breaking the law or being the victim of someone else who had broken it.

The 'fighting' entries which all concern John, probably the grandson or great-grandson of the original John, read as follows.

30 September 1588 William Rydow made an affray on John Greenynge and from him drew blode. He is in mercy. Fined 2s (shillings).
And the aforesaid John Greenynge made an affray on the aforesaid William Rydow but drew no blode. He is in mercy. John was not fined.

1 May 1598 Richard Browne and John *Greninge* were presented for *a fraye and blodeshede* upon each other. Richard was fined two shillings. John *for two several affrays upon Richard Browne* was fined twelve pence.

9 October 1598 John of Awre was presented for *making affraye with his ffyste with blode shedeyn upon John Greninge*. He was fined two shillings.

It would appear from the above that John was not the instigator in these fights.

John, James and William Greening all feature in the Awre Court Book. As residents of Awre village they were among the members of the homage sworn at the Court of Frankpledge and the Baronial Court. John was sworn in as *Tythingman* (Chief tithe or tax collector) for Awre in the Octobers of 1589, 1595 and 1597. James, who was almost certainly the brother of John, had been ordered to *Reen* (clear out) his drainage ditches in 1598 and was elected as one of the two constables for the village in 1599. There were at least two William Greenings, as both John and James had sons with that name (mentioned in a will). One of them was fined twelve pence in October 1596 for keeping too many sheep on the common fields.

From Awre, the surname spread to a large number of locations both up and down the Severn. Initially, as mentioned in the first chapter, this was to the group of villages on the other side of the river almost directly opposite. The surname also began to appear in a few other places in Gloucestershire, most notably Winchcomb. Today this is an extremely attractive small Cotswold-stone town, seven miles east of Cheltenham Spa and so about fourteen miles northeast of the City of Gloucester. Winchcomb dates from Saxon times. It was the most important destination of pilgrims in Medieval England, the draw being the grave of Saint Kenelm – the murdered boy king of Mercia – who had been buried at Winchcomb Abbey. This was much earlier than the pilgrimages to the tomb of Thomas-a-Beckett in Canterbury, immortalised in the tales of Geoffrey Chaucer.

There were Greening families in Winchcomb in the sixteenth century (there are still some there today) and I originally assumed that these could have come from Awre. I was probably wrong, as they may have been there already. There are two mentions of a Greening in this town that pre-date the Awre records by nearly one hundred years.

Historians do not agree on the origins of the British jury. Some believe the system arrived in England with the Norman invasion, others that it was here from Saxon times. The reason why juries should consist of twelve men is also unknown, as one would think that an odd number might be preferable – so a majority conclusion would always be reached. The most likely reason for the number, in a Christian country, is that Christ had twelve apostles. However twelve is a 'geometrical' number. Many items are still sold in dozens, there are twelve months, twelve constellations of the Zodiac, twelve Knights of the Round Table and even the Dalai Lama has twelve advisors.

The first jurors were not involved in criminal trials or legal disputes, which would be settled by a single Judge or a Lord of the Manor, but they were used in inquiries or inquests. These were usually called to help determine property matters, sometimes after the death of one of the King's tenants. Early jurors or *Oath-takers* would therefore be local men, of good standing in their communities, who were witnesses of fact and who would be able to speak out of personal knowledge – of the property in question or of the deceased person. In fourteenth century England all land and buildings were owned by the King, or held by the Church – on behalf of the King.

In 1397 and 1398 there were *Inquisitions taken at Wynchcombe*, which concerned the two main properties in the district. These were the Abbey (destroyed in the sixteenth century) and Sudeley Manor (now known as Sudeley Castle). The one in February 1397 was to ascertain if a proposal by a man called Richard Bushell to assign part of his tenanted property to Winchcomb Abbey, *to find two wax candles to burn every day at High Mass before the High Altar in the Abbey Church of St Mary and St Kenelm, King and Matyr*, would reduce the King's income. The one taken on the *Tuesday before Michalmas* in 1398 followed the death of Thomas Botiller, *Chivaller. The said Thomas held from the King in chief, on the day he died, jointly with his wife Alice who syrvives, the manor of Sudleye, of the feoffment of John le Rous, John de Beresford, clerk, and John Kyrkeby, the younger (to hold of them and the heirs of the body of the said), under licence from the king, dated at York 18th July …[1385]. It is held by knight service, but by what fee the jurors do not know, it is worth £40 a year clear. The said Thomas died 21st September last. John his son and heir was aged 14 on St. Margaret's Day last.*

One of the twelve *Oath-takers* at both inquests was *Henry Grenyng*. We know nothing more about him, except that he lived in Winchcomb during the reign of the young King Richard II – who in 1381, at the age of fourteen, had defused the Peasants Revolt caused by the imposition of the first Poll Tax. Henry must have been a survivor. He was probably in his thirties or forties in the 1390s, so will have lived through the most terrible half-century in English history when more than half of the population had died of the bubonic plague. The Black Death had arrived in Britain in 1348 and initially ravaged the land for two years. However it returned in 1361 (the Pestilence of Boys) and in 1369 (The Pestilence of Children) and yet again for the 'Fourth Pestilence' in 1374. There were further serious plague outbreaks in 1390 and 1405. Henry Greening was a contemporary of Chaucer and Sir John Dalyngrigge; he also lived in an era of great conflict. A year after the second inquest at Winchcomb, King Richard had been defeated in battle by his cousin Henry Bolingbrook and subsequently murdered in captivity. Only four years after this, King Henry was nearly overthrown at the battle that took place in my hometown. The Battle of Shrewsbury in 1403 was a particularly bloody affair. Because of the skill of the archers (on both sides) some historians estimate that over twenty thousand men-at-arms and many of the mounted knights, perhaps half of those who took part, were killed on the field. Many more would have succumbed to their wounds in the days that followed. Today, if the estimates are correct and over six hundred years later, no higher loss of life has occurred in a battle on British soil. Indeed the death toll would have been higher than the British Army's worst day ever for casualties – the first day of the Battle of the Somme in 1916.

There is no way of telling, but Henry Greening of Winchcomb must have been one of the earliest bearers of the surname. Possibly John, the farmer in Awre in 1493, was descended from him.

In chapter one I suggest that the earliest 'reasonably likely' ancestors, of the lines of Greening descent followed in this book, were Guy and Elizabeth Greening. I also wrote that there was circumstantial evidence to link Guy, who was living in the parish of Rockampton at the time his will was made, with the Greenings at Moreton Valence. Guy was an unusual name but there were two others living at this time (the only ones I have found at any time). These were a father and son, living at Moreton Valence. The father, a generation younger than Guy at Rockhampton, is listed in the Gloucestershire 'Men and Arms' register of 1608. At that time he was described as a tall young man in his twenties, who had received military training and so could serve the king as a Pike-man. He and his same name son were also beneficiaries in the Will of Thomas Greening, the father of the senior Guy. This will was made in November 1613, only eighteen months or so after that of the Guy who lived in Rockhampton. It therefore seems reasonable to conclude that this original Guy and Thomas were brothers. Guy had named his eldest son Thomas and his brother Thomas had reciprocated and named his eldest son Guy.

If my guess is correct, I can now look for a possible candidate to take us back a further generation. Unfortunately many of the Parish Records for Moreton Valence from the 16th and 17th century have not survived (Awre church records go back to 1538), however there is a John Greening, Yeoman of Moreton Valence, who made a will on 27th November 1565. It is quite probable that he was the father – or more probably the grandfather – of Guy and Thomas. His wife was called Jane, but the will does not list his children by name it only informs us that he had eleven of them – all still living at the time the will was drawn up. Not only is this one of the very early Greening wills it is also beautifully written, so a copy of it is reproduced in this book. This John was possibly the first Greening yeoman, the very first Greening to own freehold land. He must have been a man of some consequence. There is a reasonable chance that he was descended from that earlier John – the farmer at Mydways in the village of Awre.

When I wrote the first little book one of the early archives that interested me was the August 1608 military review, which I've just mentioned. There were twenty-one Greenings in the county at that time, in the sixth year of the reign of James the First, who were *able and suffient men in body fitt for his Ma'ties service in the warrs*. I listed their names, occupations and the villages where they lived in an appendix to the book. Although this census only listed able-bodied men and there would have been some families consisting only of women and children with, or without, elderly or infirm men – the list surprised me. There were seven men (a third of the total) living in Moreton Valence and Saul but only one in Awre (Thomas). As the records of the Manorial Court and St Andrew's Church show that there were a number of Greening families in the village in the late sixteenth century – in addition to the family at Mydways – this seemed strange. However I assumed, that for some reason, most of the Greenings had migrated to the other side of the river.

A fascinating BBC Television documentary, first broadcast in early April 2005, provided the answer to this enigma and allowed me to re-write the end of this chapter. Many, if not most, of the Awre Greenings had probably drowned.

The subject of this television programme was the worst-ever natural disaster to strike Britain in historical times. The giant wave that engulfed the low lands of the Bristol Channel and Severn Estuary on the 20th of January 1607 (1606 old calendar) is now believed by 'the experts' to have been a tsunami. Contemporary descriptions say it did not occur during a terrible storm but suddenly swept up the channel and river without any warning on a morning of clear weather. If this was a tsunami they conjectured that it could have been caused by submarine volcanic activity off the Irish coast. The wall of water was apparently between twenty and thirty feet in height and, in addition to the complete destruction of many buildings in low lying districts and the annihilation of large numbers of livestock, there was a loss of more than two thousand human lives. This was a vast number of people at that period and many of those who survived would have lost their homes, their belongings and their livelihoods. We only have to look at a map of the estuary to realise that Awre would have been one of the worst hit villages. It is on low ground and at the apex of the channel funnel. The wave here would have been at its highest.

If you visit Awre today, after refreshing yourself at the Red Hart Inn (part of which was there in the sixteenth century), take a walk from the car park at the front of the pub down pretty Woodend Lane that leads to the Severn. Just before you reach the river you will pass a fairly new house on your left hand side. This is a rebuilt and extended dwelling called Medway, which is on the site of an eighteenth century cottage that had the same name. Before the cottage there was no doubt an earlier building here and before that a wooden, mud and wattle farmstead called Mydways. This was originally in a small hamlet called Woodend, but most of the other properties have been lost over the years as the result of the erosion of the riverbank. Mydways was only a few feet above the normal flood level of the Severn. In 1606/7 it would almost certainly have been swept away with everything in it. Only very sturdy buildings, like stone built St Andrew's Church, with its parish records safe in a chest in the tower, would have withstood the wall of water.

The Rector of Awre, if he survived this tragedy, did not record it or list those who had died in the parish register. However the Reverend Henry Childe, Vicar of Arlingham a parish next to Saul and on higher ground the other side of the river, did record the catastrophe and he also tells us that later that year *there was a most extreame hott somer, in so much that many died with heat*. In 1624 a 'Survey of Winter Estate Tenancies' shows that a William Greening – the son of John (possibly the tythingman) – and who was married to Alicia, paid two shillings and two and a half pence rent for a tenement called Mydways in base tenure. The farmstead must have been rebuilt and William either survived the flood or he was a close relative from another village who had been allowed to take over the tenancy.

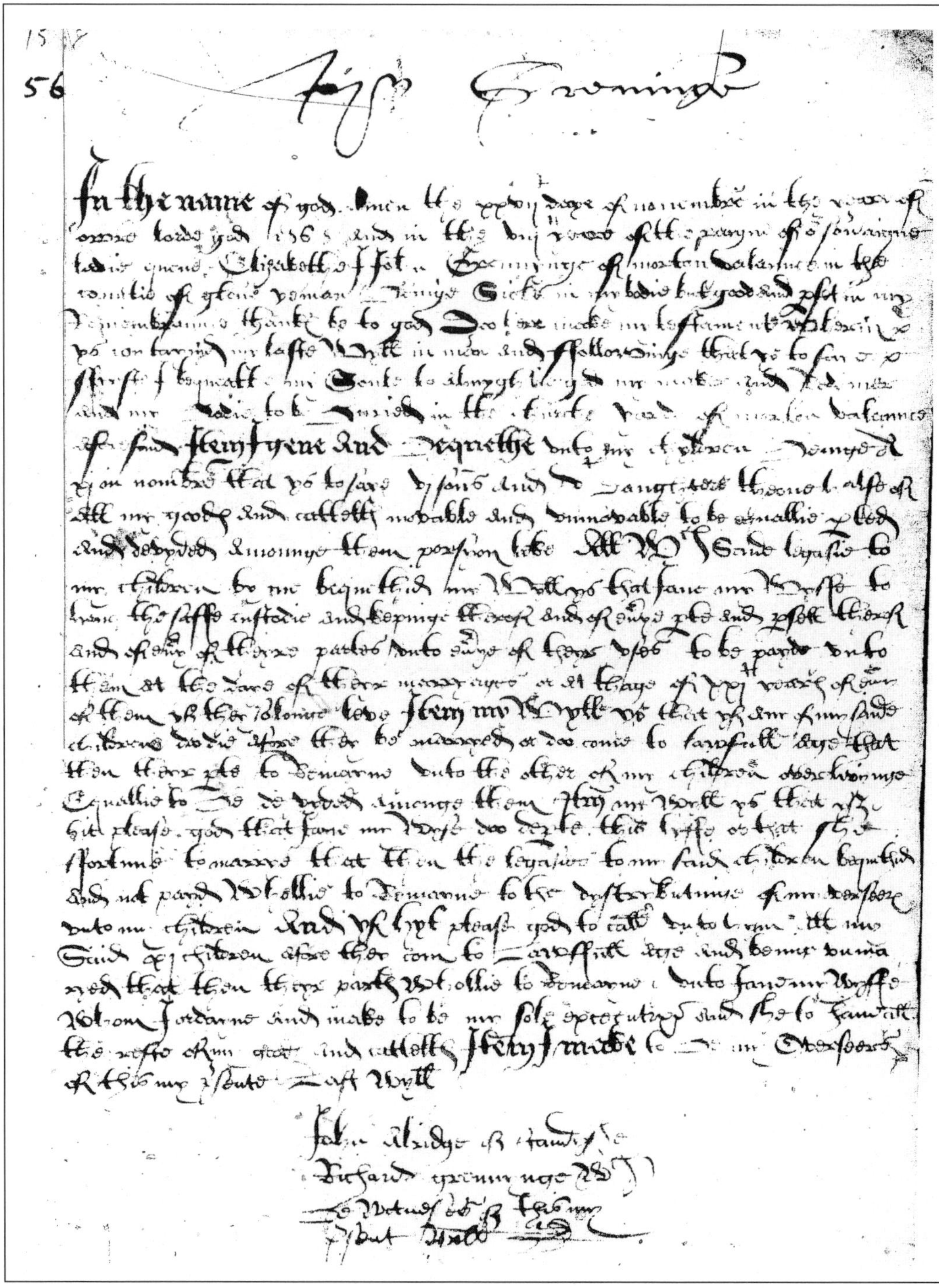

Will of John Greening (dated 27 November 1565)

CHAPTER THREE

✦

Fretherne is a small village, directly opposite Awre, on the east side of the River Severn and less than a mile from Saul. Unlike Awre, where the land bordering the river is flat and subject to flooding, the riverbank at Fretherne is precipitously high with Fretherne Cliff rising sixty feet above river level. The village is believed to have been the birthplace of 'Fair Rosamund', the fabled beauty who became the mistress of King Henry II in the twelfth century. Her family – the Cliffords – were at one time the lords of the manor here.

It was in St Mary's church at Fretherne that Nathaniel Greening and his wife Elizabeth had their son Benjamin baptised on 19 July 1756. Birth dates were not usually recorded at this time but we know that Benjamin had been born ten days earlier, on the ninth of July, because 95 years later he wrote a dated letter on his birthday anniversary. Nathaniel had married his wife Elizabeth Cowley at her home village of Frocester, about five miles from Fretherne, on 1 April 1749. The parish register entry records that he came from Saul, but that would indicate where he lived at the time of his marriage not where he was born. There is no baptism entry for him in the parish registers for Saul or in the registers of the other villages in the area. However there are three entries in the church records of All Saints at Bisley, now a Gloucestershire village but then a small market town, about ten miles east from Saul. These three facts can be woven into a feasible story, which is later confirmed by a quite different archive.

In January 1708 the Bisley Parish Register documents the baptism of Mary Moss, daughter of Thomas Moss. On the fifth of February 1723 the same register records the baptism of Nathaniel Greening, son of Nathaniel, with no mother's name given. Three months later, on the second of May, a further entry informs us of the marriage of Nathaniel Greening and Mary Moss. As there are no records of any Greening family living in Bisley, a fair interpretation of these facts is as follows. Nathaniel(1702) – who we met in Chapter One – had a relationship with Mary Moss, who was probably a servant girl (most young girls were) living-in and working at a farm or country estate either in the Saul area or somewhere else nearer her birthplace. Mary became pregnant and returned to her parents' home where the baby was born. Nathaniel, who was not yet 21, acknowledged that he was the father of the child and agreed to marry Mary. However, as it was normal for infants to be baptised shortly after birth, baby Nathaniel(1723) was baptised at Bisley with his natural father's surname. Nathaniel(1702) and Mary were then married three months later in the same church. Mary was very young, aged only fifteen if her baptism followed shortly after her birth, but marriage at fifteen was legal and not uncommon in the early eighteenth century. Also relevant are two entries in the parish records of Stroud, which was the main market town in this area of Gloucestershire and is situated between Saul and Bisley (it is in the Bisley 'Hundred'). This shows the baptisms, on 29 November 1730 of Thomas Greening (*Tho Grinning*) and on 3 April 1777 of Mary Greening. No mother's name is given in the church register for either entry, but the name of the father was Nathaniel.

The separate archive that ties all this together is an 'Overseers of the Poor' Removal Order dated 3 March 1739. This informs us that Nathaniel Greening, his wife Mary and children Thomas, aged 9, and Mary, aged 7, were to be 'removed' from the parish of Longney(just north of Saul) to the parish of Saul. This implies that Nathaniel(1702) – for it was certainly he – had become a pauper. He had found himself unable to support his family and had or was about to become reliant on parish relief. The English 'welfare state' had been in place since the days of Queen Elizabeth in the sixteenth century but, by necessity, it had to be administered on strictly parish lines. If a person or a family became in need of assistance from the community, the parish where the person or the father had been born (or was 'legally settled') could only normally provide this. In Nathaniel's case this was Saul, rather than the neighbouring parish of Longney – where he had probably moved to seek assistance from one of his brothers. Two Overseers of the Poor were usually appointed for each parish. Often one of them would be the Rector or a local Justice of the Peace – who in some cases was the same man.

We do not know the circumstances that led Nathaniel to this low point. Many people at that time were constantly in and out of poverty, in need of parish help at some stage in their lives, but Nathaniel had started out with advantages. This was the same man who, as firstborn, had been given *ye first choice* of his successful father's holdings to pick for his inheritance. We do not know if he had been unlucky or was just a feckless man. I wonder if he told his dying father, in the spring of 1722, that he was courting Mary Moss – who was to give birth to his child nine months later.

I am not identifying Benjamin with the year of his birth (in brackets), but retaining the title "Old

Ben" – the name I gave him in my first book. I used this sobriquet because not only did he become a Greening patriarchal figure, living until he was nearly 98 and having around one hundred and fifty descendants while he was still alive, but he was also the first of a long line of Benjamins. One of his sons, five grandsons and numerous great-grandsons were named after him.

Although we can conjure up mental images of Nathaniel(1679), Old Ben's great-grandfather and, to some extent, of his grandfather Nathaniel(1702), we have no personal information about his father – Nathaniel(1723). He was not mentioned in the Removal Order as he had reached the age of sixteen. He had become independent and was most likely working as a live-in farm servant, possibly for an uncle or possibly at a farm in the Stroud area – where he may have spent some of his childhood. Frocester, where his wife Elizabeth was born in 1723, is not far from Stroud. Before his marriage Nathaniel was certainly in Saul where, it is likely, his parents and his brother and sister were still living. After his marriage, he and Elizabeth moved to the adjoining parish of Fretherne where all their children were christened. Ben had two older sisters, Sarah (bap 1750) and Grace (bap 1751), a younger sister Elizabeth (bap 1761) and two younger brothers – Daniel (bap 1758) and Samuel (bap 1763). We do not know Nathaniel's occupation. Like most men he was probably an agricultural labourer, but it is a possibility that either he or his brother Thomas had been apprenticed to a carpenter. The Overseers of the Poor could have arranged this. This is pure speculation on my part but as Old Ben became a cabinetmaker, it seems likely that he may have learnt the skills of working with wood from his father or his uncle. He almost certainly lived with his uncle at one stage of his life.

Although we do not know anything about his childhood situation we do have a lot of information about Ben's later life. He was the main 'character' in my previous book, as luckily a fair number of the letters he wrote during his long span have been preserved for posterity and we are able to build up a picture of him as a man. He also left a number of his creations behind; Benjamin became the first of a long line of Clockmakers. I am fortunate to have one of his long-case clocks, which he will have made in the 1790s, in my home in Shrewsbury, England.

In Benjamin's day most country clockmakers were really cabinetmakers. They built the clock case and then fitted in a mechanism that they had purchased from the maker, usually in business in a nearby town or city. The mechanisms would be personalised by engraving the cabinetmaker's name on the face of the clock. Old Ben was a clockmaker who fitted into this category. He will, of course, have become familiar with the mechanisms and been able to repair clocks for customers as well as assemble them. Three of Ben's sons followed him in the clock-making trade and then many of their sons and grandsons after them. By this time most of them will have served out apprenticeships, with established mechanism manufacturers, and become complete master clock, watch and instrument makers themselves. These multiplying businesses had also migrated to more profitable locations. Old Ben's grandsons were not only trading in Gloucestershire and Wales, but in Bristol, London and Australia.

The Worshipful Company of Clockmakers, which has its headquarters in London's famous Guildhall, is the oldest surviving horological guild in the world. It is a London 'Livery Company' and was founded under a Royal Charter by King Charles I. The head officer of The Company is the Master, who is elected annually. Although this is a figurehead roll he is, in theory, the senior clockmaker of the City of London. Since 1631, when The Company was founded, many famous men have held this appointment. The list includes Thomas Tompian, *The Father of English Clockmakers*, George Graham – the mentor of John Harrison, the man who solved the Longitude problem, a number of Astronomers Royal and some Lord Mayors of London. In 1933 Benjamin Thomas Greening was elected to the prestigious office of Master. He was the grandson of Charles, Old Ben's second son.

Frampton-on-Severn is a fairly large village a couple of miles south of Fretherne, Saul and Wheatenhurst. In the 1770s, when Old Ben went to live there, it was a small market town and the destination of stagecoaches leaving the King's Head Inn in the City of London each Wednesday and Saturday. Frampton today is a most attractive place with many period houses and an extremely large village green (at 22 acres reputed to be the largest in England). One side of the green is dominated by Frampton Court, one time the seat of the Clifford family but in the mid-eighteenth century, the home of Richard Cluterbuck – who had rebuilt the mansion with his fortune after a successful business career in Bristol.

Cluterbuck was a common surname in Gloucestershire. A few years before Ben, his uncle Thomas had moved to Frampton with his Cluterbuck wife Hester – whom he had married at her home village of Wheatenhurst on 12 March 1749. Old Ben also married a Cluterbuck, she was Ann and their marriage took place at Saul parish church on 6 December 1779. In my previous book I speculated that Hester might have been Ann's aunt, with a little more research, this looks probable. Ann was certainly baptised at Wheatenhurst in October 1756 (she was the same age as her husband). Her father Thomas was likely to have been a half-brother to Hester as the father of both of them was named Samuel Cluterbuck. This gives us the scenario that Ben and Ann were living with their respective uncle and aunt before their marriage. Ben must have been apprenticed to a cabinetmaker at this time and that could have been Thomas. Ann was certainly expecting her first baby before her marriage, as infant Nathaniel (grandfather's name again) was baptised at St Mary's parish church in Frampton on 7 May 1780. There is another connection between Ben and his uncle. They both became non-conformists. The earlier children of both men were baptised in Frampton Parish Church and the younger ones in the dissenters' chapel. Much later in his life, Old Ben was to become a fiery free-church preacher (his letters are studded with sermons). My suggestion that this may have been sparked by Roland Hill the famous evangelical preacher, who spoke at the opening service of Frampton Congregational Chapel when Ben was twenty years old, is a plausible one.

I was interested to find Old Ben's uncle's name, among four hundred others, printed in the opening pages of a book of poetry published in 1782. Thomas Greening of Frampton was one of the subscribers who had ordered and prepaid for a copy of the book, *A Miscellany of Rhimes*, so was possibly an acquaintance of the publisher – R. Raikes of Gloucester. The name of this gentleman, one of that city's most famous sons whose statue graces the local park (as well as the Victoria Embankment in London), immediately clicked in my mind – from schoolboy history lessons. Robert Raikes the founder of Sunday Schools. This epithet, for me and I'm sure for many others, put this great philanthropist in entirely the wrong slot where he remained until I researched this connection. Raikes did not start the rather (lower) middle-class, Sunday afternoon, Bible story sessions for children that I remembered from my early days. He was the proprietor and editor of one of England's first provincial newspapers, *The Gloucester Journal*, which had been started by his father. He was also much concerned with prison reform. When visiting the illiterate prisoners in Gloucester Jail he realised that the sad state of their lives was entirely the result of deprivation as children. The gangs of ragged ill-fed boys and girls he saw roaming the poorer streets of Gloucester on Sundays, were not there from Monday to Saturday. They were working (mostly in the pin making industry) six days a week for very long hours. They had never had any of the childhood he had known and no education whatsoever. Raikes rented rooms and employed suitable teachers, from his own pocket, to teach these children to read and write (possibly Bible stories too). No child, however ragged, was to be turned away. There were others of course, at this time, also involved in this social change. Robert, as a newspaper owner, was the publicist and most well known. Perhaps the history books should be altered. Raikes should not be described as the founder of Sunday Schools but the founder of Schools – on Sundays?

A descendent of Robert Raikes makes an appearance later in this book. One of Robert's granddaughters was Julia Maria, the daughter of the Rev Robert Napier Raikes who was the Rector of Longhope in the Forest of Dean (my father was offered this parish in 1945 when he was demobilised after serving as an Army Chaplain during the Second World War). Julia married Henry Roberts (later a Major-General in the Indian Army) and their only child was Caroline Ann (Alice) who became the wife of Edward Elgar.

After Nathaniel (1780), Old Ben and Ann had five more sons and four daughters. All were born in Frampton-on-Severn. There is no record of a baptism for Priscilla (i), the original eldest daughter. She died as a baby and her burial is shown in the records of Frampton Brethren Congregational Chapel on 4 January 1791. Hester was baptised in 1794, Priscilla (ii) on 25 April 1798 (her birth is also recorded in the chapel books as 15 February – which shows that not all children were baptised within days of their birth) and Maria in 1800. The sons, after Nathaniel, were Charles (bap 3 February 1782), Daniel (bap 28 November 1784), Benjamin (bap18 March 1787), Joseph (bap 26 December 1791) and William (1796). I have found no entries recording the burial of the two youngest children; William and Maria, so this was unlikely to have taken place in Frampton. As neither of these two appear in later records we must assume they died in early childhood. This book follows the lives of the seven remaining children.

Fromebridge Mill is just off the Gloucester to Bristol main road and near the M5 motorway. It is in the old parish of Wheatenhurst (now Whitminster), a mile from Frampton and just south of Moreton Valence. It was a working mill and water powered from the River Frome until quite recently – and has had many incarnations since before the days of the Doomsday Book, in which it featured (there has been a mill here for a thousand years!). It is still very much in use today. Now, only ten or fifteen minutes from Gloucester by car, it is usually packed with people in its new roll as a large and popular pub/restaurant.

Corn was ground at Fromebridge in the first half of the eighteenth century but, in the 1760s, a brazier named Joseph Fairthorne purchased the property. He converted it into a brass works and wire mill. The production of 'Hand-cards' was one of the main uses for wire at that time. Carding – usually carried out by children – was the first stage in the production of cloth, which after farming was the most important occupation in Britain before the industrial revolution. Hand-cards were wooden 'bats', a little larger than a table-tennis bat but square. They were covered in leather in which wire hooks had been set in rows. The wool or cotton fibres were combed between the spikes then scraped off in rolls (cardings), which could then be spun into a continuous thread ready to be woven into cloth.

By the late 1770s Fromebridge was one of the largest wire mills in the country and, although we have no documentary proof of this, I think it fairly certain that this is where Old Ben's eldest son – young Nathaniel (1780) – went to work from a very early age. We know he moved from Frampton, when he was about 17 or 18, to work at another wire works at Tintern – on the River Wye just north of Chepstow – where he was regarded as a skilled worker. Possibly 'The Fromebridge Company' had some connection with Tintern or perhaps Nathaniel had been offered a better job at the wire mill which, established in the sixteenth century, was probably the earliest wiredrawing works in Britain.

Around the time that Nathaniel moved to Tintern, Old Ben and the rest of his family moved to Chepstow. The town of Chepstow, only just over the Gloucestershire border, was at that time the largest port in South Wales. It was a very busy shipbuilding centre, a growing and thriving commercial hub with far more opportunities for a clockmaker than Frampton-on-Severn.

Nathaniel could not have worked at Tintern long because a newspaper article, written many years later, informs us that at the age of nineteen he was persuaded by a copper-smelter called Captain Ainsworth to move to Warrington in Lancashire. The captain wanted his expertise to help set up a copper wiredrawing works. When Nathaniel arrived at Warrington, Ainsworth had either gone bankrupt or his financial backers had not materialised. Nathaniel decided not to return to Gloucestershire and, presumably after persuading someone to lend him some money (perhaps the captain's bankers?), managed to set up in the wire trade on his own. He started his business in small premises near the Lion Hotel in Bridge Street. This was in 1799 and Nathaniel had not yet reached his twentieth birthday.

Nathaniel could see that there was a demand for woven wire, but the manufacture of screens, sieves and wire cloth was a slow and laborious process so he designed and developed a handloom that made this production much faster. These were the early days of industry and, seeing the potential of the steam engine, Nathaniel then had his hand-weaving machine converted into a steam-powered loom. He was an innovative man and his was the first steam driven wire-weaving machine in the world.

When Nathaniel died in 1852, the business he had created had an international reputation and had won gold medals at exhibitions in America, Paris and London. By the 1870s, when his sons were running the company, Nathaniel's firm was selling its products in Asia, South Africa and South America as well as the United States and Europe. 'N Greening and Sons' was described as *by far the largest and best known makers of wire-screening in the world*.

Many people's favourite British bird, and certainly one of mine, is the Red Kite. It is a medium sized bird of prey with a very distinctive outline, swept back wings and a long forked tail. It is a beautiful bird to watch in flight and it does 'hang' in the air as though it were at the end of a fine thread. For much of the last hundred years and until quite recently it was one of Britain's most rare birds, but this was not always the case. In the eighteenth century it was widespread and – as a scavenger – it was a common sight even in the centre of London, much in the same way as its cousin the Black Kite hangs around African and Asian towns and cities today. Improvements in our western way of life and persecution had almost brought the species to extinction in Britain by the 1950s. The remaining native kite population had declined to probably less than half a dozen pairs, living in a remote area of Mid-Wales. Bird protection societies moved in, nests were guarded round the clock by units of the Territorial Army and gradually the bird began to re-establish itself. Fifty years later this is hailed a big conservation success story. There are now hundreds of kites in Mid-Wales (they stick mainly to their 'home' area – although one is occasionally seen flying over the border counties, like Shropshire where I live) and they have become a big tourist attraction to the region. A number of feeding centres have sprung up and the image of the bird appears as a logo on almost everything in central Wales from hotel brochures to direction signs and confectionary wrappers. Red Kites have also been re-introduced to a few other areas of Britain (rather than depleting the Welsh population the immigrants have been brought from Norway). Rather strangely – if you want to see a Red Kite today – the best place for a certain sighting, as long as it's not raining, is over the busy M40 motorway twenty minutes drive north from Heathrow Airport.

In January 1817 Old Ben wrote a letter to Nathaniel, from the Forest of Dean, shortly after returning home from a visit to see his eldest son in Warrington. It starts:

> Dear son, have herewith sent you a kite. Ever since I came from you I have been trying to get one but could not. I made applications to several of the keepers to shoot one, but they has never done it, but this Day some boys found one in a tree and knoc'd it Down and Catch'd it alive, and I not knowing how to skin it, I thought it best to send it alive, which I expect it will lieve till it comes to you, which I hope it will. You wanted me to get a Nighting Gale and Nest but that I cannot get.

Old Ben then continues with a wonderful description of the dire state of the rural economy in the second decade of the nineteenth century:

> Our country is in a melancholy state, all trades is very Dead, Labour of all kind is so scarse, that great numbers of Labourers are out of Employ. The Parrishes are over burthen'd with the Poor, the work houses are throng'd, wheat is a guinea a bushel, no money to be had for the little work that is done. Tradesmen are failing, many are Bankrup'd, numbers gone Theiving, and stealing others Property, some house-breaking etc., in short, the Lawyers and Magistrates has got the greatest Trade that is going. …

Old Ben had turned sixty and he was more interested in spiritual than material matters. Most of the rest of the letter consists of a sermon about the need for repentance and ends:

> Please to let know how you are going on in your Business in these Critickle times, and how your Museum do answer. I am afraid that will do you no good but let be how it may in your temporal affairs. I hope you do not neglect seeking for the one thing that is needfill, the salvation of your soul; time is short, and you and I have a great deal of work to do, thus I beg you work wile it is Day for the Night (of Death) comeith when no man can work.

Nathaniel had brought his father north to Warrington, to see his factory and how well he had prospered, to meet his second wife and also to inspect his new big interest in life – his growing natural history collection. Nathaniel, now on his way to becoming a wealthy industrialist, had time on his hands and like other successful entrepreneurs of this period was fascinated by the sciences and the world around him. Nathaniel features in a book about Warrington, written by William Beaumont and published in the 1880s – *The late Nathaniel Greening, a well-informed, ingenious person, was the first to bring before his fellow townsmen an exhibition calculated to create, more especially among the young people of the town, a love for the study of natural history, in which he was himself a proficient. To give effect to his object, Mr Greening built a very large and handsome room, which he filled with the beautiful objects of natural history, birds, beasts, fishes and insects, all well placed, exhibited, and arranged in cases, over which the student might see and admire the wonders of creation …* Nathaniel's hobby formed the starting collection of the Warrington Natural History Society, which had its inaugural meeting in 1838. Two of the founders were Nathaniel's sons, Benjamin and Timothy. Timothy was appointed the society's librarian. Years later the society's exhibits were handed over to the municipal authority and today Warrington has an excellent Natural History section in its Public Museum and Library.

A few years ago I asked the museum conservator if, somewhere in his stores, he still possessed a very old and – I presumed – rather moth-eaten stuffed Red Kite. I was assured that such an exhibit (if there had been one) could not have survived for nearly two hundred years. He told me that the oldest bird specimen in his possession then, not on general display but occasionally used by him in lectures on early taxidermy, was a House Sparrow that had been donated to the museum by an elderly Warrington lady in 1925. This lady was Mary (born 1855) the spinster daughter of John Greening, who had 'preserved' the bird on 27 March 1854, and the sister of Nathaniel 'the second' who features in a later chapter. John, who was born in 1823, had been the first Chairman of 'N Greening and Sons Ltd' and was Nathaniel the entrepreneur's youngest but one son.

Nathaniel Greening (1780)
Old Ben's eldest son. Industrial Revolution entrepreneur who built the world's first
steam-driven wire-weaving machine
(drawing by Mercedes Waters, from a 'magic-lantern' slide)

Benjamin Greening (1807)
Nathaniel's son. Grandson of Old Ben.
Wire manufacturer in England and Canada

CHAPTER FOUR

✜

The land of Wales, to the west of England, has peninsulas jutting into the Irish Sea at both its north and south extremities – creating wide Cardigan bay between them. Situated approximately half way down the bay is the coastal resort of Aberystwyth, which, although only a fairly small town, is generally regarded as the cultural capital of the province. It is home to the main campus of the University of Wales and the National Library – the joint custodians of the Welsh language and protectors of the country's separate Celtic identity.

Just inland from Aberystwyth the land rises to the Cambrian Mountain peak of Plynlimon. It is on the east facing slopes of this mountain that the two main Welsh-English rivers have their sources. Although their springs are less than half a mile apart and they both end up in the same place, they initially flow in different directions. The longer river, the 219 mile Severn, runs north-east making a large arc through mid-Wales and English Shropshire before it turns south (just after passing through the county town of Shrewsbury – in which I have spent much of my life) flowing through Worcestershire and then Gloucestershire where it reaches the wide estuary that has already been described in Chapter One. The shorter river of 157 miles, the Wye – arguably the most beautiful waterway in Britain, runs south-east through mid-Wales then meanders through English Herefordshire before turning south, where it forms the border between the two countries represented by Monmouthshire (now part of Gwent) and Gloucestershire. At the border town of Chepstow, famed for its early stone castle, the Wye becomes the last main tributary of the Severn at the larger river's mouth.

Twenty-five miles or so before they meet, the two rivers are running almost parallel and about a dozen miles apart. They then gradually draw together enclosing a rather unique wedge shaped containment of land between them. Much of this territory is covered by one of England's remaining ancient forests and, if we walk through it, we can go back in time as almost all of

England was once like this. The Royal Forest of Dean still boasts 27,000 acres of woodland and is home to a number of small towns and villages, many of which were coalmining communities between fifty and two hundred years ago. Before coal, iron ore was mined here. At that time the forest ceiling would have been broken everywhere by plumes of smoke from the fires of charcoal burners, producing the commodity needed to turn the ore into ironware. The forest itself was the region's main commercial asset; it provided much of the timber for England's wooden Navy. The Spanish had plans to send secret agents to burn it down. This never happened and Drake's fleet of Dean-timbered ships, helped by the winds, destroyed that invaders Armada.

Trees do not cover all of the area. A strip between the woods and the Severn is farming country with grazing animals, crops and orchards. It is here that the village of Awre is situated. There is also farmland just to the east of the Wye and to the northwest of the Royal Forest, where Herefordshire joins Gloucestershire. This is the location of small farms in a most attractive setting of low hills and rounded valleys. One of these was a tiny farm or smallholding called Handley. This was at the end of a narrow lane nearly half a mile from a cluster of properties known as Pontshill, itself an outlying hamlet of the main village of Weston-under-Penyard.

Two hundred years ago Handley was a holding of just over four acres, it lay inside Herefordshire – but only just. One of the property boundaries, and the lane that joins it to the hamlet, was right on the Gloucestershire border (see plan reproduced at the end of this chapter). It was at Handley that John Greening (1815), his two sisters and his brother were born.

Today Handley is a most attractive 'up market' residence set in landscaped gardens which, if put up for sale, would command a very high price for its individual charm and very private location. The attached barn and the tiny cottage, where the Greenings lived, are still there – but they have been converted and extended in all directions. The family of one hundred and eighty years ago would now have great difficulty in recognising their old home. The long muddy lane they travelled by horse and cart is now a long tarmac drive and the hamlet at the end has evolved into a small village, with modern houses inhabited by commuters from the nearby towns. Everything has not changed. The views from Handley will have altered little; the magic panorama of rolling farmland, fields, hedges, copses and – in the distance – the escarpment topped edge of The Forest remain as delightful to the eyes of those who live there now, as I believe they were to the family who lived there then.

John's father Joseph married Esther Apperley (first name sometimes written Hester), the daughter of a wheelwright, at Esther's home village of Westbury-on-Severn on the twenty-sixth of May 1806.

Westbury is two miles north of the small market town of Newnham, and so about four miles north of Awre. Handley is only seven miles – as a crow flies – to the west of Westbury but, as it is on the other side of the forest, the twisting road of eleven or twelve miles would have been a two hour journey by pony and trap.

We do not know if the newlyweds moved to this smallholding straight after their wedding or a little later. There were Apperleys farming in this area of Herefordshire, if they were related to Esther, this may have been the reason for the couple finding this rather remote miniature farm. The Greenings were certainly there in 1808 when their first child Elizabeth was born. I think it most probable that Joseph was a tenant at Handley, but he may have been able to purchase the freehold. Years later, Elizabeth and her sister were to have carved on their father's headstone the words *LATE OF HANDLEY, IN THE PARISH OF WESTON, HEREFORDSHIRE*. This indicates to me that their father had been a proud man, he had been a farmer in his own right. Handley had been the highpoint of his life and, for some period, he may therefore have been its owner.

At four acres and twenty perches, the smallholding was really too small to be a viable concern. There was a small field of about two acres, an even smaller pasture, a little orchard and the tiny cottage and barn. I would guess that Joseph eked out a partial living with raising and selling a few livestock plus whatever he was able to produce from his orchard and could grow in his garden. He then supplemented this by working for larger farmers – especially at planting and harvest time. An Acre is 160 perches, strictly speaking 40 perches long and 4 perches wide. The perch being both a measure of length (sixteen and a half feet) and area.

In 1794 a gentleman named John Clark published "A General View of the Agriculture" of this part of England. He wrote *The County of Herefordshire is equalled by few spots in the island of Great Britain for the production of every article that can contribute to the comfort, the happiness and, in some degree, the luxury of Society.*

This grandiose statement had little relation to the harsh realities of agricultural life at that time. However the early years of the new century were better ones. The price of produce had increased and consequently agricultural wages were rising (that equation was more probably the other way round).

Another "General View" of farming in Herefordshire was written by John Duncumb, "Secretary to the Agricultural Society of that Province", in 1805. He informs us that *The price of labour is seven shillings weekly in summer with liquor and two dinners. In winter six shillings with similar privileges.*

This was for casual workers hired by the day or week. The wage tariff for 'servants' employed by the year was as follows.

Waggoners	*10–12*	*Guineas*
Bailiffs or Cattlemen	*8–10*	"
Dairy Maids	*6–7*	"
Under Maids	*2–3*	"

This was an improvement from John Clark's time, 11 years earlier, when day labourers earned *6 shillings a week in Summer with a Gallon of drink for each man, 5 shillings a week in winter with 3 quarts of drink. In Harvest 14 pence a day with meat and drink. Women 6 pence a day with 2 quarts of drink all year except harvest, when they also have meat.*

Annual wages in 1794 (from May-day hiring) had been

Men	*6–9*	*Guineas*
Women	*3–4*	"
Boys	*2–3*	"

[Note for American readers. A Guinea was one pound and one shilling or 21 shillings]
The farm labourers' hours of work had not changed, they were still –

In Harvest	–	*as early and as late as they can see*
In Winter	–	*from light to dark*
In Summer	–	*from 6 to 6*

We do not know if Esther suffered miscarriages but, unlike most families at that time, there was a large gap between all her children. Elizabeth was seven before her brother John was born. He was baptised at Weston Parish Church on 10 September 1815. It was then another seven years before Ann arrived, she was christened at the church in Hope Mansell, a village the other side of Handley, so the family may have changed their religious allegiances. The youngest child, William, was born in 1827 but he died before his second birthday.

In the lean years the family will have had few comforts, but there were good years too when some luxuries might be afforded. They were self-sufficient and there was always food on the table and logs to keep them warm in the winter. Although the children would have only received their formal education in the village school at Weston, Joseph and Esther were intelligent parents who encouraged their offspring and passed on the wisdom and knowledge that they had gained in their own lives. The home was a happy one – there were books, discussions, music and poetry, as well as the tasks and chores of a smallholding in which they will have all shared. The children also developed a deep love of nature and the countryside. The girls would have been engaged in needlework with Esther and John would have received tuition in farming from Joseph. Many years later John, in a reflective mood after hearing of his father's death and in a distant place, would write … *I have my Father there, consulting with me, how to manage the cattle and crops – but I question and answer myself now, for he don't speak to me as he used to when I knew he was alive.* Ann's childhood can also be imagined from remarks made by her own eldest daughter Lucy – years later still. She described her mother as being *truly one of Nature's gentlewomen* and wrote of her *unmistakable air of good breeding.* The Greening family at Handley were undoubtedly financially hard up but, as later events show, they were rich in spirit and enterprise.

Joseph had been born in Elmore in early 1780 (baptised 6 February) and had two brothers and two sisters who reached adulthood. His father was a William Greening who had also been baptised here in 1737. Elmore is a rather scattered village, dominated by a large Elizabethan house – Elmore Court (for hundreds of years and still today the ancestral home of the titled Guise family). It is on the east side of the River Severn, three miles or so north of Epney and Moreton Valence and a few miles southwest of Gloucester city.

I have not been able to find out many facts about William (1737). He married Martha Salcomb at Elmore in July 1765 and was possibly a tenant farmer, but may have owned his own land. He certainly had a younger brother Zechariah, who described himself as a yeoman, and they were both almost certainly the sons of a man who had owned land at one time. This was Joseph (1708) who has already been mentioned in Chapter One, as one of the five sons of Nathaniel (1679) and a younger brother of Nathaniel (1702) whose descendants we also follow in this book. Joseph (1708) married Mary Bodnam at Elmore on 2 October 1733, but we know little about him except that he had at least four sons, one of which died in infancy, and at least one daughter – Mary. He certainly inherited some land or property from his father, but we are unable to tell if he retained this or if he was a successful farmer or not. As he does not appear to have left a will this may show he had little to leave. He died in 1779 and was buried at Elmore but there is no tombstone to mark his resting place. This is another indication that his family were not very prosperous at that date.

At this point in the book, I should explain that I have done my utmost not to go off in too many tangents. Joseph (1708) and his son William (1737) both had a number of siblings and I do hold some information about some of them. However, if I try to write about too many lives we would end up with so many Greenings (many with the same first names) that the book would be in danger of being flung through a window. So, other than Joseph's brother Nathaniel, I will only write here about William's brother Zechariah – who is also in this story. The other brothers and sisters of both men I must leave to others to research and write about.

Zechariah was an unusual Greening Christian name (he was not the only one, there were a number of others in another village) and he is the ancestor of quite a number of present day descendents who are in touch with me. These include at least four in Britain, two in Canada, two in the USA and – rather intriguingly – one lady in Australia who will feature later in another chapter. Zechariah was born in 1744 and married Jane Boughton at Hardwick, her home village – between Elmore and Moreton Valence, on 5 April 1774. Jane had a younger sister Elizabeth, who also married a Greening at Hardwick six years later. This was John, who was most probably the son of Thomas and Hester (Clutterbuck) baptised at Wheatenhurst in June 1750 – and so a grandson of Nathaniel (1702) who first appears in Chapter One.

Like his father we have few facts about Zechariah's life, but we do know that it was a long one and that he suffered poor health for some time in the later part of it. His and his wife's tombstone can be found in Elmore churchyard today (For some unknown reason, the parish church of St John the Baptist is about a mile away from the main part of the village). Underneath the inscription *In Memory of ZECHARIAH GREENING of this parish who died March 12th 1831 Aged 87 Years* there is a little verse:

> Afflictions sore, long time I bore
> All human health was vain
> Till God did please, death should me seize
> And ease me of my pain

A few years later the stonemason added: *Also in memory of JANE The Wife of Zechariah Greening who died November 12th 1838 Aged 84 Years* – with her own verse:

> Engrave no flattery on my stone
> Man is by nature lost
> Salvation is by Christ alone
> Of what have we to boast

The gravestone also records *JOSEPH the Son of Zechariah and Jane Greening who died in infancy*. I will write about some of Zechariah's other descendents in a later chapter.

Within a year or two of the burial of twenty-one month old William at Weston, the family at Handley started to experience severe difficulties. We do not know exactly what happened to them individually but, after the good harvest of 1827, agricultural communities throughout the midlands and southern England entered a prolonged period of deep recession. The harvest of 1829 was particularly poor and this was followed by an extremely harsh winter – with snow arriving in October. Many farm labourers were unemployed and there was a big increase in crime. There was another poor harvest in 1830 and rural unrest gained momentum. That year saw the start of the 'Swing' riots, triggered partly by a reduction in poor relief and aggravated by the introduction of new farm technology – like the threshing machine. Many small farmers went bankrupt or were forced to give up their tenanted holdings. Joseph may have been one of these.

We do not know the date but it was probably in 1833 or early 1834 that the family left Handley and moved to a cottage in the village of Claines, just north of Worcester. By mid-1834 Elizabeth was twenty-six and Ann twelve. John, now nearly nineteen, was learning a trade. He was to become a boot-maker. On 16 June 1834 Elizabeth married Francis Simmons at St Swithin's church in Worcester. Mr Simmons had taken over the tenancy of an inn in the centre of the city, the Shades Tavern, which he ran with his new bride. Probably within a year Ann had joined them as a general help. It was some years later, while working for her brother-in-law and sister, that she became friendly with a lodger at the inn – who was destined to become her husband.

On 4 April 1841 John, now twenty-five, married Maria Kelley at Claines parish church. Maria had lived in Worcester all of her twenty-three years. As a young boy John had dreams of becoming a farmer but at least, as a boot and shoemaker, he was able to earn a steady if meagre living to support his young wife. Although working in a small city like Worcester was much easier than life in a rural village, times were still bad. These were the early years of the Industrial Revolution and workingmen were at the mercy of rapidly changing market forces. If you were unable to support yourself the only option was the workhouse. Within four years John and Maria had three more mouths to feed. James (Jim) was born on 31 December 1841 and baptised two years later, at the same time as his baby sister Clara. Charles Francis (Charley) followed in April 1845. The economic situation for poor people in this country was not improving and Charley's birth year saw a catastrophe across the Irish Sea that exacerbated the unemployment situation throughout England, Wales and Scotland.

Since the turn of the century the population of Ireland had increased sharply and, as little industry

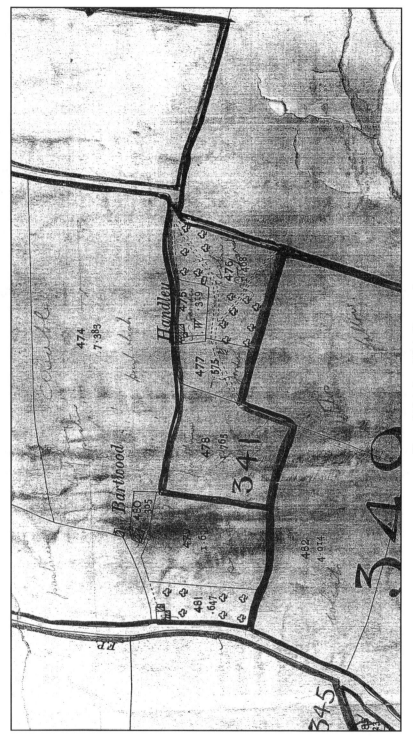

Plan of Handley (19th Century)

had been established there, the majority of the inhabitants worked in agriculture. Not only were these people among the poorest peasants in Europe, but their diet consisted almost entirely of only one commodity – the potato. When Potato Blight destroyed this single source of sustenance, as it did in 1845 and the years following, a high proportion of the population faced starvation. Hundreds of thousands, especially children and young people, died. Some starved but most succumbed to illnesses stoked by malnutrition. A slightly larger number escaped – many (perhaps the luckier ones) directly to America, the majority initially to mainland Britain. At this time the cost of a passage, from an Irish port to one on the mainland, was two old pence per person. This adds up to five pence – or a dime, of present day money, for a family of six adults (accompanied children travelled free). In some cases the fare was possibly all they owned. The effect here in England was that the already under-jobbed labour market was awash with people, who would work at anything for half pay and be prepared to live with their families in any 'dwelling' where at least the rain might be kept off their children's heads.

It was probably this last straw that persuaded John that, even if it meant leaving his ageing parents, his beloved sisters and all that was near and dear to him, if he was to have any proper life for Maria and himself – and if his three small children were to have any prospects for their futures – he would have to leave England.

As a postscript to this chapter it may be interesting to record a few Irish statistics, especially as Ireland now – in relation to its size – is one of the most economically successful countries in the world. Today, one hundred and sixty years after the start of the potato blight, the population is still less than half of what it was then. Approximately one million died during the famine years and, during that time and the half-century that followed, three and a half million people left its shores.

CHAPTER FIVE

✛

From the south, central Chepstow is still entered through an original gateway in a surviving section of its medieval wall. From this portal – High Street, Chepstow's main thoroughfare, runs downhill through the shopping area. Looking down from the arch, odd-numbered shops are on the left and even-numbered on the right. Therefore the first shop on the right at the top of the hill is number two. Although now a newer building, number two was occupied by the clockmaker Greenings for about one hundred and thirty years. Old Ben moved in around 1798 or 99 and one of his great great grandsons, William Jesse Greening, was still trading from here in the late 1920s. *TIME & TIDE WAIT FOR NO MAN*, a sign WJ's father had placed in the shop window – perhaps at the end of the nineteenth century, was still on display when the shop *GREENING Watch & Clockmakers* finally closed.

Old Ben's four sons, after Nathaniel, will have all been given an education in woodworking by their father from a very young age. Daniel, the third son, was to take his skills to the local shipyards. The other three followed their father into the clock making trade. Initially all of them may have helped their father in Chepstow, but within a few years Charles, the second son, had moved to Bristol where he was joined by Joseph his youngest brother. This left Benjamin, the fourth son, at number two High Street with his father.

At some date – possibly 1815 – the year before he made his trip to Warrington to see his eldest son – Old Ben, with his wife and almost certainly their two daughters, returned to live in Gloucestershire. Ben was in his sixties and, as his namesake son and family were filling the accommodation at High Street, he and Ann moved eleven miles north to the small mining town of Coleford in the parish of Newland. This was in the heart of the Forest of Dean. Ann was not well and Old Ben wished to spend more time preaching. He did, however, find himself a small business premises and set up trading again as a watch and clock maker. We know this because Ben's earliest surviving correspondence – starting with the Red Kite letter to Nathaniel, posted in 1817 – was written from Coleford. An entry in *PIGOTS 1830 Directory for Gloucestershire* lists among the Coleford traders, *Benjamin Greening Watchmaker*. In April 1815, eldest daughter Hester married Thomas Dowle at Newland parish church. In February 1818, nearly three years later and less than two weeks before her twentieth birthday, Ben and Ann's youngest child Priscilla married James Williams. As it was usual for a bride to be married in her own home parish and as Priscilla's wedding was at Goodrich in Herefordshire, over seven miles from Coleford, it may be that she was marrying against her father's wishes.

I have found no death or burial record for Ann, but she almost certainly died in 1821. Ben stayed on in Coleford/Newland for another twelve years. In 1833, in his late seventies, he returned to Chepstow where he lived with his son Benjamin (and Benjamin's widow after his death) until his own death in 1854. Nathaniel wrote to his father in November 1821. This correspondence has not survived but it was, almost certainly, a letter of condolence following his mother's death. Old Ben did not reply until the following spring but he made up for this with a very long letter. A lengthy section of this is an extended sermon, which I have omitted. The remainder of the letter, transcribed as it was written, follows.

> Dear Son & Dau<u>r</u>
> I rec<u>d</u>   yours of 17th Novr. With its conteree for which I return you Many Thanks, it came in a time acceptable. I should have rote before, but I waited for Benjamin to write as he told me he would (possibly Nathaniel's son Benjamin had attended his grandmother's funeral) and did intend to write in the same letter, but he has not sent it to me yet, so I would waite no longer.
>
> As you Requested me to answer your questions, as you first ask if I am in Debt. I am, I do owe more than 6 pounds now, besides what I have paid since your Mothers Death. The Lord only knows if I shall ever be able to pay it. Your next question is, what meanes I have to pay it. My answer to that is I have nothing but my Labour, which is only Jobbing and that is very fluctuating. Some times I have got pretty well enough, at other times it is very slack. Your last question is, do I get a living now. To that I answer, thro the goodness and Mercy of God to me, I can safely say that I do not want for food or raiment, and I do feel thankfull that I am here with Content and I am not running in debt. I have paid some of the old. As to your advice, at present I cannot comply with. You say it might be better if I was to have a man and his wife to live with me, which would be a great help towards the Rent, but where shall I find such that would make everything agreeable I know not

any. Besides they have or may have children, then I am sure I should be miserable. As I have gon thro a world of trouble in bringing up a large family, I am determined not to be troubled with children any more, unless I am obliged to it. I have the same woman with me now as I had and we do agree extremely well, for I do believe she is a Real Christian. She is a very Clean Decent woman, and she acts with a very good account. I find in her everything as a wife, but a wife; the which I can do without. If she is content, which I think she is, I am determined that nothing shall part us but Death or Providence, for I never enjoy'd so much Peace and Tranquillity in all my life as I have of late. The Lord knows how long I have to live but let my days be many or few; I hope to spend the remnant of them in Peace. I have to say that thro Much Mercy I am in health and, considering my age which is almost 66, I have not the least Infirmities what so ever. I have got the real use of my limbs as well as ever. I do sometimes think I am as active and nimble as ever. I am sometimes disorder'd in my Bowells with the wind, but on the whole I do enjoy a tolerable good state of health for which, I call on my soul and all my Ransom Powers to Praise the Lord for his manifold mercies bestowed upon unworthy me.

You say I gave you to understand in a former Letter that Benjamin (Nathaniel's brother in Chepstow) had commenced Preacher. He have for some years, which it appears not without effect, for he is highly esteem'd for his works sake.

I don't know if I ever said anything to you about myself. I have to say that I have been Preaching ocationly, but of late more constantly for about 14 years. I am out now almost every Sunday, some times I Preach twice and some times thrice on a Sunday, and some times I walk from 16 to 20 or more miles a day. Although my Constitution of Body is but weak, yet I can say the Lord doth support in this wonderful manner. I can say I am never better than when I am employed in this work. As I said in my last, you might not be surpris'd if you saw me in Warrington this summer, but as you have rote to me, and I hope you will again, so I relinquish the thought as it would take me a fortnight to come and Return. For if I did I must walk it, for I could not pay Coach. I have to say (as far as I know) the family are all nearly the same as when I wrote last, only Hetty have got another son. I have one thing to say before you (viz) I feel a great Desire to have a Gravestone to your Mother's Grave. I have ask'd the Price of one and to have a Neat Plain Stone it cost £2:2:0 (two guineas). I shall leave it to your Judgment, if you think well of it, I must ask your assistance or it cannot be done. Perhaps you will say you may never see it, which is most likely. If it can be acomplish'd I shall have this Epitaph on it.

> "Afflictions sore, long time, I bore,
>
> Physicians was in vain,
>
> Till God was Pleased Death should me seize
>
> And Ease me of my Pain."

(This is almost the same verse as the one on Zechariah Greening's tombstone in Elmore churchyard!)

She was afflicted more than 27 years. As it is in the Baptists Chapel yard, it will cost nothing to put it there only the man's work. If it were in the Church yard it would cost considerable …

There then follows a very long sermon (approximately 2,000 words) on the theme *"It would be better that the business of the world be neglected a little than the business of the soul"*. After which Old Ben continues:

Perhaps your wife may say I have not said any thing to her, but what I have ritten is to both. What I say unto you I say unto her – watch.

I should be very glad to see you once more, but it is very probable I never shall, unless you should have ocation to come on Business. I should very well like to come to you, but perhaps sircumstances on each parte will not permit, therefore I have wrote to you the longer, it may be the last time I may ever Rite as life is very uncertain, therefore I beg you will Rite soon and let me know what effect this will have on you and yours, and what you think about the stone for your mother. I have one thing to request of you (viz) not to read this once and then lay it aside. Read it again and again, very deliberately, consider well the Import of it. You will look for a letter I rote you 11 years ago last February. I hope you have not lost it. Put that and this together and when you read it think upon it as Legacy your Father sent you, for in future when I Rite I may not Rite so large, as I do Rite so slow, it takes me long time.

Hetty send her love to Mary, and she is glad to hear of her welfare. You must excues my failer in my Righting, as you may find I have left out words, you will put same in place as you do Read.

Coleford Apl. 18th 1822.

Hetty – Hester, Old Ben's eldest daughter, would have been living near her father in the Coleford/Newland district. We can picture her calling to see him frequently. Mary was Nathaniel's second wife and it seems likely that Hetty had either attended her eldest brother's wedding or been to stay with him and Mary in Warrington.

Nathaniel's first wife was Elizabeth Wild and the marriage took place at St Peter's Church in Liverpool on 13 February 1804 (over 150 years later the Beatles, John and Paul, first met at St Peter's Church fete!). Their eldest son George was born the same year, followed by Benjamin in 1807 and Ann in 1811. I am not sure who the first son was named after but the second was named after his grandfather. I have been unable to find any record of Elizabeth's death or burial but Nathaniel married his second wife, Mary Johnson, on 7 November 1814. This ceremony also took place in Liverpool but this time at St Mary's, Edge Hill. Mary bore eleven children, seven sons and four daughters but three of the sons died in childhood. The four surviving ones were Timothy (1816), Noah (1821), John (1823) and Nathaniel (1828). The daughters' names were Susanna, Mary, Sarah and Hannah. Susanna was given her mother's surname as a second name and, for some reason, two of the other girls were baptised with Cluterbuck as a middle name, their great-grandmother's maiden name.

Reading between the lines you can pick up a divide between the two half-families. Both George and Ben would have worked for their father when they were very young but went their own way as soon as they were able. George became an auctioneer and Ben started up on his own in the wire trade – in Warrington, in direct opposition to his father, until later moving his business to Manchester. I suspect that as a child and when his mother was alive he had been his father's favourite, but had become very unhappy when a stepmother and younger brothers arrived on the scene. When Nathaniel married for a second time he was in his mid thirties; the years of his early struggles were behind him. He was on his way to becoming a wealthy man. Mary Johnson probably had a middle class background, she wanted and he was able to afford a more expensive education for her sons than had been received by their half-brothers.

Much later in their lives, Benjamin and his half-brother Timothy were to emigrate from England and, with their wives and children, travel to Canada together. Although they had both been involved in the Warrington Natural History Society, they had never worked together. After their arrival in Canada, by chance they found themselves in business together. The partnership did not last long and they fell out severely, they had quite different personalities. Benjamin was strong minded, hard working and practical – much like his father. Timothy was more relaxed and enjoyed an easier life; he had been brought up as the son of a rich man. Benjamin never quite forgave his father; he had five sons but did not choose the name Nathaniel for any of them. We will hear more of Benjamin(1807) in a later chapter.

We now revert back to Chepstow where Benjamin (1787), Old Ben's fourth son, was running the shop at 2 High Street. Delving into family history can sometimes be very confusing and such was the case when researching this particular son. Some of what follows is my interpretation of the records I have found. My conclusions may not be correct. Ben (1787), like his eldest brother, married two wives but in his case both of them were named Ann. Further perplexity follows as one of his sons, also called Benjamin, had a wife who's maiden name was the same as that of his father's second wife!

His brother Daniel (1784) was a witness at Ben's first wedding in Chepstow Parish Church on Sunday 26 April 1807. His bride, who was also recorded as *of this parish*, was Ann Edmunds and banns had been read in church on the previous three Sundays. In the 'Banns Register' she is named Ann Edwards, but I'm fairly certain that Edmunds was her correct surname. Ann gave birth to at least four children. The baptism of daughter Amelia was in April 1808 and that of two sons, George and Henry, on the same day in September 1811. As no birth dates are given we are unable to tell if the two boys were twins or if one of then was being christened late. On 5 December 1813, Ann's last child was baptised. This was the one given his grandfather's (and father's) name. This parish entry also records that father Benjamin was *a watchmaker of Castle Parade, Chepstow* so, at the end of 1813, this family had not yet moved into 2 High Street and Old Ben had not yet moved to Coleford.

I am not certain when the first Ann died, but Ben married his second wife Ann Reynalds on the day before his 'first wedding' anniversary seventeen years later – on 25 April 1824. This ceremony took place at St James Priory Church in the centre of Bristol. I think it likely that this Ann did not come from Bristol and guess that at that time churches in this large and impersonal city may have performed a similar function to Gretna Green in our era? This was the place where couples, from villages or towns (like Chepstow) in this region, could go if they wanted a 'quiet' wedding where they were unknown. As far as I am aware this marriage was not by licence and it is possible that some central Bristol parishes, where part of the population was transient, were not too strict on marriage celebrants proving that they were 'of this parish' or in calling banns for three successive weeks before the service. As Ben's older brother Charles was living in this city – and in this parish – a local address could be provided if required. A couple of other Greenings had 'Bristol' marriages, which we will come to later.

The second Ann had a number of children, including two girls Eleanor and Hester who both sadly died as children. Her son George Wesley was baptised in the Wesleyan Chapel at Monmouth in 1836. He can be found in later records described as a mariner. As in many English and Welsh towns, the economic climate in Chepstow was harsh during the 1830s. Making a livelihood as a clockmaker was not easy so the skills Ben's second wife brought with her gave the High Street shop a much-needed diversification. In *Piggott's Directory for Monmouthshire* for 1835, Ann is listed as a *Straw Hat maker* and the first detailed census of 1841 shows that there was an *Assistant Bonnet maker* also in residence at number two – as well as a maid.

The first Ann's son, Benjamin (1813), had been trained by and worked for his father from early childhood. By the early 1830s he had become a watch and clockmaker himself. Although still young he appears to have gone to Coleford/Newland to take over his grandfathers small business and remain there, enabling the old man to move back to Chepstow. Young Ben's older sister, Amelia, had most likely been living at the Forest address for a few years – looking after her grandfather. She had her wedding at All Saints' church Newland on 22 February 1830. She was nearly 22 and her husband was Thomas Meredith.

On 28 October 1834, Ben (1813) – following his father's example – married in Bristol. This time the wedding took place at St Augustine's, another central parish. Like his father he also married a Reynalds, in his case Sarah Elizabeth. Circumstances and the Bristol location seem to suggest that this may have been against his father's wishes. In my previous book I suggested that this Ben's wife and his stepmother were probably related. Although I have no documentary proof there is some circumstantial evidence. Ann Reynalds had named her eldest daughter Eleanor (she had died aged five), Sarah Elizabeth's mother is recorded as Eleanor and she had called her own eldest daughter – who had already been born – Ellen. The two Benjamin's wives were not mother and daughter but they could have been sisters. Although not breaking Biblical rules, perhaps the relationship was too close for parental approval.

Ben and Sarah Elizabeth produced twelve or more children, with ten of them reaching maturity. At least six of them were born in the Forest. Ellen was baptised at Newland in September 1834, a month before her parent's wedding. First son, yet another Benjamin, was baptised at the Wesleyan Methodist Chapel in Newent (a town north of the Forest of Dean) on 28 June 1836. As this was a non-conformist christening, Benjamin's birthday – 18 April – is also recorded. The next four were baptised at the Wesleyan chapel in Monmouth (where Ann number two had baptised her son), Nathaniel Augustus in May 1840 (born Nov '39) followed by Amelia and Eliza Ann (possibly twins) in1844 and Frances Elizabeth in 1846. Benjamin and Sarah Elizabeth had moved back to Chepstow and were living in Welsh Street by June 1841, the time of the census. They must have been keen members of the Wesleyan chapel congregation to have their later children christened there. Although not too far from Coleford, Monmouth was seventeen miles from Chepstow. We have now reached the arrival of Civil Birth Registration (from 1 July 1837); so baptismal records lose most of their importance for the family historian. My files do hold the names of many more Greening children but I feel I must pause at this point. Although this is a family history there is an ever-present risk of it becoming flooded.

Old Ben, back in Chepstow and living with his fourth son, was still writing letters. In May 1850 he penned a reply to George, Nathaniel's eldest son, who had written to him at the start of that year. George was an auctioneer, residing in Frodsham near Chester. The letter commences:

> Dear Grandson and Family
> I have to say I recd   your letter which bears date Jany 7th –50, for which I thank you. In that letter you wish to know if I was yet living and what age I am. I have to say through the mercy and longsuffering of God, I am still living a monument of his mercy and if he do prolong my life to the 9th of July I shall be 94. I have a good hope through grace I am travelling towards that eternal rest, that rest that remains for the people of God. I do hope that you and yours are travelling in the same, as it is very likely we may never meet again on Earth, we may all meet in heaven, amen and amen.

Ben then asks about John's father and other members of the family.

> I am now going to ask you about your father, whether he is living or not. As it will be 24 years since I was with you, in July, and I have recd only one letter from him in all that time. That was in Augst 23 – 1830. I have written to him but I have not recd any answer. If he is living, I shall thank you to tell me what state he is in body and in circumstance. Please to tell me about your brother Ben, and your sister Ann, and where they are and how they are, and if your son is married and how many children he have. I very much wish to know for that will be the fifth generation. I shall thank you if you will tell me how many children your father have by your step-mother, and where they are and what they are doing.

The letter then continues:

> I shall give you an account of myself. Through the mercy of God I do enjoy a very good state of health and am free from pain, and my sight is remarkably good, I have written

this without glasses. I am living with my son Benjn, I have been with him more than 17 years. I am past labour, my intellect is very well at my advanced age. – All your Uncles and Aunts and all your relations are all well as far as I know. As I have given you an account of myself and all my family, I do hope you will favour me with all the particulars to the above, for which I will thank you. – Your uncle Ben is (like yourself) very fond of flowers. He will feel much obliged to you if you will send him a few roots or cuttings of Pansies, and send the names of them. Please to send them per post. I shall conclude by saying and now dear friend a long farewell, for we shall meet no more, till we are raised with Christ to dwell on Zion's happy shore. God grant we may, amen –
Benjn Greening

Old Ben adds a postscript:

I beg you will not be offended, I beg you will write very plain as I have, for I can't read your writing. I beg you will not delay to write.

George must have replied to his grandfather, suggesting that he visit the family in Lancashire and Cheshire. This may seem rather strange to us today, especially considering Old Ben's very advanced age. Why didn't they go to visit him? Why also had Nathaniel still not written to his father? On 9 July 1851, on his birthday, Old Ben writes again to his eldest grandson.

My much esteemed Grandson and Daughter
It is with shame I take my pen to write to you; when I think of what you have written to me, wherein you have given me an account of your family and all your relations, and where they live. I am glad to hear that they are all doing well. I beg you will forgive my neglect for not writing to you before now (but it's a family case of neglecting, it runs through the whole family). Now I have to tell you that, through great mercy I am in a good state of health for which I am thankful to the Lord for it. But I cannot walk but very little now, my feet is tender and corns, and I have no strength. It is enough for me to walk a mile, but this is no more than may be expected for I am this day 94 years of age.

Old Ben had made a mistake it was his ninety-fifth birthday. His letter continues:

... it is twelve months ago I wrote to you last. If you can make it convenient to see your father, you will tell him that his greatly neglected father is yet alive and tell him he have not written to me but once since I was with him, which is 25 years this month. I have to

tell you that your uncle Joseph is gone to South Australia, he have been there going on 10 years and I have received but one letter from him since he has been there. I have written several times to him but cannot have an answer. You see now the truth of what I said before that this neglect runs through all the family. Now, as you said in your letter, you very much wish I would come to see you. I have been talking about it many times, having a great desire to come, but the want of the means which I have not its that which keeps me from coming. I have been thinking, as you say that all your relations are all doing well, – if all of them would contribute something it might put the means in my way to come to you, but if you cannot do it you will not offend me. I have to say that all my children are greatly interested for my welfare with exception of two (viz) your father and your uncle Joseph. I do not ask them for anything, neither do I want anything of them, all I want of them is that they should write to me. I should be glad to have one letter more before I go hence and be no more seen. I have to say that I have been living with my son Benjn 18 years last November but for many years I have not done any work, but thank the Lord he have provided for me. ... I thank him for all that is past and trust him for that's to come. I can say no more, only I can say that my son and daughter sends their respects to you.
I remain your ever affectionate Grandfather – Benjamin Greening

As far as we know Old Ben never did receive a letter from his eldest son. Nathaniel had become a rich and successful man but had forgotten his roots. Less than nine months after this letter was written Nathaniel had died. He had reached the age of 72 but his ancient father had outlived him.

CHAPTER SIX

✛

Wisconsin is one of the northern United States, just below Canada and tucked in to the south and west of the Great Lakes. Although not a state until 1848 this area of North America saw an Indian uprising in 1832, when Muk-a-tah-mish-o-kah-kaik or Black Sparrow Hawk – the warrior Chief of the Sauk and Fox Nation – rallied his tribes in a bid to free his land from encroaching white settlers. After a number of skirmishes the uprising was brutally put down by the US military at the battle of Wisconsin Heights and the episode is recorded in American History as the Black Hawk War.

At the small settlement of Blue Mounds a fort was built in 1832, to protect settlers from Black Hawk's scalping parties and ten years later it was a tract of land, twelve miles north of here, that British lawyer and land agent – Charles Wilson – thought would be suitable for settlement by members of a newly formed society in England. The British Temperance Emigration Society and Savings Fund was inaugurated on 26 December 1842 at Samuel Robert's Temperance Coffee-house in Liverpool. It was principally the idea of three men who, as employees of a firm manufacturing nautical instruments, had come into contact with seafaring men from various parts of the world and had become interested in emigration after 'reading the London and Edinburgh papers'. One of the items agreed in the society's constitution was that ' no woman should be allowed to hold office'. The in vogue word Temperance was, no doubt, included in the Society's title to give it an image of respectability.

The declared object of the society was to raise a fund by weekly contributions, to buy land in Wisconsin and 'to secure for each settler a farm of eighty acres with improvements, the whole not to exceed the value of £40'. Shares in the society could be purchased by a payment of one shilling per week and the names, of those wishing to emigrate, were to be put into a bag so that lots could be drawn for the limited number of farms available. The 'improvements' were that each farm was to be fenced, have five of the eighty acres put into cultivation – under the direction of the Society's agent – and have a log house. This cabin was to be 14 feet by 20 feet and a story and a half in height.

The land chosen by Charles Wilson was an 'unbroken wilderness' about twenty miles square and did not contain a single white settler in 1842. When he moved there in 1844 he was initially obliged to live in a deserted Indian wigwam. Bands of Potawatomi and Winnebago Indians roamed the country hunting and fishing. There was a large variety and an abundance of game. Deer, duck, geese, partridges and fish existed in vast numbers. There were countless songbirds in the forests every summer and flocks of pigeons numbering thousands were often seen. Bears, wolves, foxes, otter, mink and muskrats were common. Charles Wilson purchased land at one and a quarter dollars per acre from the United States Land Office at Mineral Point, a small town about 30 miles away, and work started on the creation of the first settlement of Mazomanie. This was the name of an Indian Chief, meaning 'Iron that walks', and coined from the railroad that was being built across the state. In October 1844 the Argus newspaper of Madison, later the state capital of Wisconsin, carried an advertisement:

> The British Temperance Emigration Society are desirous of receiving tenders for the building of thirty log houses on their settlement between this and the first day of April 1845. Full particulars may be obtained from the agent, after 20th of October, at the English settlement, Gorstville, near Cross Plains.

In 1844 a US Dollar was worth approximately four shillings (twenty pence in today's money), so the cost of the land for an eighty-acre farm was £20. This left another twenty pounds to fence the property, cultivate five acres, build a log house and cover the agents fees and expenses!

Fifty-six people from Britain arrived in that first year 1844 and, between 1845 and 1847, a further eighty-two members of the society came as settlers. The United States census of 1850 shows that the town of 'Farmville' (a name later dropped), made up of Mazomanie and Black Earth, had a population of 105 males and 101 females. Mazomanie and its surrounding 'townships' had a total population of 691 people. The majority of these had arrived from England under the auspices of the British Temperance Emigration Society. Other parts of Wisconsin were also receiving a large influx of British immigrants arranged by other organisations. The town of Mineral Point, in the centre of a mining region, had expanded very rapidly. It is believed that about seven thousand Cornish people settled in this area between 1835 and 1850.

One of the English groups who arrived in Mazomanie in 1847 came from Worcestershire – John

Greening, his wife Maria and their three young children Jim, Clara and Charley. At some time between 1843 and 1846 John must have become a member of the British Temperance Emigration Society and been chosen to take up a farm there. He and his family sailed from Liverpool on 2 April 1847. His elder sister Elizabeth travelled with them to Liverpool and saw them off at the docks. John had already said his goodbyes in Claines to his parents and to his younger sister Ann, who had become friendly with a lodger at the Shades – a young piano tuner named William Elgar – whom she married the following year. John and Maria had four more children after their arrival in North America.

A full transcript of John's 1847 journey, by sailing ship from Liverpool to New Orleans and then by steamboat up the Mississippi to Wisconsin, is printed at the end of this book. Although John would never see his parents or sisters again, America did provide him with a new life. In October 1847, not long after his arrival at his new home, he wrote in his journal:

> I must have a cross plow so went to the maker and gave directions for one to be made and stopped to see it partly done. I had a coulter made for it (they don't use them here) and had it made a little stronger than theirs. I had it brought home and then got a home made wooden wheel and fixed it to the beam for breaking sods, to be taken off for cross plowing, and this day, 11 Oct 1847, I struck the first furrow in <u>my own land</u> [He underlines these three words] It works admirably with two yoke of oxen. Oh, it was happiness to me.

The Emigration Society had been a little over-optimistic in their 'improvements' budget. John's land, although no doubt his boundaries had been marked, had to be fenced by him. After the piece about ploughing his first furrow, his journal continues:

> The land must now be fenced in and that involves a very great deal of labour, for the rails are laid in a peculiar manner on the ground that I cannot describe to you. It takes a good wagon load of heavy oak rails, cut and split 10 ft. long, to make a fence of 16 to 18 yards. When done it is a perfect wall of wood 7 feet high, yet the cattle jump over it with ease after the green corn in summer.

In November that first year, John wrote to his parents and sisters in England describing his new surroundings:

> I wish I could send you some of our prairie flowers, they are very beautiful and in such

variety and profusion. All shapes and colours, they succeed each other in rapid succession. Their numbers, colours and beauty baffle all my powers of description. We have no singing birds here but their loss is made up by great numbers of crickets and grasshoppers that we can hear sing and creak for half a mile night or day. Just before rain they make a wonderful noise, but they don't annoy us at all. We have a curious variety of game for those that can spend their time with a gun. Raccoons are whimpering around the house nightly and may be shot if you have a good dog, on moonlight nights. I have heard wolves howl in the edge of the woods at night and then the neighbour's dogs begin to bark, all up the settlement. I have lain in bed and heard the most horrible din between the two for hours together. There is no fear of them coming to us, no one ever sees one. They only carry off a young pig, if they stray off a mile or so in the woods. There has been but one bear seen in this whole country round, and that was two years ago. He shuffled off in double quick time when seen. Our Robin Redbreasts are quite as large as a blackbird, and just the same domestic favourite as in England. Crows are quite the same (and just as black). Wild pigeons are larger and very numerous. Blackbirds are of two kinds, one smaller, one larger than yours. Prairie Hens are the size of Pheasants and very numerous.

John must have been given a shotgun, as a parting present from his brother in law at the Shades Tavern. In another letter he writes:

wild ducks are plenty just now till frost comes. Tell Brother Simmons the first shot I fired out of his gun killed five ducks, but I could only get three off the lake. The next killed four and I only got three of these. I want a dog for that but I have a pup and that is something.

Before Christmas that first year, John had decided that the log cabin was too small for his family. His journal entry for 21 December 1847 reads:

I am busy now cutting logs for building my new house. I am going two miles to the Wisconsin riverside to cut them, then haul them 5 miles to the sawmill. They take half the boards and all the slabs for the sawing. I have cut and partly hauled about 6,000 feet, as my house will take about 3,000 feet. Tis to be 24 feet long and 12 wide up to the square, with a T roof with a six foot pitch and three windows below stairs. The oaks I have cut down for the purpose would bring 700 pounds in England, at 2/6 per cubic foot. I cut a tree 40 or 50 feet long and just take the butt length off, and leave the rest for the prairie fires. The winter has set in the beginning of this month. Snow fell 3 or 4 inches deep and has stayed with us ever since with frequent additions. We don't expect to see the ground again till April.

The following day, 22 December, John describes his visit to a deserted Indian village:

> ...I found an Indian village of wigwams, just left by some of them two or three days, in a thick forest almost impenetrable. You must imagine with what pleasure I examined their sleeping places and their stage for drying venison meat. I counted deer's legs by the dozen. The Indians belong to the tribe of Winnebagoes. I could almost wish they had been there that I might have smoked the pipe of peace with the Chief, but I shall visit the spot again some day...

By 1849, Mazomanie had become an organised township in Dane County and all the male population had to meet to elect local officers; Magistrates, Town Clerk, Superintendent of Schools, Constables etc. When the poll for Justice of the Peace was closed John came out top with almost twice as many votes as any other candidate (Charles Wilson, the original land agent, came bottom with only a single vote).

> ...and that gives me the title of Esquire by Law. Squire being the only title recognised in this country and can only be acquired by being chosen Magistrate. The office takes away the Christian name in American parlance, and tis not John or Mr. but Squire Greening, at a word. Each Justice's office is his own log cabin and his powers are these: To solemnize marriages, adjudicate in cases of assault, issue summonses, to administer oaths, to award fines etc. for trespass, to decide in cases of contention between any parties who become amenable to the law, and to give judgement against all debtors under the sum of $200. Also the various other duties incumbent on Magistrates in England. We are elected for two years and eligible to re-election if we please the constituency,

John only a boot and shoe maker in Worcester two years before, had not only become a self-sufficient farmer in America – cultivating virgin land and building his own house, he was now the most respected man in his community. Like his sisters in England, he was largely self-educated. He was a very fine example of the strong, intelligent, humane and wise men that the Victorian age produced.

The creation of this new community was not without its many problems and, before John and his family arrived, there were already complaints being made to England against the emigration society's agents. Charles Wilson and his associates, in turn, had accusations against some of the settlers. Most of the arrivals still owed subscription instalments to the Society and many of them *were without money and found themselves in a country where money was scarce, and when farm produce was raised the markets were distant and the other wants of the settlers were numerous and pressing.* Charles Reeve, Wilson's assistant, wrote to the Society in England in November 1846 explaining that there was... no *medicine, no provisions, no money, and whole families lying sick not able to help each other. The county commissioners have aided the poor but we have many deaths here...* He also pointed out that most of the settlers, having been trades people in England, knew little or nothing about farming. Some of the emigrants had left England but never arrived in Wisconsin and a small number, presumably those with funds, had returned to their homeland.

In December 1847 Reeve wrote to Peter Heyworth, one of the Trustees of the Society in England, who had visited the settlement the previous year.

> I firmly believe there are many men here that would not scruple to sacrifice either me or Mr Wilson in the event of us turning them off their farm ... a proposition was made at one of their meetings to assemble a force to attack Mr Wilson and me for the purpose of drawing us off the Prairie, it is but justice to state it was negated.

Reeve also explained the difficulties experienced with the arrival of American squatters.

> Since you were here we have had a great many of the lowest Americans from Illinois come in among us, they have taken claims, or as they term it 'squatted on the prairie', between us and the town site. These men have pursued this plan all their lives, setting down on government land, improving until they find a purchaser and removing to other claims. They are averse to pay for anything ... enemies to us because we purchase the land that would otherwise be left for them to settle on. They get among our members and persuade them it is a great shame to pay rent in a free country, and promise them their assistance in repelling any attempt to turn them off the land justly forfeited. You may judge of our situation and feelings among such a nest of hornets.

In addition to being the senior Justice of the Peace, John Greening was also appointed Chairman of the Supervisors for the township of Mazomanie. As the leading citizen in his new home he must have been a very busy man. John was not only creating his own farm and supporting his young and growing family, but also trying to sort out some of the problems of his embryo world. A victim of all this was his journal, as there are no further entries or drafts of any more letters to England after 1849. John will have kept up his correspondence with his sisters but unfortunately none of these communications have survived. The last paragraph in his journal is the end of a draft letter to his sister Ann, dated 8 April 1849, a request to his brother-in-law for some sheet music for an Independence Day party:

> Ask Brother Elgar to send me Julien's old Polka, just the melody for the flute, to be here by the 4th of July. And if he could add a bass, it would be thankfully received.

John was a man of many talents, he could read music and played the flute.

All the Indians were friendly, by the time John took over his farm in central Wisconsin, although the English settlers had little contact with them. However in 1851 the Greening children would have enjoyed a most memorable sight that we, today, can only witness in the cinema or on television as part of some Hollywood epic. Jim, Clara and Charley, perhaps with their new little sister Lizzie, watched a very colourful, if rather poignant, pageant that passed through Mazomanie – possibly across John's land. Between six and seven hundred Indians, Chippewa, Potawatomi, Winnebago, Stockbridge and Huron – escorted by United States marshals – were travelling to reservations that had been prepared for them on the western side of the Mississippi. A military band led the procession and there were numerous banners of the Stars and Stripes floating in the breeze. It was later reported that, before these original Americans arrived at their destination, half of them had crept away after nightfall preferring their Wisconsin homes to the unknown territory to which they were being moved.

Some notes on Mazomanie and its founders are included in the "History of Dane County" published in 1906. This tells us that John's farm was in 'section seven' and that he later acquired one hundred and sixty more acres of the same section, where he built a house in which his eldest son James was then still living. John had passed away on 22 February 1900, in his eighty-fifth year. Maria had died nearly three years earlier in June 1897. The four children born in America were all daughters. All four of them and their eldest sister Clara married and, between them, they will certainly have many descendents living in the United States today. Clara married Charles Kerr who was probably the son of John Kerr, a member of the first group of settlers who emigrated from England in 1844. Elizabeth (Lizzie) married William Parr and Anna married Frank Warner, both from Mazomanie. Amelia married L C Oulmanm of Minneapolis and the husband of Laura Greening, the youngest of John and Maria's children, was the Hon W A Nolan of Grand Meadow, Minnesota – for ten years an elected representative of that state's legislature. In 1906 John's younger son Charles, or Charley as he was always known, is described as a merchant of Grand Meadow. We will hear more about him, another remarkable Greening, in a later chapter.

For the benefit of her children and grandchildren, Clara Caswell – the schoolteacher Charley married – wrote down part of the story of her life, in about 1915 when she was in her mid sixties. This includes the happy report of her first visit to her in-laws, after her wedding party on 28th December 1869.

> We left the train for Mazomanie, Wisconsin, to visit Charley's people. It was after midnight when we arrived. Charley looked out when opposite his home and we saw a lantern swinging frantically. He said that was Jim, his brother.
>
> We found his father and mother at the depot to meet us as they lived a mile from town on a farm. At that time there were at home, besides his father and mother, his brother Jim and sisters Lizzie, Annie, Amelia and Laura. His oldest sister, Clara, was married and lived only a very short way away. We had some very jolly times and his people were very kind to me.

Maria (Kelley) and John Greening (b. 1815)

CHAPTER SEVEN

✛

After the Queen, the most published portrait in England and Wales today is that of the composer Sir Edward Elgar. His profile has appeared on the reverse of all Bank of England twenty-pound notes since 1999 (Charles Darwin is featured on the back of ten-pound notes). Many biographies have been written about Sir Edward, so I do not intend to cover much of the ground that writers with far more knowledge and ability than myself have already presented to the public. He was the fourth child of William and Anne Elgar and was born in June 1857 in the little village of Broadheath, a few miles to the west of the city of Worcester. The cottage in which Edward, his parents and his siblings lived is now part of a study centre, library and museum devoted to his work, his life and his memory.

In partnership with his brother, William Elgar ran a small music shop at No10 High Street, Worcester and the Elgar family moved into the flat over this shop when Edward was six. All the children were musically gifted and their early education in this came, of course, from their father. The children were also encouraged to appreciate poetry and literature and study the wonders of nature. Here their greatest influence was their mother who was an amateur poet herself.

In my first little Greening book I quote one of Anne's short verses, written when her son Edward was 21. I include it again here for reasons of its simplicity and natural beauty.

> Only a sprig of heather
> But it grew upon the wild
> When you and I together
> The summer day beguiled.
> When the skylark high was singing
> Above the yellow broom

And the cool hill-breeze was bringing
The sweet scent of its bloom.

Sir Edward Elgar's Greening roots, through his mother Anne, did have a profound influence on his early life. Although his maternal grandparents had died before he was born, his biographers tell us that – as a teenager – he often walked to the village of Claines, a couple of miles to the north of Worcester, with music scores from his father's shop so that he could study these in peace beside his grandparent's tombstone in the churchyard there. I'm sure there was an additional reason for his frequent walks to Claines, which I will come to shortly. Edward also never met his maternal uncle; Anne's brother, John Greening whose story is told in the previous chapter, had left England for America ten years before his birth. At this point in this narrative I publish – for the first time – the draft of a letter from John taken from his journal. This was written to his sister shortly after her marriage to William Elgar. I find this a beautiful and moving letter, which encapsulates the spirit of the composer's mother's family. The letter was written from John's log cabin home in north Wisconsin on March 14th 1848.

My own dear Sister Ann

I suppose long ere this, you are a wife. May heaven shower its choicest blessings on you. May an over-ruling providence guide you through the mazes of a chequered life. May you enjoy a long life, and more happiness than usually falls to the lot of mortals, is the sincerest wish and prayer that was ever breathed by your only Brother. You must imagine my feelings towards you, to describe them is impossible. Tell the man you have chosen to travel life's weary journey with, and whom I now call Brother, to love you for me. Aye for me, who has deserted two of the dearest Sisters that ever Brother had. But they shall never be ashamed to own me as a brother, that link can never be broken, only by death. And though one third part of the earth and an immense ocean separates us, still we are the same, aye the very same, only more so. Brother and Sisters, I have a deal to tell you, but not now. Time presses, I shall certainly see you all again if ever I can find some cargo to pay my journey. At present I must be content and wait patiently. God knows how long, keep my dear parents alive till then. Once get 6,000 miles to separate you and faults are lost. Their names are sacred and thoughts of them are Holy. God bless them and all of you.

The cold is still intense, it freezes water to ice in a minute, still I work out in it and it is endurable. We are so far inland and so great elevation above the sea that we breathe a different air to you, tis almost all oxygen and hydrogen, very little nitrogen, consequence everything dries up instantly. Salt never gets damp, iron don't rust and wood decays with dry rot. We use much salt and the animals must have some often for, being so far from the sea, we have no saline particles in the air like your little Island, which is saturated with salt . . .

John was never able to return to England and never saw his parents or sisters again. His journal ends with the draft of a further letter to Anne, written a year later after he had received the sad news from her of their father's death, this is printed at the end of his journal – at the end of this book.

In his later life one of Elgar's closest friends was Sir Ivor Atkins, for many years the organist at Worcester Cathedral and conductor of the Three Choirs Festival there. Sir Ivor's son Wulston, who was a godson of Elgar's and who became a major patron of the Elgar Society, published a biography of the composer in 1984 – half a century after Elgar's death. In this book Wulstan reveals that only a year or so before his death, Elgar had confided in his father the details of an early romance that, although it had taken place some years before his marriage, he had made Sir Ivor promise not to make public until fifty years after his demise. Although this may seem extremely strange to us today, we must only assume that this was the way a very correct gentleman of Elgar's generation would arrange to protect his only daughter from the knowledge that her late mother had not been the only lady in her father's life. There could be another reason.

Sir Ivor asked his son to publish this revelation in the due course of time because he was of the opinion that it was important. He had gathered from his friend that this lady had not only been Elgar's first true love, but that she was also the inspiration behind some of his early and most important work. Most musicologists think that the 13th of the Enigma Variations was dedicated to one of Elgar's friends, Lady Mary Lygon, but Wulstan's father was sure that because of *its depth and tenderness* it was really dedicated to this lady. He also thought that the later Violin Concerto, dedicated by Elgar to *Herein is enshrined the soul of ******, was for HELEN rather than other friends with five letter names – as believed by Elgar's wife and others. Some, but not all, of the composer's more recent chroniclers and 'experts' on his life accept that this first love probably was a major inspiration. The lady was Helen Jessie Weaver.

Wulstan's book relates how Helen, an accomplished young violinist, had met Elgar through her brother Frank Weaver, who was a fellow musician with Elgar in a Worcester musical group. Helen and her friend, Edith Grovenham, had become students at the conservatoire in Leipzig – and that Elgar, although unable to afford to study there himself, was able to journey there for two weeks of the concert season in the first two weeks of January in 1883. Here he arranged to stay in the same lodgings where the girls were living and, after escorting them both to various concerts, he fell deeply in love with Helen and she with him. Helen was unable to complete her studies in Leipzig because she was needed back in Worcester to nurse her terminally ill mother. In England she met up with Elgar again and they became engaged.

Eighteen months later the engagement was over. Elgar, corresponding with his best friend Dr Charles Buck, writes of a broken heart. The biographer tells us that the reason they decided to end their relationship was because Helen's family were non-conformist whereas Elgar's were Catholic. They are said to have returned each other's letters and destroyed them and we are informed that Helen, now broken in health as well as in heart (Wulstan thought she had contracted smallpox), sailed off to New Zealand where she died.

Part of this story may be true but not all of it. It seems unlikely that the parting was due to a difference in religion. Neither family was particularly devout nor would they have become engaged in the first place if this had been an obstacle. The reason may have been simple economics. Edward realised he could not afford to support a wife and Helen, sensing that he was destined for greatness, did not want to be a burden on him. Did she sacrifice her happiness for his art – or was there a completely different reason?

A little research has revealed some other discrepancies and misconceptions. Helen and Edward did not first meet in Leipzig or shortly before in Worcester. They knew each other and were probably friends from early childhood. Helen was the youngest child of William and Jane Weaver who, in December 1860 when Helen was born, lived in the flat over William's boot shop and manufacturing premises at 84 High Street, Worcester. This was not, as some Elgar chroniclers have written, at the far end of the High Street from the Elgar brother's music shop but almost directly opposite. In Worcester High Street property numbers do not alternate, with odd numbers on one side and evens on the other, they run consecutively up one side of the street – then turn and run back down the other-side. Number 10 and number 84 faced each other. Not only must the Elgar and Weaver children, who lived above shops on opposite sides of the street, have known each other but they also grew up together and must have played together. Both families were musical and some of the children in both were talented musicians. With just over three years between them, it is a fair guess that Edward and Helen were childhood sweethearts.

William Weaver was the leading boot maker in Worcester and his business was expanding. In the 1871 census he is recorded as the employer of 8 men, 4 girls and 3 boys. With business going so well he was able to afford to move his family, out of the flat above his shop, to a small-detached house in a village just north of Worcester. You've guessed it – Claines. Perhaps Edward did walk there frequently with scores from his father's music shop, but did he call on the way at Helen's house, or meet her in Claines churchyard – where they could talk endlessly about their mutual love of music and possibly about their future together? Perhaps it was Edward who suggested that Helen might become a professional concert violinist – and encouraged her to enrol at Leipzig, where he would have liked to have been able to go himself. Helen's father, now a successful businessman, was able to support his young daughter in this endeavour.

Why did Helen decide to leave her family and friends and make a new life in New Zealand? This would be a difficult enough decision for a 24-year-old single woman today. In Helen's time, when it was most unlikely that those who made the journey would ever return, it is almost impossible for us to understand how such a decision could have been contemplated. Unless some letter of Helen's survives and sees the light of day, we will never know the full reason why she wished to travel as far away from Worcester as was earthly possible. Her decision may have been helped a little by new technology. Prior to 1883 all travel to New Zealand was by sailing ship. A fast ship, with a good captain and a little luck with the winds, would make the journey in three months. Frequently ships took a month or more longer and some never arrived at all. It was a long and perilous journey and an extremely uncomfortable one. Many passengers became ill on the voyage and some died.

Although sailing ships would continue to make this journey until the turn of the century, Helen's voyage coincided with the arrival of steamship travel and she sailed on one of the first of these vessels on the New Zealand run. The S.S. RUAPEHU was built at Dumbarton on the Clyde, from where its maiden voyage began at the end of December 1883. The ship's first voyage to New Zealand was made in a record 45 days. By today's standards the Ruapehu would be regarded as a very small ship at just over four thousand tons with a passenger capacity of 165. Helen left Plymouth in the second half of October 1885. We do not know who came to the quayside to wave her goodbye.

Helen reached New Zealand but she didn't die. She found some happiness there but some sadness too. The SS Ruapehu arrived in Auckland on 7th December 1885 and less than five years later on 9th August 1890 she married John Munro at St Paul's Church in Auckland. Both she and her husband were 29, although John was a few months younger than his wife. He had been born in Glasgow and had emigrated from Scotland to New Zealand with his parents and sisters in 1873. After working for his auctioneer father for four years, he had joined the Bank of New South Wales and, after his marriage, the bank appointed John as manager of their branch at Patea. Some years later he was promoted to be the manager of a larger branch at Stratford.

Helen had two children, a girl and a boy, but sadly both of them and her husband pre-deceased her. Helen herself died on 23rd December 1927, four days before her sixty-seventh birthday. Helen's will is full of small bequests left to her friends, her neighbours and some charities. They include £50 to a society for the prevention of cruelty to animals, £50 to her late daughter's godson and all her books to Nelson College in memory of her son. There is no mention of a violin in her will; perhaps she had not possessed one for many years. Her gramophone and records she left to her friend Bertha. We do not know if Elgar's music was among the recordings, but I suspect it was.

You may ask yourself what this story has to do with a book on the Greening surname. You may also wonder why I carried out research into Helen Weaver's life, both in England and New Zealand. The answer is coincidence.

My first little book produced a flood of letters and emails from Greenings and Greening descendants all over the world. Many of them asked my help in finding links in their family trees and some of them gave me fascinating new information to expand or change what I had written. Some have become regular correspondents and two of them – from different ends of the world but linked by chance – have given me two of the major stories in this volume.

Charles 'Chuck' Greening lives in Orange County California and he kindly gave me a copy of his great-grandfather John's journal, which – with his permission – I publish in full at the end of this book. This is a compelling document about a family's journey to make a new life in America in 1847. In addition Chuck has given me a lot of background information about the new township where John settled and became the first Justice of the Peace. He also gave me notes on his grandfather, John's son Charlie; including copies of Charlie's letters home from the American Civil War in which he served as a Yankee soldier. I will come to this in a later chapter.

Chuck is a decade and a half older than myself but, when we met up in California earlier this year (2004), we found we had much in common. In addition to our interest in family history, Chuck is a widower like myself and we both enjoy bird watching and jazz. John Greening, Chuck's great-grandfather, was the elder and only brother of Ann Greening – the mother of Sir Edward Elgar.

How intriguing then, at the same time as I was corresponding by email with Chuck in Orange County, I was also in communication with Jane Woodall in the Blue Mountains of New South

Wales in Australia. Jane, the daughter of Col Dr Charles Llewellyn Greening, was born in Britain but married Michael Woodall and went to live in Australia over twenty-five years ago. Jane had read my book and was interested in finding out more about her Greening roots. With quite a bit of research and more than a little bit of luck I was able to trace her Greening ancestry back to a Thomas Greening, who was a servant in Worcestershire in 1841. This Thomas was possibly a great-grandson of Zechariah of Elmore (see chapter 4). What made this more exciting for me (and Jane) was the sentence she used in one of her first letters to me, "my husband's grandmother was the illegitimate daughter of (Sir Edward) Elgar". If what Jane wrote was correct, she and her husband Michael would quite likely have distant blood ties. Michael would also be a fairly close natural relative to Chuck in America. I detail Jane Woodall's ancestry at the end of this chapter.

Michael Woodall's paternal grandmother was adopted as a baby and, my research soon found, was living as a small child in Worcester in 1891. As her name was Dorothy Weaver, you can now understand my fascination with this story!

First of all I should write a note about illegitimacy in Britain. This has been common throughout our history, far more so than many people imagine, although in the past the figures were only a fraction of today's, when approximately a third of all children are born outside marriage. Illegitimate births are believed to have made up an average of 5% of the total, in the country as a whole, during the 17th and 18th century. This percentage is sometimes disputed, as it is based on rather unreliable statistics and there were large regional and annual variations, but it is generally accepted that there was a marked increase when the Victorian period arrived. This era brought a new mobility in society with, of course, little in the way of birth control. Quite a large number of Victorian men, of high and low estate, would have fathered children from women other than their wives.

Is it of interest, does it matter and does it demean their stature in any way if a famous man is later discovered to have been the father of an illegitimate child? I don't feel it really matters and, in today's more enlightened age, it certainly does not alter our perception of that person. However it can be of interest. Not of much interest if the person was a statesman or a scientist or a soldier, but interesting if he was an artist. The work of creators – be it in literature, the visual arts or music – is all part of their private existence. Their compositions and their lives are indivisible. With all of us the main influences on our life story, after the genes with which we were born, are the early years. Elgar would have been no exception.

Sir Edward Elgar, who – in a recent poll – was voted the most famous English Midlander after

William Shakespeare, is universally regarded as Britain's and especially England's most loved native composer. His music seems to resonate with the spirit of the English shires. Some of his greatest compositions are frequently described as sad and melancholy, but I believe that nostalgic is the adjective that best expresses their mood. His most loved music is of memories of the past, of lost loves, lost hopes and lost dreams. I do not know if Elgar had an illegitimate child or not and it is not my intention to do more than report what I have been told and what my research has discovered. A proof may be possible but is this really of any importance. Before we start, it was not possible for Helen Weaver to have been the mother of Dorothy. The story is rather a slender one but here it is.

On the fifth of November 1910 a smart wedding took place at All Saints Church, Carshalton, Surrey. The bride was twenty-two year old Dorothy Weaver, spinster of 'Butter Hill', Carshalton, and the groom was Charles Woodall – aged thirty-two. He gave his profession as 'Merchant'. The first witness was Dorothy's father, at that time a prosperous Corn Dealer and Miller. He had been born and brought up in Somerset, where his father had owned a small mill. However as a young man, like his new entrepreneurial son-in-law, he had been involved in a number of business ventures.

One of the guests at the wedding reception would have been Dorothy's only and younger sister Erica. Although good sisters they were extremely unalike, not only in temperament but also in looks. Erica was quite small and very dark, like her parents. Dorothy was a fairly tall light brunette. Although it was a taboo subject for discussion, both girls knew that they were not – in fact – blood relatives. William and his wife Lavinia had adopted Dorothy when she was a baby. In 1888 or 1889 the Weavers, who were then in their thirties, had been married for some years but had not been blessed with a child. So, when given the opportunity, they were delighted to give a home and their name to an attractive baby girl. They were more than surprised when, just over a year later, Lavinia found herself pregnant and gave birth to another little girl of their own.

Charles and Dorothy made their home near Epsom, where their three sons were born. Charles, like his father-in-law, had become a mill owner and the family lived well. Dorothy liked tennis and parties and entertaining the couples many friends, who included artists and playwrights. Charles, with his financial success, was able to pay the bills. Many years later their youngest son, Tony, told me that he thought his father had made a lot of money during the first world war but that, after the war, there had then been a lean period when the authorities caught up with him as he had "forgotten to pay some of his taxes"!

In early January 2004, with his family's permission, I visited Tony at the private nursing home in St

John's Wood, North London, where he was being cared for. Tony, then in his eighties, still had much of the charm I'm sure he possessed in his younger days and still had a sparkle in his eyes. However, although he could recall parts of his childhood and his youth, much of his memory failed him. The names of places and many people and dates eluded him. The one date I had hoped he might have retained in his mind was the annual one on which his mother celebrated her birthday. Unfortunately this could not be conjured up. We passed a pleasant hour or so over tea and biscuits and Tony agreed that I could call again for a further chat. Sadly this was not to be, Tony was diagnosed with cancer and passed away last summer. Both of his older brothers, Basil and Peter, had died some years previously.

One of the stories that Tony could remember was the one his mother had repeated to him on a number of occasions, both when he was growing up and afterwards. He thinks that this important recollection, which his mother spoke about, occurred when she was a pre-teen girl. The Weaver family had emigrated from Britain for a few years and gone to live in South Africa (Durban?). It seemed likely that this incident happened shortly before that period.

Dorothy had been taken to afternoon tea, possibly by her mother, to the garden of an imposing house. Their host, to whom the young girl was introduced, was Mr Elgar – the composer. It was a summer's day and, while a maid served tea in the garden, Mr Elgar made a 'big fuss' of Dorothy and encouraged her to tell him about herself. It was after they had said their goodbyes that an adult turned to Dorothy and said 'that very nice gentleman is your real father'. Dorothy had told Tony (and no doubt his two brothers – for this is a family legend) that this was the one and only occasion she met Elgar, but she understood her parents were acquainted with him.

Certainly at the time of the 1891 census, when Dorothy was aged two and Erica was two months old, the Weaver family were living in a large Regency residence called Lansdowne House in Lansdowne Crescent at the north of the centre of Worcester (Civil Parish of South Claines). At that time this was a most prestigious address and the house still stands, on high ground, overlooking the city and the cathedral. William's age is given as thirty-two. He is described as a *Flour Miller and Corn Merchant*, who was born at Spaxton in Somerset. Lavinia is shown as being four years older than her husband. In addition to the four family members, living in the household there was a *Companion Housekeeper* – aged 49 – and a 22 year-old *Domestic Servant*.

During the three generations of Dorothy's life; when she was a child, during her own marriage and then through the adult lives of her three sons, the subjects of illegitimacy and adoption were rarely discussed. The Victorian stigma, relating to children born out of wedlock, still pervaded this period and the topic would not be raised in case it caused embarrassment. For this reason no questions were ever really asked, and no speculations made about the identity of Dorothy's natural mother.

As I have already stated Helen Weaver could not have been Dorothy's mother. Ages given in census returns are frequently incorrect but not usually so for young children. Dorothy's age is given as two in the 1891 census and this is confirmed by the 1901 entry where she is recorded as being twelve. As the earlier census listed the people in every dwelling on the night of 5th April, Dorothy's date of birth should lie somewhere between 6 April 1878 and 5 April 1879. Helen had left England for New Zealand two and a half years before the earlier date. There is also no apparent link between the William Weaver, who lived in Lansdowne House in the Civil Parish of South Claines in 1891, and Helen's father also William Weaver who lived in Claines – less than a mile away – in 1881. Weaver is a fairly common surname and there were seven separate Weaver families living in Claines in 1881. Dorothy's William was the son of a Somerset miller who had also been born in Somerset. Helen's father's ancestors came from Warwickshire.

Census returns also give a person's place of birth. This information is often notoriously unreliable, as in Dorothy's case. When she was two and living in Worcester her place of birth is given as Worcester. In 1901, when she was twelve and living in Bath, Somerset, her birthplace is recorded as Croydon, Surrey. When I met Tony he had a vague recollection that his mother had said she had been born in Wales. She could have been born anywhere. There was no formal adoption process in Britain until 1927, so Dorothy's would have been a strictly private arrangement with probably never any written record. There were 157 female births registered in England and Wales, during the twelve months from April 1888 to March 1889, where Dorothy was given as a first or a second name. She might have been one of these or none. As a newly born baby she might not have been recorded as Dorothy or recorded at all. Although fines for non-registration and late registration (after 42 days) were introduced in 1875, a small percentage of births were never registered. To avoid the late penalty some birth dates were recorded incorrectly.

Further research could be done on this subject but I will leave that to others. As I have already written, this story is a slender one and Elgar's involvement is based on a family legend. For the record, the composer first met his wife – Caroline Alice Roberts – in October 1886 and they were married at Brompton Oratory, London, on the 8th of May 1889. Edward was not quite thirty-two. Both parents of Caroline Alice (she liked to be called Alice – although her original middle name was Ann) had passed away before her wedding but at the time of the 1881 census she was living with them at St George's Square, Claines, which is quite near to Lansdowne Crescent. Alice was over eight years older than her husband.

Dorothy Woodall (Weaver) with her three sons (taken circa 1918)

Earlier in this chapter I promised to recount Jane Woodall's Greening roots. Jane's father, Dr Charles Llewellyn, was an Army medical officer in India. His middle name, which he has also passed down to Jane's brother (another Charles Llewellyn), derived from his mother's surname. Mary Llewellyn who was the daughter of a draper married Jane's grandfather, William Charles Oswald Greening, at Cadoxton Parish Church (not far from Cardiff) in February 1909. At the time of his marriage the groom was a Railway Carting Agents Clerk. William Charles Oswald was a little difficult to trace back through the census files as his first name kept changing. In 1901, when he was living in lodgings in Pontypool, he was 'Chas'. In 1891 when he was fourteen and already working as a clerk for the Great Western Railway, but living at home with his parents Thomas and Fanny, he is listed as William C. Ten years earlier, when he was first mentioned at the age of four, he is called Charles. Thomas, at his son's wedding, is described as an 'Aerated Water Manufacturer's Manager'. Before that he had some ups and downs in the grocery trade. In 1871 he was a grocer's assistant in Hinckley in the county of Leicestershire. By 1881 he had married and moved to Monmouthshire in Wales. Here in Wye Bridge Street, where William Charles was born, Thomas ran his own Grocery and Bakery business. The shop must have failed, as by the time of the 1891 census he was a grocer's assistant again. Thomas was born in Upton-upon-Severn on the first of July 1849; he was the youngest of five children including his stepsister. Upton is a small riverside town in Worcestershire, a few miles north of the Gloucestershire border.

When Thomas was growing up the main influences in his life would have come from his mother Ann, who appears from the records to have been a strong woman. His father, who was also named Thomas, died when he was quite young. Except for some information on his marriage certificate (his father was yet another Thomas) and a census return where he gives Gloucestershire as his birthplace, we know very little about Ann's husband. He was born before the days of birth registration and I have found no record of his baptism (he may never have been baptised). It is likely that his Greening ancestors lived in the villages just south of the City of Gloucester and it is possible that he was descended from Zechariah of Elmore. I suggest how this might be so in the last chapter of this book.

CHAPTER EIGHT

✝

Perhaps you can join me and picture a woman struggling up the hill from Chepstow Back, where the ferries berth. She is poorly clad in a long ankle-reaching dress and a shawl, which have both seen better times. The shoes on her feet are very worn and we can see that she is impoverished. The woman is in her thirties and, although her face still has strong features, her once good looks are now beginning to fade. She looks worried and exhausted. In her one hand she carries a heavy bag containing all her worldly goods and the other holds the hand of a six-year-old boy. He is thin and small for his age but his mother has dressed him to the best of her ability. The pair have arrived in Chepstow on the daily steam packet from Bristol, the fare having cost the woman most of the coins that had been in her purse. She is proud and will do anything to avoid the indignity of appealing to the overseers of the poor for relief. She is making her way to a house in Priory Row, where she knows she will not be very welcome. However the people there cannot surely refuse help for her son, they are his grandparents.

It is late summer and a little over two years since the twenty year old Queen ascended the British throne, but these are troubled times. The previous year the London Working Men's Association had launched a 'People's Charter', which called for radical changes in government and the not unreasonable demand that there should be frequent elections and that all men, regardless of wealth, should have the right to vote. Within weeks this movement – The Chartists – would be broken at the nearby town of Newport, when thousands of supporters from surrounding iron and coal-mining villages would march on the town to demand the release of some of their leaders, who had been arrested and were being held in a local hotel. Soldiers guarding these prisoners would lose their nerve and fire into the crowd. Twenty-two Chartists would be killed and more than twice that number wounded. Later some of the leaders of the march would be sentenced to Death, have this sentence commuted to transportation for life and be brought in chains to Chepstow docks for the sailing-ship that would take them to Tasmania (sixteen years later the main Chartist leader,

John Frost, would be given a pardon and receive a hero's welcome on his return to Newport).

The woman reaches the house in Priory Row and, although she has no proof of her marriage to their eldest son, the middle-aged couple accept that the child is his and take the boy in. The woman is relieved; although the people in Priory Row are not rich they are part of a well-known local family. She knows her son will be well cared for. She is very sad to leave her child but realises that in this harsh world she has a better chance of survival on her own and the boy may have a better life with his father's parents. The year is 1839.

The woman remains in Chepstow, to stay near her son, but well before the end of the year she realises that she has given herself a big new problem. She is pregnant again and this time the father is a married man; her missing husband's younger brother. Sarah, for that is her name, had been brought up as a Roman Catholic so the mortal sin of abortion has not even been considered. So, on the twenty-sixth of May 1840, she gives birth to her second son. This takes place in a decaying and damp lodging house at Davis Court, a slum area in the centre of Chepstow. She is lucky to have a friend, Margaret, who helps her with the birth. Civil registration having become law in July 1837, Sarah herself registers her son's birth on the fourth of June. He is registered as Richard, son of Sarah Greening, formerly Couchman. Dashes are entered in the two spaces left for the father's name and occupation. On the thirtieth of August Sarah takes her baby to the parish church for his baptism. Here he is recorded as Richard, the illegitimate son of Sarah Greening.

As you will now have guessed, part of this chapter is pure fiction. My story and the reality of what happened may be quite different. I have just given a possible interpretation of the facts so far known to me. We only get a few glimpses of Sarah Couchman's life and her visit to St Mary's church is the last one. A year later England had its first detailed universal census. Sarah had vanished from Chepstow and I can find no other Sarah Greenings or Sarah Couchmans in England and Wales who appear to match her details. This census missed a few people and she may be one of those, or she may have died, or she may have left these shores, or it is even possible that she remarried and is registered under a different surname. I would be most interested to find out what happened to her, as she was certainly my great-great grandmother. Richard was my great-grandfather.

As well as not being able to find out what happened to Sarah after Richard's christening, I have found no record of her birth or baptism. Her parents must have been John Couchman and Sarah Tarrant, who were married by licence in St Mary and St Peter's church at Tidenham on 23 December 1798. Tidenham is a village only a couple of miles from Chepstow but just over the

English border in the southwest corner of the county of Gloucestershire. Sarah, no doubt named after her mother, may have been the couple's second child but she could have been much younger. Although I have not uncovered any documents that show where or when she was born, there is information about three of her siblings. John Couchman's first child was not baptised at Tidenham, so it seems that John and his wife moved from the village shortly after their marriage. James was born within a year of his parent's wedding, as he was aged sixteen when his funeral took place at Tidenham on 2 July 1815. Two other children were born in Bristol and were christened there, at St Joseph's Roman Catholic chapel in Trenchard Lane. RC baptismal records were written in Latin and are more detailed than those of the Anglican Church. They give the actual date of the child's birth and the mother's maiden name. John, probably named after his father, was born on 15 October 1803 and Mary on 7 September 1806. Mary, like her eldest brother, did not achieve adulthood. She was buried at Tidenham in July 1816. She had not reached her tenth birthday. I have not seen a record of Sarah Tarrant's death, but John senior died and was buried at Chepstow in May 1834. He was sixty-two.

These few recordings do give us quite a bit of information about the Couchmans and their rather sad history. They were the only family with that surname in Gloucestershire, Monmouthshire or Bristol at that time; so we have nothing to confuse us. The licence to marry and the christening of the two children in Bristol show that they were Roman Catholics. Chepstow did not have an RC church, which gave Catholics in that town no alternative to Anglican baptisms and burials. Prior to 1837 all marriages of Roman Catholics had to take place in the Church of England to comply with an act of parliament (Hardwick's Act). John was a labourer and we know the family lived in Bristol for some years, where he would have moved to find work. We also know they returned to Tidenham some time between September 1806 and June 1815. The family is not mentioned in any Tidenham poor records so John was able to support them. More than probably he worked in the Chepstow shipyards, the main employer of Tidenham men.

At the same time as the Couchmans were living there, the now small but then quite sizeable village of Tidenham was also home to the Watkins family and the Greening branch of 'Old' Ben's son Daniel. Some members of these families moved backwards and forwards from Chepstow a number of times and it is quite a task keeping up with them. Although only walking distance apart, the two locations are in different counties and in different countries. Their archives are kept in separate places. Tidenham documents are held at the Gloucestershire Record Office in Gloucester, those for Chepstow either at the Gwent Record Office at Cwmbran or in the public library at Newport.

Daniel's eldest son Frederick was nearly twenty-four in 1830, when he and Sarah Couchman crossed the Severn to get married. As this was a 'Bristol' wedding it seems certain that it was a union without parental approval. Sarah could have been as old as twenty-eight or as young as eighteen. No ages were entered in the church register and the few details we have of her life give us no clues. The ceremony took place in the mediaeval church of St John the Baptist, which stands on a section of the old city wall at its northern gate. I believe the couple only had one child who survived infancy and, as he was probably born in 1833, Sarah and Frederick must have spent at least two years together. I do not know what happened to Frederick. I have been unable to find a record of his death or burial in Bristol, so it seems probable that he deserted his wife and moved elsewhere. Perhaps some day a record of him will be discovered. The fact of this couple having a child is only conjectural, but it is based on strong circumstantial evidence. In the first census of June 1841 the youngest member of Daniel Greening's household in Priory Row, Chepstow, is named Frederick Greening aged eight. Unfortunately this early census did not give the relationship between members of a household, but this boy can only be the one described in my short fiction. He must have been Sarah Greening's legitimate son, who had been named after his father. Later in this story I explain how I have found confirmation of this.

I think the father of Sarah's second son, the illegitimate one and my certain ancestor, was Daniel's second son Benjamin. Again the evidence here is circumstantial and, I admit, a little flimsy. If Richard's father was not a Greening then, although my line carries the surname, we are – of course – impostors! The strongest evidence is the certificate of Richard's own marriage, which took place in Bristol when he was twenty-three. Richard himself supplied the details that were given to the clergyman, about his father's name and occupation. However I'm sure, *Benjamin Greening – carpenter,* would have been based on what he had been told as a child. Although a busy town and port, Chepstow only had a population of three and a half thousand and the truth of his parentage would have been known by a number of people. The other evidence is very much my own projection of events.

Daniel's second son was seven years younger than his elder brother. He also married a Tidenham girl, Winifred, the daughter of John Watkins a close neighbour of the Greenings. Winifred was nearly five years older than Ben and this wedding had the approval of both families as it took place in Chepstow Parish Church in June 1835. Sarah was the first child of the marriage and she was christened in Chepstow in April 1837. By the late summer of 1839, Winifred was heavily pregnant again with second daughter Harriet who was to be born on the seventh of October. Ben and Winifred were living at this time in Priory Road, Chepstow. This was not far from Priory Row, the home of Ben's parents. It is possible that Sarah (Couchman) Greening was living with them and had been invited to do so to help with the immanent birth. Winifred's mother was dead and Ben's mother was an invalid. There was probably not a great discrepancy in the ages of Sarah and Winifred and, both having been Tidenham village children, they would have known each other well. In compliance with the new two-year old law, Harriet's birth was registered eight days after her arrival in the world. The Registrar notes that Sarah Greening, who was *present at the birth,* gave the information. We do not know if this was Winifred's sister-in-law or her mother-in-law as they both had the same name. If it was Sarah 'Couchman', this may have been during the period when she got amorously involved with her brother-in-law. Ben was a hot-blooded twenty-six year old man at a time when his wife would not have welcomed his advances. It is interesting to note that not long after this second child's birth, Ben and his family moved back to Tidenham from Chepstow – maybe at Winifred's insistence. Perhaps I am reading too much into this but, if it was Richard's mother who was present at Harriet's birth, the scenario is a possible one. Benjamin was not strictly speaking a carpenter. He was employed as a Sawyer, most likely in the shipyards. His father Daniel, the shipwright, was an accomplished joiner as was his elder brother. It is likely that he also possessed some of their skills.

There were three other Benjamin Greenings in the Chepstow district in 1839. These were the two clockmaker/preachers, 'Old' Ben (sawyer Ben's grandfather) and his son Benjamin (sawyer Ben's uncle), who could hardly be in the running. There was also sawyer Ben's same age cousin, 'young' clockmaker Ben, who might be put on the suspects list. This Ben was probably still living in the Forest of Dean in 1839, but could have been back in Chepstow as he was certainly there by the time of the 1841 census. However he would have been described as a clockmaker not a carpenter, so it is most unlikely that he was Richard's natural father.

On the night between the sixth and seventh of June 1841, when eight-year-old Frederick Greening was recorded by the census enumerator as resident in a house in Priory Row, Chepstow, his half brother, twelve months old Richard, was also recorded as living where he had been born at Davis Court. His mother was not there. We do not know how long she had been absent before that date, but it seems likely that she would have been with her baby for most of his first year of life. Sarah's friends, Margaret Course and her husband John were looking after Richard. They were in their forties and had four children of their own with ages ranging from five to fifteen. Nearly three months after this Sarah had not returned to Chepstow or, if she had, she had left again. The Courses, who would have been very poor, had no alternative other than to take Richard to the Workhouse. The Minute Book of the Chepstow Board of Guardians (now in the County Archives at Cwmbran) was meticulously kept and fifteen-month-old Richard Greening is recorded as being admitted as a workhouse inmate, in the week ending 28 August 1841.

Luckily Margaret Course was not a 'baby farmer', an insidious profession that had sprung up in

Victorian Britain. It was virtually impossible at that time for a workingwoman without a husband to support herself and her child. Illegitimate children and their mothers were not only ostracized by society, they were unable to qualify for parish relief or be helped by charitable organisations. In 1836, Muller's Orphan Asylum in Bristol ruled that illegitimate children could not be admitted. The Asylum was only open to *lawfully begotten* orphans. A New Poor Law had been passed in 1834, which made an illegitimate child the sole responsibility of the mother until the child reached the age of sixteen. For a hundred years prior to this law, putative fathers had been responsible for such a child's maintenance and could be imprisoned if they failed to provide it. Unmarried fathers would be forced to marry the mother. However in 1833 the Government commissioned a 'Report on Bastardy'. This came to the conclusion that the then current arrangement only encouraged licentiousness and so the law was changed.

Baby farmers were unscrupulous older women who took advantage of the new law for the purpose of making money. They would advertise 'nursing' or 'adoption' services in newspapers. Desperate girls, who had given birth outside wedlock, would some how raise the fifteen to twenty shillings a month that was required to have their baby 'nursed' or persuade the child's father to find between ten and fifteen pounds to have the baby 'adopted'. Although most of the fathers would be young working-class men, some would be the sons of tradesmen or employers who had seduced their employee – perhaps a young maid. These would be pleased to find the adoption fee rather than be named and shamed. If the child was 'nursed' it might last a few months until the girl was unable to keep up the payments. If 'adopted' its life would be much shorter. The baby would simply be starved to death or even poisoned. In those days, infant mortality was so high in the married population that a few more baby deaths would not be regarded as abnormal. Although there were a few notorious court cases, in the main the authorities turned a blind eye to this practice. Many thousands of poor children of unwed mothers must have ended their lives in this way.

Infant mortality in some workhouses was also high but Richard was lucky. Chepstow Workhouse appears to have been a well-run institution and, as Richard was the only baby there when he was admitted, it is possible that he was initially cared for by the wife of Joseph Lewis, the workhouse master. Life outside the workhouse in 1841 was a precarious one for many children. Richard would at least be fed and have a roof over his head – and, when he was old enough, be sent to school.

In late June 2005, as I was finalising the text of this book, quite by chance and from a recently available source I was excited to discover some more information about my great-great grandmother – Sarah Greening (nee Couchman). Rather than re-write this chapter, I have left it as it stands and give the following postscript to her story below.

Richard Greening (b. 1840)
Great-grandson of Old Ben, great-grandfather of author.

Postscript

Sarah Couchman, who became Sarah Greening on her marriage to one of Old Ben's grandsons (Frederick, the eldest son of Daniel), had – at least – three separate families. The first one comprised of son Frederick who I presume was her eldest child. He was the small boy at the start of this chapter, who was brought up by his grandparents and later became the inventor I write about in Chapter 13. The second was Richard, my own great-grandfather, who spent his childhood in Chepstow workhouse. Finally she was the mother to a third family who were born and raised in the City of London. On 9th January 1844 Sarah gave birth to twins at 64 Dorset Street, St Brides. They were a boy and girl, William and Elizabeth, and on this occasion the father's name was recorded as William Greening. I'm guessing again, but it seems likely that Sarah had not remarried or found a new Greening protector. We are now in the very centre of London where the registrar would accept whatever he was told by the informant. The father's occupation is given as *Seaman*, which means he was not there and Sarah is the only person who would be able to tell us who and where he was.

This time the children did stay with their mother; perhaps there was nobody she could leave them with. I have not been able to find out where they were in 1851 but at the time of the 1861 census they were living in Harp Alley in the City. Sarah, described as a widow, was then occupied as a *Tentmaker*. 17 year-old William was working as a *Litho Printer* (most probably in Fleet Street, just round the corner) and Elizabeth was a *Valentine maker*. Harp Alley is still there today. It is a small street near Ludgate Circus. Perhaps in remorse for deserting her two earlier sons, in 1861 Sarah was also providing a home for two other children. These were her niece, 14 year-old Harriet, and nephew 11 year-old Charles. Although they were not a sister and brother, the surname of both of them was Couchman. It is possible that their four parents had died. Harriet was the daughter of John (no doubt Sarah's brother born in Bristol in 1803) and Charles was the son of Charles, who must have been another of Sarah's brothers and who's occupation is shown as *Surveyor*. I have not yet found out what happened to any of these four young people.

Sarah died in Bart's hospital, very near to where she had been living, on 1st June 1866. She was 54. In the space on the Death Certificate left for occupation is written *Widow of Frederick Greening a Ship's Carpenter*. This at least is true. Frederick's father Daniel had also been a ships carpenter before becoming a shipwright. Although both job descriptions are carpenters the first one is for a man who goes to sea. With this information we know that Sarah would have been eighteen years old when she married Frederick in Bristol and, if the 1861 enumerator was correct, the census tells us she was born in Somerset. Most probably Frederick did go to sea, which is the reason I can find no record of his death. Perhaps he lost his life on the ocean or he may have decided to start a new life in some distant port.

CHAPTER NINE

✛

In the spring of 1910 a firm of Minneapolis architects were commissioned to design a new bank building for the Exchange State Bank. One of the partners in the firm, that later became well known for designing church, civic and commercial buildings throughout America, was William Grey Purcell. The bank was to be situated on a prominent corner site in Grand Meadow, Minnesota. It was to replace a small brick-built property attached to a building of wooden construction, where the bank had first opened for business in the early 1880's.

An account of William Purcell's first meeting with the Bank's President is preserved in the American Northwest Architectural Archives at the University of Minnesota.

> On the first visit to Grand Meadow, Elgar Greening and I were standing by the old wooden bank, reviewing the building to be, when a wheelbarrow came bump-bumping over the railroad tracks pushed by an old man in a sloppy sweater and oversized overalls. "Here comes the President, my father". The old fellow was genial and hearty, made me welcome, but left banking to his slim quiet son. When we went "up to the house" for lunch, he took me out to the apiary, and I was then told that this unknown and unsung farmer had solved the hitherto unsolvable, and could control bee swarming on a schedule.

The Bank's President, and indeed the founder of the Exchange State Bank, was Charley – the two year-old toddler who had sailed across the Atlantic with his father John Greening in 1847. In the account that Charley's wife Clara wrote for her children, she describes the bank's early days

> Charley gradually worked into the banking business – I don't know how for he had very little education. At first he had a little office in one corner of the hardware store.

Afterwards he sold the hardware and built a little brick building, which he used as a bank until he had the building built which the bank now occupies. He worked very hard and long hours. He never came home to sleep until after midnight. Trainmen who used to get in here at midnight used often to run up to the bank to get their checks cashed, for the bank was never closed until he locked the door after midnight to come home for a few hours sleep. He needed help badly, so he sent Elgar to the cities [a Minnesota colloquialism for the twin-cities of Minneapolis and St Paul] for a few months schooling in a commercial school and then took him into the bank as cashier. Elgar was the youngest cashier anywhere around the country at that time.

Charley was a man of many parts. He first met Clara, on the first day of his arrival at the small town in Minnesota where she lived and worked as the town's schoolteacher. *Charley and I seemed attracted to each other from the first* Clara writes, and they were soon going out together. Charley was employed as a 'tinner' (a maker of tin-ware) at the town's hardware store but, within a year of his arrival, there was a serious fire in which the store was burnt down. This threw Charley out of work. Across the road from the hardware store one of the town's leading citizens had just opened a new brick-built hotel, to replace his small wooden hotel (*he had hired men to make the bricks*). The hotel's owner, who was Clara's father, asked the man who he already viewed as his prospective son-in-law to come and work for him as the hotel clerk. *It was while he was acting as hotel clerk that we were married – December 28, 1869, at noon.* It would also have been during his time as a hotel clerk that Charley taught himself how to keep accounts.

Elgar Greening, born in 1873, was Charley and Clara's second child and their eldest son. He had been named after Sir Edward Elgar in England, who was Charley's first cousin. After finishing high school, Elgar attended business school for a year. Then, at the age of eighteen, he joined his father as cashier in the bank. Although Charley remained President until his death, Elgar gradually took over the day-to-day running of the bank and – by the time he reached his thirties – was in full control of the enterprise his father had started. Years later Elgar's only daughter, Dorothy (today a retired teacher in her nineties living in Los Angeles), remarked that her father had nearly killed himself, with work and worry, getting the bank into shape so that it could be granted a Charter as the Exchange State Bank. This had been achieved. Charley died in 1914 and shortly after that Elgar persuaded his youngest brother, Elmore, to join him in the family business. Elmore, sixteen years younger than Elgar, had been a late and unexpected child for Clara and Charley. Like his eldest brother, his first name also had an English connection. He was named after the village in Gloucestershire where his great-grandfather had been born. Elmore had graduated from college with a degree in Botany and then taught science in high school for a short period, before his brother converted him into a banker. The two brothers ran the Exchange State Bank with modest success until 1932. The great American depression arrived that year and the bank, like many of its competitors large and small, was forced to close its doors. Elgar and Elmore were left with a pile of debts and uncollected loans to farmers.

The bank building, designed and built in 1910, is still standing. It features on the US Department of Transport's "America's Byways" website, where it is described as *an architecturally significant and attractive bank building in downtown Grand Meadow.*

Although born thousands of miles away in England, Charley had only been a very small boy when he arrived in Mazomanie – the small pioneer town in Dane County, Wisconsin, where his parents settled. He had grown up as an American farmer's son. The family farm was not far out of town. If you take the West Hudson Road out of Mazomanie today you will need to cross the Wisconsin River tributary, the Black Earth Creek, on one of the few remaining 1911 'Pratt truss' bridges in the State. This river crossing still bears the name Greening Bridge and is situated six hundred yards from the old family homestead, where Charley spent his childhood and teenage years.

As elder brother Jim would one day take over the farm from their father, Charley, as a young man in his early twenties, decided he would try his luck in the adjoining state of Minnesota. The experience of two previous years had changed the farm boy into a confident young man, who knew that America was entering a new age. Circumstances had broadened his horizons. He had spent time in Louisiana in the 'deep south' and had met and mixed with people from all walks of life. With the intelligence with which he had been born he wanted new challenges. The catalyst for the evolution of Charley's early maturity was the Civil War.

Just after Near Year's day in 1864, at the age of eighteen, Charley had enlisted in the 11th Infantry Regiment of the Wisconsin Volunteers. The war between the Union and the Confederate south, or as Charley would have known it – between the United States and the Rebels, had already been raging for three years. He had at last persuaded his parents that, as their younger son, it was his duty to volunteer and fight for his country.

Like his father before him, Charley decided to keep a journal of this traumatic period in his life. He also exchanged many letters with his brother Jim, his parents and his sisters. Their correspondence to him has sadly not survived, but his letters home and his journal – pages of which he posted with his letters to his brother – have been preserved. These provide a fascinating insight into the life of a private soldier in the Union Army and of conditions in part of America at that time. I would like to thank Charley's same name grandson (Chuck) for giving me a full transcription of these.

Charley's Civil War service did not involve him in any of the more famous set-piece battles of the history books, but his formation took part in a number of the lesser known confrontations and skirmishes – especially in the Red River Campaign. He fought at the Battle of Monett's Ferry on Cane River in April 1864, in which there were six hundred casualties. He was also at the Battle of Yellow Bayou the following month, where eight hundred and fifty lost their lives. Both of these actions were Union victories. Although *a shot went within twenty inches of my head*, Charley was lucky to emerge from the conflict unscathed. Although many soldiers on both sides were killed and many more badly wounded, the biggest cause of death (as in most armies before recent times) was illness and disease. In both his journal and his letters, Charley tells of a number of occasions when more than half of his unit were incapacitated by illness and he gives moving accounts of the deaths of a number of his close comrades. The soldiers were often soaking wet for long periods of time and Charley himself was laid low with fever on a dozen or more occasions. Although many of his friends and acquaintances never saw their homes again, a combination of his strong constitution – with his diet bolstered by food parcels from Wisconsin – and good fortune kept him alive until the early autumn of 1865, when he was *Mustered Out of Government Service* and was able to return to his loved ones at Mazomanie.

The United States and Union Army postal services come through the Journal as very efficient organisations. Charley – like many other soldiers – received a constant supply of parcels from family friends as well as from his Mother and sisters, which helped to supplement the often meagre military rations. In early December 1864 he received an English Christmas pudding from Mazomanie. It had not travelled well. His thank you letter, written from Brashear, Louisiana, starts:

> Dear Mother, I received your two nice presents (the cans I mean) about 4 o'clock. They were in good order & I thank you very much for them. Now about that pudding, when it came it was very mouldy. So I cut it off & rubbed it well with sugar & made it stick all over & thought it would then keep. I looked at it 4 days after & it was worse than when it came. So I cut it off again & buttered it well, scalded the tin, wrapped up the pudding & put it back once more. Yesterday I looked at it and found it all mouldy again. So I said it is just three weeks from tomorrow until Christmas & if I keep it until then, there will be nothing to eat left. So I said, Charley, you must eat your pudding tomorrow (Sunday) & think on Christmas how good it had tasted. So eat it I did. I boiled it a little to heat it through. I had to cut away one third of it for the mould eat in so deep. I made some brandy sauce for it & oh, didn't it slide. I'll give you my way of making brandy sauce on

a slip in this letter or, at least, how I made it and it didn't go very bad either. I am very sorry I could not keep it, but it was best to eat it while there was some left ….

As the eldest son, Jim was not expected to enlist in the Army. He was needed to run the family farm with his father. However, in May 1864, he also decided that it was his duty to volunteer for service. He signed on as a 'one hundred day man' – a short service reserve. His Regiment, the 40th Infantry, in which he was appointed a First Sergeant, was not involved in actual fighting and for much of his service Charley's elder brother was orderly sergeant at a camp near Memphis, Tennessee. I notice, in the Rolls of the Wisconsin Volunteers, that there is a John F Greening who is listed as a private soldier serving in the 3rd Cavalry. He was not related to the Mazomanie family in this book and is recorded as coming from Baraboo, then another small frontier town only a little over twenty miles away on the other side of the Wisconsin River. Perhaps he was also from a British immigrant family.

James H Greening was married twice. His first wife, Ella Richards of Platteville, died a few years after her 1879 wedding. Jim married again in 1890 and his second wife was Leora Laws, whose parents came from Vermont. Leora and Jim had four sons, James Claude (born 1891), Paul Edgar (born 1892), Frank Russell (born 1894) and Wilbur Charles, born in 1895. I'm sure that these four Greenings are likely to have many descendents living in the United States today but I have no information about them. I hope some of them may come across this book and I would be pleased to hear from them. Jim took over the Mazomanie farm from his father and the 1906 *History of Dane County* tells us that *for thirty-three years Mr Greening made a good deal of sorghum, the superiority of which is vouched by all who try it.*

After Charley's marriage to Clara, and before he became a banker, he resumed his occupation as a tinsmith. The account Clara wrote for her children describes some of the early years of their marriage:

> For the first year we lived in two very small rooms back of the hardware store. The tinner's bench was against the partition and it surely made plenty of music when Charley made tin ware. Nanna (their first child) became used to it. She would sleep through any amount of noise but, when the noise stopped, she would often wake up.

> The second year, Charley built a hardware store and also a small two-room house. The house stood where a machine shed now stands. It was in this little house, in that location, that Elgar was born. That summer Charley bought some lots on the south side

of the railroad track, in what was then a wilderness. We had our little house moved onto those lots. The same lots we have lived on ever since. I took the two children over to the farm and stayed while the house was being moved and two small bedrooms built on. We now had four rooms in our home. In this little home both Josie and Charlie junior were born.

Clara's account later continues.

Charley was elected to the State Legislature in 1876 and served for one year. I sent Nan and Elgar over to the folks on the farm. I took Josie, who was a baby, and spent a few days with him while he was there. I remember that I had quite a time getting my meals. I did not dare take the baby to the table in the hotel. I was afraid to go alone myself while Charley stayed with her and we couldn't always get the chambermaid to stay with her.

We spent many happy years in the little house. We had trials of course, and much hard work, but we were happy most of the time and usually well. As our children grew, our house seemed too small and we decided to build a larger one. Charley and I spent many evenings working on plans for that house. I told him I had had enough cosiness and now I wanted *room*. We built the foundation one summer and the next, the house we still occupy.

I shall never forget the lonely, dreary feeling of the first night in the big new house. It seemed so big and empty and the children so far away from me. They were upstairs and we had no upstairs in the old house. We divided up the work. Nanna was to help downstairs as she liked to clean; Josie was to do the upstairs work. Both girls were to do dishes. The one who wiped dishes was to sweep the kitchen floor and they were to take turns at washing dishes. They knew that the sooner their work was done, the sooner they could play. Elmore was born in the new house. He was seven years younger than Charlie.

Frank Warner, Charley's brother in law who was married to his sister Annie, became a partner in the hardware store.

He built a little house just across the street from ours. He did much of the work on his house and he and Charley even did the plastering. Annie was a wonderful woman, educated, cultured and very companionable. Their children were born to them in this little house, Leon, Alice and Lewis. Our two families had wonderful times together. Spent all our holidays together, first at one home and then at the other. Annie was quite a

Charley Greening in Civil War uniform

Exchange State Bank building, Grand Meadow, Minnesota
Built in 1911 (photo 1972)

musician. She gave Nanna her first music lesson when Nan was very young. Annie's health failed and she went to Minneapolis to a hospital. She left Leon with Mrs Stewart and Alice with me, taking Lewis who was eight months old. She found she could not manage the baby while having her operation, so Frank brought him back to me. He was a very good baby, but all her children had whooping cough and I had my hands full. Soon after this Frank decided to leave us and go into business in Minneapolis with his brother Lewis. We missed them sadly.

After his brother in law's departure, Charley sold his hardware business and started his new career as a banker. He somehow also managed to do a little farming and beekeeping. We must conclude this chapter, on this remarkable Greening, with a little more of the report by the Architect, William Grey Purcell.

There is another really paradoxical circumstance of great interest arising from this building operation. To get its full force, one must turn back to the world-old problem of bee swarming. Even in ancient Egypt, those wise and clever agriculturalists knew the loss involved when the bees swarmed away from their hive – without only an occasional chance of retrieving them or capturing in turn the swarm of some neighbour. If they could only know what made them swarm and when they would do it, the useful bees and their delightful product could become a very dependable part of an organised agronomy. But no one ever found out, and for five thousand years this problem remained as much a mystery as the language of the Etruscans.

The idea, like all such deep secrets of nature, was too simple. As long as there were unfilled cells above the queen bee, the colony stayed with the old home. The minute this storehouse was filled, the colony split and a part moved out to find and build a new city. When Mr Greening wanted a prosperous hive to swarm, he replaced partially filled tiers with trays from other hives in which the honeycomb was all filled, and then waited for the hive to swarm, which they promptly did. If a colony was not too vigorous and needed building up, he removed the tiers of honeycomb as fast as the bees filled them up, and replaced them with tiers containing empty comb, and the bees kept on contentedly working. It was just as simple as that, and let no man imagine that this old man's contribution to world economics is a slight matter. The saving in time alone to orchardists the world around, running all over the countryside trying to find and capture runaway swarms, is unbelievable. The saving in actual bee colonies, which would otherwise be lost, must represent a quarter or a third of the living capital of the industry.

The family of Charles and Clara Greening (photo taken in Minnesota c. 1895).
L. to R.: Nanna, Charles Jr., Clara, Elgar, Elmore, Josie and Charles (b. 1845)

CHAPTER TEN

✝

Although declining by 1800, the white slave trade of the North African Barbary Coast had been operating for at least 350 years. It has been estimated that the fanatical Muslim corsair pirates had captured and enslaved over one million Christian Europeans during this period. These were not only from the crews and passengers of waylaid Western European and North American vessels but also the inhabitants of villages near the sea, from Southern Spain to the English West Country and the coast of Ireland, who had been snatched from their homes. A few of the captives had been released after the payment of ransoms; the majority had ended up with a life of bondage and misery and never saw their homes or families again.

Although – over the years – many attempts had been made to stop this outrageous practice, it was not until 1816 that the British Government decided to finally bring this 'barbaric' part of the world to heel. Today it would be described as the War on Terrorism! By 1816, the fight with Napoleon had come to an end and also Britain's two- year conflict with the United States. However the Royal Navy's strength was still very high, it had not yet decommissioned many of its ships and was the most powerful fighting force in the world. Rear-Admiral Sir Edward Pellew, Lord Exmouth, was the man chosen for this retributive task. He sailed his punitive fleet of eighteen warships – joined at Gibraltar by a Dutch squadron of five frigates and a corvette – to the principal city and port of the most powerful Arab ruler in North Africa, The Dey of Algiers.

The Algerians were prepared; they had strengthened their defences and brought in thousands of reinforcements. *On nearer approach*, wrote a British officer, *the defences became visible, and the batteries were discovered to be studded with artillery, as thickly as space permitted, amounting to several hundred guns. Numerous clear red flags formed a sparkling contrast to the whiteness of the houses. Flags variously striped were also seen on the walls; these were the banners of different Moorish chiefs, assembled to defend the Crescent. In 1816 the Dey's Palace was in the centre of the city, a very large crimson flag, the largest*

I ever saw, waved slowly and majestically over it. It was said to be composed of silk, decorated with silver stars and crescents. For a while it looked as though the expedition would end in failure, as some of the British ships began to take heavy casualties from the shore batteries and accurate sharpshooters. Sir Edward himself was slightly injured and was lucky not to have been killed. As the afternoon progressed the massive firepower of the British fleet began to turn the tide and, by the end of the day, over 50,000 cannon balls had reduced much of Algiers to rubble. The corsair fleet was in flames and the notorious Barbary Coast slave trade destroyed. The immediate result of the victory was the liberation of 1,200 slaves. Among these were 18 English, 28 Dutch, 226 Spanish and 2 French. Most of the rest came from the states of the Italian peninsular. The first clause agreed by the Dey in the conditions of peace was *"The Abolition of Christian Slavery for ever"*. Lord Exmouth and his men became national heroes and he was showered with decorations and honours from many European countries as well as his own.

In this one-day battle, fought on 27 August, over two thousand North Africans had been killed. The British casualties numbered 215, made up of 141 dead and 74 wounded. The highest losses were on *Impregnable*, one of the largest British Men-of-War at Algiers and the ship in the centre of the bombardment. Twenty percent of its crew of 750 were either killed or injured. *Impregnable* was built in 1786 and at 2,200 tons was slightly smaller but almost indistinguishable from Nelson's flagship Victory. It had three gun decks and 90 cannons (the *Victory* had 100 guns).

25 year-old William Greening, who also suffered burns, was one of the wounded on the *Impregnable*. He had been in the armed forces for a number of years and had seen the end of the Napoleonic campaign. He had fought in the Second American War of Independence; serving on the sloop *Fairy* – one of the smallest ships in the Royal Navy, which had 16 guns and a crew of 125. In August 1814 William had taken part in the sack of Washington, when the original White House had been burnt down, and in September had been present at the battle of Baltimore, where the British commander General Ross had been killed. He was also involved in the war against the French in the West Indies. The *Fairy* had been one of the ships that seized Guadeloupe from France in 1815, two months after Wellington's victory at Waterloo. The sugar island was restored to the French after a peace treaty the following year.

William returned to England with the fleet and had a honourable discharge from the service in November 1816, because of the wounds he received in action. Thirty-two years later a Naval General Service Medal was issued with an 'Algiers' clasp. This had to be personally claimed by those who fought in the battle (and were still alive). The Naval medal roll confirms that William did this. He also received a pension for life of twenty pounds and twelve shillings a year, which seems especially high for someone without a rank. This would equate to half pay for a senior non-commissioned officer at that time.

In William's day, quite a high proportion of sailors were not volunteers. Many in the Royal Navy were there against their will or better judgement. The life was a hard and dangerous one and the pay of an ordinary seaman only one pound a month. In the early 1800's many British and foreign ratings had enlisted as a result of the 'Press'. This term derived from the word Imprest, meaning money paid in advance for State or Government service. A 'press gang' consisted of a detachment of between six and a dozen sailors, under the command of an officer, who toured the streets and taverns looking for suitable recruits between the age of 18 and 55. Their job was to persuade likely candidates, preferably merchant seamen, to join the navy. A few may have been convinced by the rhetoric, to fight for King and Country. Most were converted after they had been plied with alcohol and knocked unconscious or physically threatened.

William recovered from his injuries, although he must have been partly disfigured by his burns, and returned to Gloucestershire. Most probably because of his serviceman's contacts, he was able to land himself a very steady civilian job as a shipping agent on the River Severn. William was to hold this post for fifty-four and a half years, so was over eighty when he finally retired. After retirement he went on to live for another decade and did not die until his 92nd year. At the time of his death, he must have been one of the oldest ex-servicemen pensioners in the country.

William's civilian job, which he held for so long, was as an agent at Bullo pill. The word *pill* is a Welsh term for a tidal inlet and there are a number of them in the Severn Estuary. Bullo is just north of the parish boundary of Awre – the old Greening stronghold – and two miles south of Newnham-on-Severn. This inlet had originally been used for boat building but in 1810 had been selected, by the Forest of Dean Transport Company, for development into a small port for the export of coal and stone. A large dock basin was built, with tidal lock gates and an upper basin for water storage. Wharfs and stone revetments on the riverbank were constructed and coal chutes installed. Then a tramway was built from Cinderford, which was completed in 1833. Although small, Bullo had become one of the most important ports on the Severn. Other businesses, like a marble works, a brass and iron foundry and a builder of railway carriages and wagons sprung up in the area. In 1854, during William's time there, the horse-drawn tramway was superseded by a broad-gauge rail link, which connected to the Great Western Railway. This increased Bullo's importance and at its height, in the second half of the nineteenth century, it was handling over one thousand tons of cargo a day. Bullo began to decline after the turn of the century and was finally closed in 1926, after which it began to silt up. In recent years the upper basin has been repaired and there are plans to install new lock gates to give the tiny port a fresh incarnation as a marina. These proposals have not yet materialised.

William, of the *Impregnable*, appears in this book not only because of his long and interesting life and because he was among that small group of men – including the pharaohs – who went to the trouble of creating their own tombs before their death. He also appears because he is mentioned in a number of books as an old sailor and the great-uncle of Sir Edward Elgar (in one book more erroneously as the uncle). This mistake was, I believe, started by Dr Percy Young in his biography of Elgar published in 1973. In Dr Young's first chapter, entitled *Greenings and Elgars*, there are a number of errors. I accept that this biography was written before the much easier present-day access to public records, but some of its assertions should have been qualified.

William was not – in fact – the brother of Joseph, Elgar's Greening grandfather. His father was a William but one who was the husband of Hannah not Martha and he had been born in the Severn port of Lydney, five miles south of Awre, rather than in the village of Elmore. His branch of the family most likely ties in with other Greenings in this book, but he was not closely related to Joseph (1780). Elgar's grandfather did have a brother called William, or rather two of them. The first one, born in 1776, died as a child of seven so the name was used again for another brother baptised on 4 December 1785. This William probably spent all his life in Elmore. He was, almost certainly, the William – shown as a gardener and widower living on his own there at the age of 65. This was in the national census taken in March 1851. The garden in which he was employed would have been Elmore Court. Joseph had another brother named Daniel who is also recorded in this census. He was then aged 69 and living with his wife Jenny at Broad Street in Little Dean, a small town on the Forest edge, where he was a shopkeeper. *Pigots 1852 Directory* describes him as a *Grocer, Dealer in Sundries and Seedsman*. Daniel had been baptised at Elmore in 1782.

William, of Algiers, was also not in the Royal Navy. Researching seafarers' records at Kew is not an easy task for a layman and the naval expert, who I asked to do this for me, found no trace of a seaman called William Greening in the early nineteenth century. After almost giving up, he finally discovered that William had not been a sailor. He had been a Royal Marine. He had enlisted on 8th April 1812 at the age of twenty and, at five feet four and three-quarter inches was slightly above the average height for marines at that time (many were only 5ft or just over). He had hazel eyes, brown hair and a fresh complexion and had been enlisted by a Major Arnett at his hometown of *Lidney in Gloster* – where he had been a labourer. My researcher assured me that all Royal Marines were volunteers, there was no need for press-gangs in this Service. On the ships that went with Lord Exmouth to Algiers there were not only sailors and marines but also soldiers of the Royal

Marine Artillery, Sappers, Miners and the Royal Rocket Corps. Instead of hats, some of these troops wore – for the very first time – the *big-topped Shako with brass plate and worsted tuft*. This was possibly in imitation of the headgear that had been worn by Napoleon's army. They must have made an impressive spectacle.

William was baptised at St Mary's Church in Lydney on 23rd January 1791. His father, who was also called William, had married seventeen year-old Hannah Winter at the same church in October 1784. Hannah came from Lydney but her husband was most likely from another parish. We have nothing to corroborate this, but he was possibly the son of Thomas and Hester who was baptised at Frampton-on-Severn in April 1760. If this was so, William – who had taken part in the burning down of the White House – would have been the son of Old Ben's cousin and so a member of one of the main lines in this book. In August 1827 the ex-marine married Mary Green at Abenhall, which is a small Forrest village where she had been born. Initially the couple may have lived at Bullo but, by the time of the first census in 1841, they had moved to the little town of Newnham. Here they lived in Newnham Street with their four small children and a thirteen year-old servant girl. William is described in the census as a *wharfinger*. A year later, in *Pigots 1842 Directory*, his name appears among the traders of Newnham as the Agent for the *Churchway Coal Company at Bullo Pill*. Newnham-on-Severn was a typical small Gloucestershire market town, not too busy as the directory also records that a sloop named *The Newnham Market* only left the town's quay *for Bristol with passengers and goods once a fortnight.* By 1870 this connection had increased to once a week. Newnham tried twice to become a more important centre. In 1810 it was proposed that a tunnel be built under the Severn from the town to Arlingham and, in 1877, plans were drawn up to build a bridge over the river here. Neither project got beyond the discussion stage; they would have been extremely costly.

By the time of the 1851 census Mary Ann, then nineteen and the eldest of William and Mary's children, had become a dressmaker. Seventeen year-old William, their only son, was an errand boy and his two younger sisters Louisa (13) and Harriet (12) are simply listed as being *At Home*. The following year Mary Ann married local tailor John Wooles. Thirty years later, when William made his will, his wife and all of the children except Louisa had died. His first bequest was *My Silver Ware Medal*, which William left to his eldest grandson Walter Wooles. Walter later became a railway engine driver. Son William had married Ada Edmonds and had been a dispensing chemist in Bristol. However he had died in his forties and I have no record of him having any children.

I do not know why William received such a large pension for most of his life, as he had only served as a private soldier in the Royal Marines. The amount must be correct because it is inscribed on his tomb, together with the full details of his four and a half years in the military (you might not tell the truth on a paper tax return but you would in a statement carved in stone). If this book creates a 'Greening Trail', around the villages in Gloucestershire that I have written about, Newnham-on-Severn should be a main stopping point on this route. Not only is it an extremely attractive small town, with a wonderful view down the Severn from the high ground of the graveyard to the south of St Peter's Church, it also holds the most spectacularly carved small tombstone I have ever seen. This is William's, which not only tells his life story but is also a marvellous testament to the stonemason who carved it. It lies a little in the shade under a yew tree (a few paces from the river view) but it does not photograph easily. The snapshot reproduced in this book does not do the stone justice and it is certainly worth visiting. Apparently William, when in his nineties, sat for many hours in the stonemason's yard with a critical eye. He was watching the craftsman carry out this very individual assignment that he himself had commissioned. We do not know the name of this very skilled workman, but I note that in 1861 William and Mary had a lodger. He was stonemason, Frederick Hopkins. Perhaps it is this man's artistry.

CHAPTER ELEVEN

✢

We now live in an age of exact timekeeping throughout the 'civilised' world. There are internationally recognised time zones and the official clocks within those zones are kept in check with radio time signals. This was not always so, the worldwide synchronisation of time is a relatively modern phenomenon. In most of the nineteenth century, 'public' time would vary from place to place. Timekeeping was in the hands of the official who was given the task of maintaining the clock outside the city centre post office, on the town hall or in the village church tower.

The city of Melbourne, Australia, was established in the late 1830s and the civic leaders had an official clock erected on its first Post Office in around 1842, from which the citizens of this then frontier town were able to adjust their business and personal timepieces. This coincided with the arrival in Melbourne of that city's first clock-making family, the Greenings. They, first the head of the family and then his eldest son, were given the task of maintaining the clock and time in this new colonial outpost.

Benjamin James Greening (1814) took over the maintenance of this important civic mechanism, from his father, in the later part of 1846. At first he *was unable to ascertain the precise time of day, in consequence of the impossibility of taking observations without the aid of an artificial horizon, which he could not procure.* In February 1847 he was able to make the required observations and *discovered that the town time was fast by 18 minutes and 7 seconds.* Benjamin James adjusted the clock and the citizens of Melbourne were advised to alter their watches and clocks to conform to this new official local time.

In 1895, following an inter-colonial conference, Australia was divided into three separate zones of standard time. In this new age, with the arrival of the telegraph network, time throughout Australia was adjusted again. In Sydney it was made to stand still for five minutes. In Melbourne the clocks had to be advanced by twenty minutes, wiping out the adjustment Benjamin Greening had made 48 years earlier.

In my first book, I wrote that the Greening emigration group had started their journey from Cork in Ireland and numbered twenty-nine people. This derived from a note on a family tree that had been sent to me – from Australia – many years ago. This information was not correct. Bill Brand, who lives in Melbourne, has done extensive research in the Victoria archives and I am indebted to him for the emendations.

The Greening party, which we now know consisted of thirteen people, may still have been the largest family group to have sailed into Port Phillip Bay, Victoria, on the Sailing Ship *Samuel Boddington* on the 13th of January 1842. Their ship, which had taken four and a half months to reach Australia after leaving Gravesend in Essex on the first of September 1841, was a three-masted barque of 670 tons. The *Port Phillip Patriot* newspaper of 17th January reported that the Master of the vessel was Captain Edward Noakes and that there were 28 cabin Passengers (most of them named) with twenty children. In addition there were 226 Immigrants, *under the superintendency of Doctor Belcher.* The paper also reports that three infants died and two new ones were born during the voyage. It would appear that all the Greenings survived the journey.

'Our' group was made up of Joseph and Frances Greening, their five youngest children – Elizabeth 13, Joseph 11, William 8, Mary 5 and Richard 2 plus three 'grown-up' daughters and Eliza (their eldest married daughter) with her husband Henry Daw and that couple's three year-old child Caroline. The three older girls are listed in the index of Assisted British Immigrants, held in the archives of the State Government of Victoria. These were Frances and Joseph's third, fourth and fifth children – Caroline 21, Frances 18 and Anne 17. The handwritten schedule records that all three could read and write and were Protestants. As three respectable young ladies of marriageable age, they were part of a commodity much in demand in this predominantly male-populated embryo society. As assisted immigrants, the State of Victoria paid a £19 'bounty' to the shipping company towards the cost of each of their fares. Their parents and their married sister with her husband will have had to pay for their own passages and for those of the children. Joseph's financial situation must have been fairly desperate. He could not afford cabins, so he and his family were obliged to endure the hardships of the cheapest quarters on board.

Steerage accommodation on immigrant sailing ships, at this date, is almost impossible for us to imagine today. A couple would be allocated a partitioned space six feet by three feet, with a straw mattress, blankets and a bolster. Small children would share their parents cubicle, those over twelve travelled separately. There was a toilet for women and girls, but men and boys had to relieve themselves from the 'heads' on the lee side of the ship. One lamp by the main hatchway was kept burning all night but passengers had to be in their beds, with all other lamps extinguished, by ten pm. Unless pronounced sick by the ships surgeon they had to rise at seven am and, when dressed, roll up their bedding and clean the decks before breakfast was allowed to commence. For their three daily meals, steerage passengers were divided into groups of six who appointed a 'mess captain'. He or she would then collect the issued rations, take them to the galley and cook them if required (usually into stews). The passengers were supplied with a metal plate, mug, cutlery and a cooking pot. These would be washed and put away until the next meal. Vinegar was added to drinking water, which frequently turned foul between ports of call.

Although no Greening journal of this voyage survives a rather brief diary, kept by a passenger named Joseph Wilson, has been preserved in the State archives. This confirms that the Greenings were on the ship from the start of the voyage in Essex, the same county where they had been living prior to their journey. Although a number of Irish immigrants will have joined the ship at its first port of call in Cork, this was a few years before the start of the Potato Famine. The terrible events in that country, at their height when John Greening sailed from Liverpool to New Orleans six years later (travelling second class), were still in the future.

The following entries from Mr Wilson's diary give us just a little insight into the voyage to Australia.

1841 – SEPTEMBER
Wednesday 1st: By cab to London Bridge Wharf, thence to Gravesend. Luggage on board and then returned to Water's Hotel. 'Samuel Boddington' got under weigh and anchored again about 4 miles down river. Moonlight evening – Twenty or thirty small children.

Friday 3rd
Weighed at half past 6 a.m. – nearly becalmed off Dover at 9. 4 p.m. a squall with violent rain and thunder and lightening.

Saturday 4th
Nearly all the passengers sick.

Sunday 12th
Off Lands-end, light wind, fine morning but turned wet. Divine Service in the Steerage conducted by Mr. Greening, Steerage Passenger, at 12 a.m. Made Cork Harbour in the

afternoon – took on a Pilot and got in and anchored just at dark.

NOVEMBER – Monday 1st
Crossed the line today.

Wednesday 24th
Almost calm this morning, a little more wind by 12. Spoke to a ship at 2 p.m. bound for Sydney with 260 Emigrants, left Dundee on September 17th. One of the sailors found in bed with one of the young women.

DECEMBER – Thursday 2nd
Wind West – much warmer – going about 6 (Knots). The Captain much displeased by some groans and other expressions of discontent (about half-past 8 p.m.) on account of the Salt fish, a quarrel among the Intermediates arising from the same cause.

Friday 3rd
Very cold 30 degrees at 7 a.m. Wind S.W. going 9 at 10 a.m. All the Steerage Passengers mustered aft at 9 a.m. and reproved by the Captain for their conduct last evening and invited to arrange their difficulties by three Deputies – one for Captain, one for Surgeon and one for steerage passengers. This was agreed to and Mr Greening, Mr Forsyth and Mr Dickins appointed to inspect the fish which was condemned by them (in writing) and 6 oz of beef or pork ordered to be served out to each person instead of it.

These records indicate that Joseph Greening was the leader and most respected steerage passenger on the ship. It also confirms that he was a lay preacher like his father and two of his brothers. Although the last leg of the journey was accomplished in record time (38 days from the Cape of Good Hope to Port Phillip) I am sure that, after more than a third of a year at sea, all the family must have been overjoyed to set foot on dry land in Victoria.

Benjamin James, Frances and Joseph's eldest son, did not travel to Australia with his parents. Although Bill and I have found no record, it seems likely that he and his family followed about four years later – in late 1845 or early 1846. Benjamin had married Angelica Sophia Kirk at Stepney in London in late 1839 and the first two of their children were born there. A daughter, Frances Claire, had her birth registered in Stepney in the spring of 1845. So it was after that date, but before taking over responsibilities for the Melbourne clock, that the journey must have been made. Angelica gave birth to later children in Australia.

Joseph was the fifth and the youngest surviving son of Old Ben and, like his brothers, had been born in Frampton-on-Severn. He had followed his father into the clock-making trade and will have left Chepstow for Bristol as a young man, where it seems likely that he initially lived and worked with his older brother Charles. In January 1814 he married Frances Pritchell James at St Paul's church, Bristol, and it was in this city that his three eldest children were born, commencing with Benjamin James that same year. His fourth child was baptised in March 1823 at Frampton-on-Severn, so was probably born in Gloucestershire. The next two were born in London and the youngest four in Essex. Although Joseph had started out as a clockmaker and sailed from Gravesend to Australia – at the age of fifty – as a Watch and Instrument Maker, he seems to have been on the move for much of his life and had tried other professions. When he lived in Essex he described himself as an Optician.

Some of this information comes from a large family tree showing the descendants of Elizabeth (1828). She married Francis Messenger and echoing her mother also had ten children. The late Joan Pickering compiled this chart in the 1970s. Joan was one of Elizabeth's many great-granddaughters. I received another tree from Robert Findlay in New Zealand. He is a grandson of Royal Naval Lieutenant Robert Joseph Greening who was a grandson – in turn – of Joseph James (1831). Bill Brand, my correspondent from Melbourne, is a great great grandson of Anne (1824) and I am in email contact with Ted Greening who lives in the North Island of New Zealand. Ted is surprisingly Frances and Joseph's great-grandson. Most descendants of Ted's age are two or more generations further down the line. Ted just happens to be the youngest and late son of the second wife of the youngest son of Frances and Joseph's late son – Richard James (1839).

On the twelfth of August 1852 a letter was sent from Chepstow in Wales to Melbourne, Australia. Old Ben was then ninety-six but still wrote with a strong hand.

> Dear Son, Daughter & Family,
> I have to say I recd your short letter on the 8th of October. You say you have written a long letter to me and sent by a Clergyman, but I have not recd it yet. I have not seen the Gentleman and I expect I never shall. I was glad to hear you and yours are well.
>
> I will give you an account of myself, and all the family, as for myself I can say through the goodness and mercy of God I have enjoyed a very good state of health.
>
> I am now going to tell you some sorrowfull account of what has taken place in the Family, that is, your Brother Nathaniel is no more, he departed in March last, he was from home at his Daughters.

Your Brother Benjn he is gone he departed on June 21st, he went to carry home a clock he had been cleaning, he cald at his Brother-in-laws about nine o'clock in the evening and he said I must give it up, I can't do it, he said no more then he was taken in a fitt – he said O Lord! and never spoke after. In about ten minutes he was gone. This happened so sudden, and from home, this took so great effect upon me that I was very unwell for a month or more, my appetite was gone I could take but very little food, and I could have very little sleep at night, but Thank the Lord I am better now. We'd believe these sudden Deaths was sudden Glory! These events is a loud call to you, me, and all of us. Be ye also ready, for we know not when the son of man cometh.

Your sister Hester and Husband and Family are well. And also your sister Priscelia and her Husband and her 2 sons (these are all she have living) are well. I have given you an account of all the Family, so no more on that subject. I have herewith Presented you with a Dozen of my tracts, if you will accept of them, I do think you will approve of them when you have read them. I can say they are very much approved of by most people that have had them with us, now if you give it a fair reading, and duly meditate upon it, you will find a great deal Included as not Expert, in short I do. I will explain 2 places to you, and that is the Bay. Now this bay is the Christian's Dying Bed, and as I have said in the tract, how long we shall ride there is uncertain. So it is, some do linger a long time and some are taken away suddenly, so it is uncertain. Now the next is the Boat called the Dispatch, that is, Death. You know that Death do dispatch the soul from the body, and land it safe (not on the beach or the seashore) but in Heaven itself – there the Christian's voyage will end –

I shall now turn to another subject. (viz) to ask you how you are getting on as to this Life, if you are able to say having food and raiment you are contented. This is as much as the body can contain, then be thankful. – now I ask, how are you getting on towards the other world, I do hope you are seeking the Lord with full purpose of heart, that you are forgetting the things that are behind and pressing forward toward   the mark and prize of your high calling which is of God in Christ Jesus our Lord. – as I gave you an account of your 2 brothers, I forgot to tell you about Charls, he was putting up a large clock in the County Prison in Glos and the scaffling gave way and he fell and hurted his ribs very bad, and one leg. He is getting better, but it is very likely he will never be right well. And his wife is quite blind, and been so a long time. Daniel is a very great sufferer indeed, and has been for 40 years last march and could never have it cured, and a fortnight ago he had a fall and hurted him very much. But Thank the Lord he do bear it with great

Patience, and his wife have been very unwell for many years. Now I have given you a full account of all the family–

As for the tracts I sent you, you will find in one a Crostic. I wish you will keep it in Remembrance of me as long as you live.

Do not be offinded, if I do ask you a few Questions are you living in the Enjoyment of the love of God in your soul, which I hope you do, but if not, then seek with all your power, seek by prayer and faith, if you do you will be sure to find it, you will find it to your present comfort here and to your Everlasting salvation in the world to come. –

I thought to have written more, but my time is limited, I have sent by a Mr Thomas, a young man that is come to reside in Melbourne from Chepstow, – I am going to ask you to send me an account of all your Family, how many sons and daughters, and daughters-in-law, and sons-in-law and how many Grandchildren, I very much wish to know. –
Now I do most earnestly beg you will not delay not a day. For you know the time of my departure is at hand, may the Lord fully prepare me and you for that solom day, is the sincere prayer of your Ever affectionate parent –

Benjn Greening – fare ye well.

As this letter would have taken at least four months to reach Australia, Joseph had already passed away before it arrived. He and his brothers Nathaniel and Benjamin had all died within the same twelve months. Their very ancient father had outlived them. Luckily Joseph's family preserved this letter. I'm not sure where the original may be. Rob Findlay sent me this transcription many years ago.

After Joseph's death, Benjamin James carried on the clockmakers business in Melbourne that his father had started. In 1851 he had a go at gold prospecting and was a member of a six man 'fossicking' party that found 'payable' gold in Andersons Creek (now Warrandyte). Bill informs me that the Victoria State Government set up a Gold Committee, which offered substantial rewards to those who found gold. They were keen to retain population that was being attracted away to recent discoveries in New South Wales, New Zealand and California. The party of which Ben was a member was one of the two main finders and were awarded £1,000. This resulted in a population explosion. When trade in the clock business fell away, Ben worked for the *Melbourne and Hobson Bay Railway Company*. He was initially employed as a clockmaker and later, according to railway company records, as a Mathematical Instrument Maker and Electrician.

In Australia and New Zealand today there will be literally hundreds of descendants of Joseph and Frances, as their children presented them with over sixty-five grandchildren. Some of these have probably migrated back to Britain or moved elsewhere in the world. As this book is overburdened already with far too many names (that is what family history is about) I don't want to add too many more here. However, for anyone researching in this area, it is incumbent on me to give the names of Joseph's children's partners. Three of them have already been mentioned. The husbands of the three 'respectable young ladies of marriageable age' were Oliver Parnham (Caroline), William Hartnett (Frances) and Frederick Wood (Anne). Twenty children were born to these three Greening daughters. The other two siblings, who stayed in Australia, were William James who married Ellen Dwyer and had at least eleven children (nine of which were boys) and Mary who married Walter Watkins and had two children (the smallest family). The remaining two boys Joseph James and Richard James, the baby of the family, both moved on to New Zealand. Joseph was married to Ellen Anderson and Richard to Catherine Lane.

Richard James Greening and his wife Catherine Selina Ann were married in Victoria in 1860 and immigrated to the South Island of New Zealand, in 1864. Richard was a very colourful character and had at least two business failures. He first became a publican in the recently established settlement of Kaiapoi, a dozen miles north of Christchurch, but he was declared bankrupt in 1866 and was unable to pay any dividend to his creditors. He then became a self-employed stagecoach driver who, after borrowing two hundred and fifty pounds from a Mr Maxwell, took the mail contract between Charleston and Westport on the west coast. He failed again, and is recorded as having no assets and liabilities of four hundred and thirty-one pounds. A New Zealand Biographical Index tells us that *he organised the Kowhai Pass Sports in January 1873,* and *in '74 he was driving the coach over the hill to Akora and did so well that he was presented with a gold watch and chain by Garwood representing the people of Akora.*

Following his failures in the South, Richard moved to the North Island. Here he earned the nickname 'Dare Devil Dick' as the stagecoach driver from Featherston to Wellington, which had to travel along the treacherous Rimutaka Hill road. After one journey he was commended for saving passengers from a certain fatal crash. I included the newspaper report of this incident in my earlier book. Catherine was only 35 when she died in 1878. She had borne her husband eleven children. Her youngest child was Ted's father Charles Herbert Greening.

In 1893 the Reverend James Stock wrote an interesting history of Kaiapoi, the small town where the

Greenings first settled. This was located near the remains of a Maori fortress that had been the site of a siege and battle between the local tribe and warriors from the North Island. He was fascinated by the fact that 'civilisation', which had taken thousands of years to evolve in Europe, had blossomed in New Zealand in little more than half a century.

> So rapid has been the process of transformation, that persons who have come to these shores within the last twenty-five years have found everything about them so like what they left behind in the Old World, that the change of residence has proved to them more like a removal from one English county to another than removal to a foreign land.

> But, he mused, that persons still living have only to close their eyes to the scenes around them to recall to mind the appearance of the country when there was not a sign of civilised life to be found anywhere within a thousand miles of it, when everything was in a state of nature, and the only people to be seen were fierce, untamed barbarians.

Kaiapoi's first European building, a thatched wattle and daub cottage, was erected in 1855 – less than ten years before Richard and Catherine arrived. Ted's grandparent's lives took place during the metamorphosis of this pioneer country, which is not easy for him or for us to imagine.

Although Parson Stock may have regarded the Maoris as *untamed barbarians,* that was not the opinion of Captain James Cook and his famous naturalist companion, Joseph Banks, when they circumnavigated the North and South Islands a hundred years before. Although they found the Maori a very warlike people who, with their isolation from the rest of the world and without the advantages of Western European technology, had evolved a completely different culture than their own – they recognised them as their equals. The word Maori means 'normal people'. Unlike the Aboriginal People of Australia, who had been on that continent for at least 50,000 years, The Maori had arrived in New Zealand comparatively recently. They had come in a series of Polynesian migrations that had started not all that long before the Normans had invaded England. Some historians believe they supplanted a previous indigenous race, the Moriories, who it is thought came from a different area of the Pacific and whose remnants only inhabited the outlying Chatham Islands when British colonisation began. Other historians dispute this.

Another man who regarded the Maoris as equals was John 'Happy Jack' Greening (sometimes known as 'Sir John Greening'). In a North Island weekly newspaper *The Hawke's Bay Times,* published on 18th May 1868, there is a news item under the heading 'Anchorage at Wangawehi'. This informs us that:

Mr Greening alias "Happy Jack" keeps a light burning in his window, every night the wind is blowing from a southward direction, without any remuneration whatsoever. This is the only beacon between Auckland and Wellington a distance of within 500 miles. Perhaps the poor man could be reimbursed with oil used or even the Government look to a lighthouse on the East Coast.

Happy Jack knew well the perils facing sailors off this very treacherous coastline.

I have had correspondence with Donna Greening, who is a direct descendant of Sir John down the Maori line. She informs me that she is one of hundreds of her people who regard John and his Maori bride, chief's daughter – Wikitoria Teheiawairangi, as their ancestors with some pride. Many, of course, have different surnames but Donna comes from one of the main lines. Her grandfather, Henri Te Rito O te Rangi Greening, was the grandson of William Henry Te Paihou and Metekete Christie. William Henry was John and Wikitoria's only son. This makes my correspondent John's great-great-great granddaughter.

Donna has given me a little background information about John from Maori sources, but I have not yet discovered who his father was or if his roots originated in Gloucestershire. It is believed that he was born in Islington, London, in about 1806 and joined the Royal Navy as a boy sailor at a very early age. He served on the *Galatea*, which was a large 36 gun 'Man of War' (a '5th Rate' wooden-hulled Battleship) that ended its days in the West Indies. John left the service in Jamaica and joined a Captain Ellis, who was going whaling in the Southern Oceans. They arrived in New Zealand waters in 1836 or 37 and John harpooned his first whale off Waikakopu on 24th June 1838. This would have been from a small open boat – Captain Ahab style.

After some years John, who earned the appellation 'Sir John' from some white settlers he had helped rescue from a massacre at Poverty Bay during a raid by a Maori War Chief named 'TeKooti', gave up the arduous and dangerous life of a whaler and set up home with Wikitoria on the still very wild coastline of the Mahia Peninsular. Here he ran a store and started his amateur 'lighthouse'. Donna tells me that the New Zealand government finally paid him twenty pounds a year for this service. For many years it was the only beacon guiding mariners sailing off the east coast of the North Island. It probably saved many lives. When John died in August 1880 he was buried with full Maori honours and a large 'Tangi' was held.

Today the language of all New Zealanders is changing. The prominence of many English words has declined and there are now hundreds of Maori words and expressions in daily use by everyone

Joseph Greening (1791)
Old Ben's youngest son
Sailed to Australia in 1841

Benjamin Greening (1814)
Joseph's son, grandson of Old Ben
Changed the time in Melbourne in 1847

– both in speech and print. About one person in five has some Maori ancestry and Donna, who admits that she is usually taken for a Pakeha (white person) and – as well as English from Happy Jack – has Viking ancestry through her mother, is fiercely protective of her Maori heritage. She teaches the Maori tongue and traditions to her children but she is also proud of her Greening surname.

CHAPTER TWELVE

✛

Power Boat racing in North America had its Golden Era in the Roaring Twenties. The controlling body of that sport, the APBA (American Power Boat Association) which was founded in 1903, was asked in 1923 to change its rules and allow a racing boat of clinker built construction to compete in the annual race for the Gold Cup – which was held on the Detroit River. The boat *Rainbow IV* (the fourth in a series) was inspected and the Rules Committee agreed that it was eligible. On 30th August 1924, this boat easily won the Gold Cup race. With an average speed of 46 mph and top speeds exceeding 60 mph on the 'straight-aways' it comfortably outdistanced the other competitors. However, an objection was raised by the owner of a losing boat and after much deliberation, *Rainbow IV* was disqualified. This was because some of the officials thought that this design – although technically permitted by the APBA – did not really comply with the spirit of the rules, as it did not have a proper water 'displacement' hull. The power boat racer, owner and designer of *Rainbow IV* reckoned that if the 'clinker' planking of the boat was run diagonally from the keel across the bottom, instead of longitudinally, the one inch steps would make the boat travel much faster. His design, which incorporated eleven steps, would reduce Rainbow IV's wetted surface to about one ninth of her total length. She was the very first craft of her kind – a multi-stepped hydroplane.

This innovator, whose originality resulted in the development of the hydroplane, had an active racing career spanning twenty-five years from 1904 to 1929. He was the holder of many world records for speed and endurance and, in 1928, won the Sir Thomas Lipton Trophy – becoming powerboat champion of North America. After retiring from active participation, he became a leading member of the sport's governing body and later the Chairman of its Racing Commission.

Harry B Greening was a Canadian, rather than an American and, as powerboat racing was (and still is) a rich man's sport, he was also an industrialist. He was a co-founder of International

Airways – which became part of Canadian Pacific – and also had interests in early Automobile Racing. His 'day job' was Chairman of the Board of Directors (later President) of his family firm – The B Greening Wire Co Ltd of Hamilton, Ontario. Although known to most people as Harry, this Greening's Christian names were Herold Benjamin. He was named Herold (not Harold) after his mother's surname and Benjamin after his Grandfather. His grandfather had also been named after his grandfather – 'Old' Ben, the Chepstow clockmaker.

The B Greening Wire Company was founded in Hamilton in early 1859. Benjamin (1807), the youngest son from the first marriage of Nathaniel (1780), had arrived in Canada eighteen months before. All but one of his children had come with him. He was fifty years old when he arrived and had already owned – and sold – a successful wire manufacturing company in Manchester, England. He had not intended to start up in business again. However he could not have chosen a more fortuitous time, the rapidly expanding economy of this young 'Dominion' ensured that its first wire manufacturing plant, which Benjamin had set up following a string of chance events (described in my first book), could be nothing but an unqualified success.

Benjamin ran the company until his death in 1877 when his second son Samuel Owen, who was in charge for the next 34 years, succeeded him. Benjamin had been an entrepreneur whereas Samuel was a salesman. It was during S. O's time at the helm, that the business grew to be not only a supplier of wire products throughout Canada and parts of the United States but also an international competitor to the Warrington firm being run by his cousins. A copy of one of the early letterheads of the Canadian company is reproduced in this book. This incorporates a line drawing of the Victoria Wire Mills, the firm's first factory in Hamilton. It heads a reply, handwritten by Samuel to his older brother in London, regretting that he was unable to accept an invitation for him and his wife Jennie to stay with his brother during Queen Victoria's Diamond Jubilee celebrations. This brother, the only member of the family to remain in England when his father emigrated, was Edward Owen. I have written about this most illustrious holder of the surname in another chapter.

In 1841, when Joseph Greening and his family emigrated from England to Australia their sailing ship took four and a half months. As steerage passengers their voyage would have been an extremely arduous one. Six years later, in 1847 when John Greening and his family left Britain for the United States, the journey from Liverpool to New Orleans took seven weeks and two days. This sailing voyage is described in John's journal at the end of this book and, as he and his family travelled second class, the passage would have been a little more comfortable than that of his distant relative but – as you will read – far from an easy one. Ten years later, in 1857, another Greening family left Liverpool to cross the North Atlantic. This time it was two of Joseph's nephews, half-brothers Benjamin and Timothy Greening with their wives and families. They enjoyed a much more pleasurable journey, not only had the era of the steamship arrived – making the crossing to Quebec only twelve days – but Ben and Tim did not have to count their pennies, they travelled first class.

Benjamin (1807) and Timothy's steamship was the very first owned by the Montreal Ocean Steamship Company (usually known as the *Allen Line*). It was the 277 foot iron hulled *Canadian*, which had been built in Scotland and had its maiden voyage to Canada in late 1854. In 1855 it was used by the British Army as a Crimean War troopship but, by the following year, was back in civilian service with accommodation for 80 First Class and 350 Third Class passengers. After Quebec the Greenings were going to steam up the St Lawrence River to Montreal – a journey that could only take place during the summer months. This was June 1857 and, although there was no heavy ice, the ship unfortunately hit a rock and began to sink. Fortuitously as they were near to shore everyone was rescued. The Allen Line replaced the Canadian with another slightly larger ship of the same name three years later. This one was crushed by an iceberg, when steaming through the Belle Isle Straight to the Gulf of St Lawrence. This also happened in June and there was a loss of 35 lives. Earlier the same year (1860) another Allen steamship, the *Hungarian* on the same Atlantic route, sank with the loss of all lives off the coast of Nova Scotia. So the Greenings had been lucky. Timothy describes the sinking of their ship in a letter to his brother Noah in England.

> …We are now a shipwrecked company of four hundred persons and eighty-four crew but thank God there has not been one life lost. At 20 minutes past one o'clock this morning, Martha, me and the children, were all fast asleep in bed, when a tremendous grind – bang – crash and roar waked us from our sleep and nearly pitched us out of bed. The screams and rush was frightful … The scoundrel Pilot had run the steamer at full speed on to a rock scarcely covered with water within 150 yards of Rock Island on which there is a brilliant lighthouse and situated about 40 miles from Quebec … The 1" and 7/8" wrought iron plates were ripped up as an old tin can would have been, and a great hole in the bottom that you might drive a cart through. The Pilot attempted to drown himself when the ship struck.

While Samuel Owen Greening – who would have been about ten at the time of the shipwreck – was building up his firm to be one of the main manufacturers of wire rope in North America, his first cousins in England were expanding their company to be *"by far the largest and best known makers of wire-screening in the world"*. At the end of the nineteenth century the original Warrington business was being run by two cousins Linneaus and Nathaniel (1855). These were respectfully the only sons of Noah and John, who had been in charge of the family enterprise before them. Linneaus and young Nat were probably more like brothers than cousins as for much of their childhood their families lived next door to each other.

Nathaniel, *'the second'* as he was known, also had private interests. The Cheshire County Archives hold a personal letter file of his for the year 1900, which makes fascinating reading. Nathaniel was a very precise man and, in addition to his business correspondence, he hand wrote a number of private letters almost every day. Quite a number of these are in respect of having electricity installed in a private house. In 1900 this was far from the simple matter today of making a single telephone call. A hundred years ago electricity was a very costly and very complicated addition to a home. You would first need to build an Engine Room, Accumulator Room and Boiler House in your grounds (perhaps in the stable yard). Then have your own engine designed, built and assembled (*...to run dynamo, our high-pressure horizontal steam engine will run at 135 revolutions, have a flywheel 7 ft diameter & 8" face. It will give off 45 effective Horse Power, as a maximum, with 100 lbs Boiler pressure... etc.*) before you even got to the stage of having your house wired and the new 'electric lamps' installed.

There is an interesting exchange of letters between Nathaniel and his eldest daughter's boarding school. Although a wealthy man, Elsie's father was very careful with his money and objected to the school charging him for part of a term when she was ill and at home. He was also upset that his word, as a prominent citizen, needed to be supported by a note from Elsie's doctor. On 30th March 1900 he wrote to the Secretary of the North West Methodist School Association in Liverpool, concerning the fees for his daughter at Penrhos College, Colwyn Bay. *...You ask for the Dr's Certificate, which apparently means you doubt what I say on this subject.* He must have received an answer by return post as three days later he wrote again. *...In reply I think the way – the extremely arbitrary way – in which you propose to deal with this matter is very unsatisfactory...* The school must have won as in July he sent them a cheque for £75 – *for school fees in advance for the May term* – to be followed by another cheque for sixteen pounds, one shilling and seven pence which, I guess, was the amount he had deducted from their previous term's bill because of Elsie's indisposition. The short final letter from the school is preserved in Nathaniel's papers. *Dear Sir, I am sorry you have taken such offence at what is merely a business transaction, but doubtless you will see it more from our point of view later on. Yours etc C H Marshall, Secretary.*

There are a number of other interesting personal letters, but by far the largest number concern Nathaniel's main passion in life – or certainly his main passion in 1900. Whereas his cousin Linneaus (like his father and grandfather) was more interested in Natural History than wire,

Nathaniel's big private obsession was cycling. Almost half the letters he wrote that year are in connection with it or refer to it. On 26th March 1900, Nathaniel wrote a long letter to Messrs Singer Cycle Co Ltd, Coventry. It begins

> Dear Sir, On Friday last week I forwarded to you per L & NW (London and North West) Railway Co. Carriage paid (at Co's risk) one bicycle No 102,463. I shall be much obliged to you if you will be good enough to overhaul the bicycle and let me have it back again this week without fail, as I want to take it on a long journey.
>
> Loose Spokes. With the exception of loose spokes I have never been troubled in any way with the machine since I first had it, but the spokes have been a constant source of annoyance to me, breaking and coming loose – even as much as twice in a week.

He then goes on to ask if the tyres could be 're-enforced' (he had read an article about this) and explains, in great detail, adjustments he would like made to the Brake, Rear Case, Front Fork and Back Fork. He concludes the letter:

> I shall take it as a particular favour if you will please oblige me by sending the machine back without fail on Thursday or Friday, that I may get it on Saturday Morning. P.S. Please do not delay the machine on account of payment. I will pay your charges, which please make as reasonable as possible. When returning the machine please consign to N Greening, Bank Quay Station, Warrington at Company's risk carriage paid.

The 'long journey' was Nathaniel's first Continental bicycling holiday and all seems to have gone very well. The vacation must have taken place in April as in early May he writes to a friend.

> Just a week today I returned from the South of France where I have had the best cycling trip I ever had. My friends and I took the train as far as Lyons and we cycled from there to Monte Carlo. The weather and roads simply perfect. We stopped at each place of interest 'enroute' and visited all the Roman remains to be seen. The country is most beautiful I never enjoyed a holiday more in my life.

Other letters show that some of his cycling companions continued on to Genoa, but Nathaniel had to return to England for business meetings. He put his bicycle on the train at Monte Carlo but it was unfortunately damaged on its way back to Warrington. In a letter to Mr Moore, The Station Master of Victoria Station, London, *Nathaniel* writes:

...I can prove beyond doubt that the bicycle was delivered to the P.L.M. Co at Monte Carlo in an absolutely perfect condition ...I am of the opinion that the damage was done in transit from Dieppe to London..On enquiry from your cloakroom you will find that I signed for both bicycles, and after my signature (N. Greening) I wrote "not examined". Awaiting the favour of your immediate reply, as I wish to get the machine repaired as quickly as possible.

In 1900 Nathaniel was 45 so must have been reasonably fit. He had not been taken in by the joys of a less demanding mode of travel, the Motor Car. Two letters in his business files of 1903 give me the impression that he was probably not too impressed by these new-fangled devices. As well as his family business, Nathaniel was also a director of a number of other companies. He had been asked to join a few 'Boards of Directors' because of his business expertise (or perhaps his capital). One of these companies was owed money by an Automobile manufacturer and it had been proposed that this business be taken over. Nathaniel asked a colleague to inspect the firm on his behalf and received the following reply.

My dear Greening, I was down at Worcester last week and have come to the conclusion that the Monarch Motor Car is worth a small D -. There is nothing in the stock worth a £5 note. The modern Petrol Motors weigh one-fourth for the HP developed.

The "Monarch", like many early motor manufacturers, bit the dust and a few days later it was in the hands of the official receiver. There is another letter of a similar date from a Mr Rockey, who was the wire companies representative in South Africa. He writes from Johannesburg.

The Motor Car is a hopeless Failure – It's all the more galling since all the others are behaving quite nicely and getting good results. It has sickened me of motor cars more than I can tell you. I will hand the derelict over to Newman for his special and sole use, he might be able to manage it, no one else can. It starts when it likes and goes when it likes. In fact worse than a gibbering horse whose hunger will sooner or later get the horse moving.

The Warrington museum was refurbished in 2005 with the aid of a National Lottery grant. It is a most interesting place to visit. If you walk from Gallery 4, *Warrington in Close-up* – which depicts some of the town's more recent history, in the direction of Gallery 5 – the prehistory room complete with model dinosaur – you pass through a fairly dimly lit corridor that has been called the *Time Tunnel*. Here scenes of Warrington life in the Georgian and Victorian eras are displayed by

Harry, Hattie, Mabel and Edna Greening
The children of Samuel Owen Greening (Hattie was the grandmother of Averill Ambrose)

tableaux. Half way down the corridor there is a glass-panelled door, which used to be and is still signed *Curator's Study*. There is a white time switch by the door that, if pressed, will illuminate the small room. Behind the curator's desk, the wall is lined with ceiling high display cabinets filled with dozens of glass preservation jars of various sizes. These contain small reptiles and spiders. This forms part of the Natural Sciences collection of Linnaeus Greening, which was left to the museum – with his meticulously kept notebooks and microscopes – after his death at the age of 72 in 1927. Obituaries reported that, at that time, his was the finest collection of reptiles, frogs, toads, batrachians and spiders in the country outside that of the British Natural History Museum.

Although a local Town Councillor, Magistrate and Chairman of the family firm, Linnaeus was chiefly celebrated in his hometown as one of Cheshire's foremost naturalists. Like his Grandfather Nathaniel and father Noah, he had had always been fascinated by the natural world and lived up to the famous Swedish scientist's name with which he had been christened. In an appreciation of his life, written by a Dr Lowe, there is a recollection of an 1890's outing by the Warrington Field Club.

> Linn Greening, as he was invariably called, was an outstanding figure, and his geniality and love of a joke made him the life and soul of every expedition. I can see him now, armed with a huge net, sweeping vigorously through the herbage and bushes of King's Wood, Abbots Moss and other parts of Delamere Forest (our favourite hunting ground) in active quest of the insects and spiders in which he was so deeply interested.

Other reports tell us that, as a young man, he had met and been inspired by Charles Darwin and that during his life he had written many books, papers and pamphlets. These had titles like *'British Snakes'*, *'Air breathing Anthropods'*, *'Wings of Insects'*, *'British Newts'* and *'What is a Bird?'*. Colin Taylor, the present museum curator (who has found himself a new study), kindly showed me a large accumulation of postcards and letters that Linn had sent to his friend George Ellison over many years. A few of these are reproduced in this book.

Both Nathaniel *'the second'* and Linnaeus were Directors of *N Greening and Sons Limited* and took their turn as Chairman, having taken over the firm from their respective fathers. Although both married and had children, only one male heir was born to Nat. He was yet another Nathaniel but was always known as Jack. He became a director of the company in 1928 and his was the last Greening surname on the board. The firm became a Public Company (N Greening plc) in the 1950s and part of a large international conglomerate in 1975.

CHAPTER THIRTEEN

✝

> I was much complimented on my speech and one old gentleman, an old army officer, told
> me there was a great future before me if only I did not allow myself to be spoiled by flattery.

So wrote the most prominent Greening in British public life – from London to his wife in Manchester in 1866. Among his papers, preserved in the Co-operative Society archives, is an extract from another letter he wrote to his wife – three years later.

> I am sorry to hear you had an unpleasant dream of me, although I hope you will not be
> put out when I say that I do not think death so very dreadful. Although I feel that I have
> much to do for myself, for you, for my children (and for England too) I feel often as
> though it would be pleasant to be at rest. I fall so far short of my own aims and desires
> and am ever working with such poor apparent results. However I am not going to give
> up as long as I am alive. Of that be assured.

The Co-operative Society College in Manchester holds the collections of the three revered 'giants' of the cooperative movement. They hold over four thousand documents of Robert Owen (1771-1858) – the saddler's son from Mid-Wales who became known as the father of cooperation and British socialism; about seven thousand items of George Jacob Holyoake (1817-1906) – the great cooperative propagandist (usually also described as a Secularist who – in 1842 – was the last man in England to be convicted of blasphemy) and, by far the biggest archive, over eleven thousand papers of Edward Owen Greening.

Edward Owen was born in Warrington in 1836. He was the eldest son of Benjamin Greening (1807) and Ann Owen, and so a grandson of Nathaniel – the wire weaving entrepreneur and a great-grandson of Old Ben. When he was a young boy the family moved to Manchester, where his father's business – Greening and Company, manufacturers of iron and wire fences – operated from the Victoria Works in Market Street. He was educated at Manchester Quaker's School until the age of thirteen, when his father made him an apprentice at his factory. Although the son of the owner, his father exhibited no favouritism and Edward worked a twelve-hour day the same as the other employees.

Edward made his first public speech at the age of sixteen, at a meeting of the Manchester Anti-Slavery Society of which he later became secretary. He was a founder of the Union and Emancipation Society and during the American civil war a keen advocate for the Yankee cause. He was a founder of the Manchester Suffrage League and, although he was not elected, he obtained the highest socialist vote when he stood for parliament at Halifax in the 1868 election as a Working Class candidate. Involved in the cooperative movement for most of his adult life, he was responsible for the first Co-operative Congress convened in 1869. He started the Agricultural and Horticultural Association in 1868 and was its managing director until 1915. He was also one of the founders of the Labour Association, a member of its first executive and its first treasurer in 1884. He became its President in 1893.

Edward Owen was an outstanding public speaker and a lucid writer on many subjects, from the reform of the Army to parcel post. He carried on a voluminous correspondence with many influential figures of his day, including Earl Grey, Lord Leverhulme and (interesting for me – my favourite childhood author) H Rider Haggard.

Edward Owen Greening died in his 87th year in March 1923. On the card attached to the wreath sent by the Central Board of the Co-operative Union were the words – *He was the oldest and the youngest member of the Board. He sought harmony in life; he has found it in death.*

Today on the front of a block of flats in Belmont Grove, Lewisham, South London, there is a plaque marking the site of the house where Edward Owen lived during the later part of his life. He is described as a Co-operator and Social Reformer.

Edward Owen was married in the summer of 1860 at Salford, Manchester, to Emily Hepworth. Emily, a free thinker like her husband, was later to become an active member of the suffragette movement. They had four sons, Edward William, Frederick Benjamin, Arthur Hepworth and Walter Morrison – and two daughters Emily and Annie.

Edward William married Lillian Alice Palmer in 1886 and in the 1891 census is shown as a co-op factory manager living in Thames Ditton, Surrey. They had a young son who they named Edward Owen after his grandfather. Frederick, the second son, did not marry and appears from his father's papers to have spent part of his life in a mental institution. Arthur married Sybilla Williams in 1893 and is described as a shipbroker's secretary in the 1901 census. Walter, the youngest son, married Mary Alice McVay in 1900 and in the following year's census is recorded as being an advertising agent. He was living in Mortlake, the hometown of unrelated John Greening who appears in another chapter. Walter wrote his father a letter in September 1918, a couple of months before the armistice, as he was about to lose his job due to the former holder of that post returning from the war.

> I am afraid I have poor news to convey. I shall soon be leaving Oxo – I understand that the man whose place I took is returning …… enclosed you will find a letter of application to Lever Bros. As you are friendly with Lord Leverhulme, will you do me a great favour of forwarding the letter on to him with a few lines from yourself? With love from May and the boys – your affectionate son – Wall.

Edward Owen did not make a copy of his reply to his son.

It seems more than likely that Edward Owen has a number of descendants living today. It would be interesting to know what they are doing.

One interesting archive I have looked at is the worldwide database for patent applications. This goes back just over one hundred years and most of the early Greening applications were from Nathaniel Greening or 'N Greening and sons'. For example *Improvements in and relating to Conveying Bands and Belts* (September 1895); *Improvements in and relating to Conveying Bands for Minerals and the like* (April 1896) and *Improvements in Wire Gauze Sampling Sieves* (April 1897). This Nathaniel, then the chairman of the company and whom I wrote about in the last chapter, was a grandson of the first wire-weaving Nathaniel. He also made foreign applications such as *Perfectionnements aux metiers a tisser la toile metallique*, which has a Swiss reference dated March 1890.

There is also a joint patent application from Edward Owen Greening and his son Edward William. This was made in September 1894 and was for *An Improved Method of Utilizing and Means for Treating Yeast*. Edward Owen was a keen horticulturist and, among his many activities and responsibilities, he was the editor and publisher of the *Agricultural Economist*.

Intriguingly for me, another Greening appears as the inventor of an application made in August

1901. This was for *The Manufacture of an improved Material for Insulating Electrical Conductors, Waterproofing Fabrics, and for other Purposes*. This applicant was Frederick Greening, who gives his occupation as Inventor and Patentee (Electrical Appliances) in the 1901 census. In my first little book I guessed that this man was my great-grandfather's half brother. The son of Sarah Couchman and Frederick, the grandson of Daniel – Old Ben's third son – and the little boy I describe trudging through Chepstow with his mother in my fictional story in an earlier chapter of this book. I based this on the one word, Monmouthshire, which he gave as his county of birth in the 1881 census (I speculated that he may have been born in Bristol but, as he spent part of his childhood with his grandparents in Chepstow, he probably assumed he had been born there). There is a little uncertainty about his age. In the 1841 census (taken on 6 June) he is shown as eight. So, if this is correct, he should have been 68 rather than 70 at the time of the 1901 census. However, my calculated guess has now been confirmed.

On 3 April 1881 Frederick was living at 2 Kingston Villa, Norwood in South London. He shared his home with his wife Maria, shown as having been born in Belgium, and their two sons Fred – aged twelve – and 'Lugia' aged ten. Both boys were at school and are recorded as being born in Poplar, Middlesex. Frederick's occupation was Manufacturing Chemist. Ten years later the family had moved to Mill Hill Grove, Acton in the Borough of Ealing. Frederick and his son Fred, now twenty-two, are both listed as Manufacturing Chemists. The household had a new member, Maria's brother 'Peka' whose occupation is given as Tallow Melter. Maria had anglicised her name to Mary and both she and her brother give Breda in Holland as their birthplace. Breda is very near the Belgium border and coincidently only a few miles away from Tilburg, where my wife of Belgium/Dutch ancestry was born.

'Lugia' was not with his parents in 1891, but I have found him in that year's census. He is the John L Greening, age twenty and born in Poplar, who was living as a lodger in Brighton. His occupation is recorded as Naturalist. Ten years later he had dropped the 'L' and – in the census of that year – is the John Greening, living with a wife Margaret and one year-old daughter Dorothy at 17 Capstone Road, Bournemouth. The clue that enabled me to confirm that this was the same man, Frederick the inventor's youngest son, was that Margaret's birthplace was shown as Neath in Glamorgan. This pointed to a possible wedding in southeast Wales and I was able to obtain a copy of the Certificate of Marriage of Maggie Holbrook, twenty-four year old spinster, to John *Lucian* Greening. The wedding took place on Christmas Eve in 1896 at the Parish Church of Saint Dyfrig in Cardiff. John was twenty-five and gave his occupation as Naturalist, his father's name and profession as Frederick Greening – Chemist. Five years later, when the couple and their daughter were living in Bournemouth, John records his occupation as *Bird and Animal Preservation Worker*. I would be very interested to discover what the responsibilities of his employment were. It would seem that in late Victorian England, John Lucian was an early wildlife conservator.

In 1901, Frederick senior was still living with his wife and eldest son but they had moved to 1 Arcadia Parade, Plumstead. Fred junior's occupation had also changed to an *Assistant to Inventor* and he had been joined by a wife, Kathleen, and two sons of his own – Victor (age 4) and Bernard (age 1). Frederick senior's place of birth is clarified, as Chepstow, and his daughter-in-law would have been Kathleen Hugh Cooke who married Frederick Victor H Greening in the March quarter of 1896 at Hackney, London. I have obtained a copy of the Inventors Marriage Certificate. Frederick Greening married Maria Van Der Steenstraten in June 1866, also at Hackney Parish Church, Frederick's occupation in the register is shown as *India Rubber Manufacturer,* Maria's father's rank is given as Gentleman and Frederick's father's name and profession is also recorded on this certificate. As I had guessed a few years ago, his name was Frederick and he was a Shipwright. This confirms that the inventor's father was indeed the Frederick, born at Tidenham in 1806, the eldest son of the shipwright Daniel – the fourth son of Old Ben.

I would be extremely fascinated to discover any living descendants of Fred (1869) or his brother John Lucien (1871). Like my family – we are all descended from the enigmatic Sarah Couchman.

A road, originally built by the Romans after their conquest of Gaul, lies between Albert and Bapaume in Northern France. These are two small towns, less than twenty kilometres apart, which lie just northeast of the city of Amiens. The countryside here is not unlike parts of the Gloucestershire Cotswolds. It is an area of gently rising slopes and valleys, sprinkled with small villages and farms and patches of woodland.

It was here that one of the worst and in the words of most chroniclers; one of the most pointless battles in the history of Western Europe took place. The River Ancre, which ran through the northern part of the battlefield, starts near Bapaume and then flows in an arc north of the Roman road until it reaches Albert. It then becomes a tributary of the larger river that formed the southern border of this area of conflict. This river, which flows west through Amiens before turning north to reach the English Channel, gave its name to the battle. Now used as a word to sum up the futility of war, its title is the Somme.

In the summer of 1916, the British Army held Albert and the German Army held Bapaume. At 7.30 in the morning of the first of July of that year, after a massive bombardment that had been expected – yet had failed – to destroy the German defences, British and French forces attacked the German front line. When heavy snow brought the battle to an end in mid-November, the Allied front line had only advanced twelve kilometres at its widest point. Albert was still held by the British and Bapaume was still behind the German lines. All this had been at the cost of well over a million casualties, with a British total of approximately 420,000 killed or wounded.

On 1st July, the first day of the battle, 19,240 men of the British Expeditionary Force lost their lives and there were more than twice that number seriously wounded or captured by the enemy. That date is still regarded as the worst day in the history of the British Army.

Many soldiers died of their wounds after the Somme offensive had been brought to a halt. One of these was Company Sergeant Major Harry Greening, who succumbed to his battle injuries at the 9th Casualty Clearing Station at Contay on 9th December 1916. Today his body lies at rest with 1,100 others in the quite small but beautifully maintained British military graveyard in the tiny village of Contay, a few kilometres to the west of Albert. This is one of a vast number of cemeteries, maintained by the Commonwealth War Graves Commission, that dot this area of France.

The following obituary and tribute to Harry appeared with his photograph in a Bristol newspaper shortly after his death.

BRISTOL & THE WAR

————

SERGT – MAJOR GREENING
KILLED IN ACTION

————

FINE TRIBUTE FROM A COMRADE

————————

It will be learnt with very considerable regret that Co. Sergt. Major Greening, a well known Bristolian, has died from wounds received in action. In many regards the deceased non-commissioned officer occupied a unique position in regard to service rendered, and the tribute to his worth as a soldier and a man, conveyed in the following letter addressed to us by a friend, is well merited:

At the outbreak of war the late Co. Sergt. Major Greening voyaged from Australia to rejoin his old corps. Before proceeding to the front he was promoted to the rank of company sergeant major, having received the rank of sergeant on his rejoinment. Whilst the battalion was in training in England he had a great influence on the ranks because of his vast experience, and had a large share in the training of recruits and drafts for France. When his battalion left for the front, Co. Sergt. Major Greening once more proceeded on active service. It would be impossible for me to express my admiration for his fearlessness, his coolness, and his extensive knowledge. It has been generally acknowledged by all ranks that he was the backbone of his company; the company stood on him so to speak; it was build around him. He was a man who has never been known to say "Go"; "Come" was ever his order. However dangerous the work, however risky, our company sergeant major, without exception, went with his men. When work was hard he was with us; when times were hot he was here and there and everywhere, bucking up his men by his fine example of courage.

Many men of the drafts sent out to us will remember him, and the manner he would help them undergo their first time in the trenches, exposing himself at great risk to his own life to show them by example how they must do their duty. His company commander, Captain R. A. Young, son of the vicar of Pucklechurch, has expressed his grief at his loss. His words were: "The finest soldier I've ever met with." All our sergeants are more grieved than we care to admit with the loss of our mainstay, our hero in action, our chum when out. A man who could control a regiment single-handed. He could sing a good song at our smokers, and he was a man "on the spot" every time. He will be badly missed and mourned by all officers and men of his corps. One other battalion will regret his death, remembering him as the man who organised a party to bring in the wounded and the dying. Again and again he brought men in at grave risk to his own life. It was Co Sergt – Major Greening who "brought in" the late Captain Ayre and Sergt. Coleman on the 19th July last; it was he who went out again and again to try to find other well-known Bristol officers. Co. Sergt. Major Greening was about to return to England for his commission. He leaves a widow and three sons, the eldest of whom is 13 years of age, and they live at 94 Victoria Avenue, Redfield.

*　*　*

Harry, or Richard Henry as he was registered at birth, was the eldest son of Richard and Mary Greening – my great-grandparents. This would also make him a first cousin of Frank and John Lucian. He was born in Adelaide Place, Bristol, on the 27th of May 1872. My great-grandfather's occupation at that time is recorded as Tobacco Packer. Harry will have joined the army, as soon as he was old enough, and had reached the rank of Sergeant in the Gloucestershire Regiment by the time of the South African War at the turn of the century. He must have been an excellent marksman as on the back of a photograph of him, posing with other non-commissioned officers, my grandmother has written that 'he won the cup for shooting at Bisley (value 200 guineas), which is in the Bristol Art Gallery, and fought in the Boer War under General Buller'.

As the newspaper tribute had informed me, Harry had left the army and – with his wife and family- had immigrated to Australia some time after the end of the South African conflict. He had probably not been there long before returning to Britain to re-enlist at the outbreak of the Great War. When I produced my earlier family history, I had found that Harry's wife's name was Elizabeth and that she kept a shop (possibly a Fish and Chip shop) in Bristol during the war. However I was unable to find out any more about their family. I speculated that they may have returned to Australia, and wrote in the book that I 'would be pleased to hear from any of their descendants'. Within a few weeks of the book's publication I had found them. My hunch about Australia had been correct and these, not so distant, antipodean relatives are now in regular correspondence with me.

Harry had married Elizabeth Alice Bowden at Bristol in the early months of 1903 and they had four sons. These were Harry Leonard (known as Len), Ernest Richard and twins Frank and Wilfred. A photograph of them appears in this book but Wilfred died shortly after this picture was taken. The information that follows comes from my second cousin Leone Ferrier, who is the daughter of Len, and Leone's daughter Jane Van Balen.

Widow Elizabeth and her three surviving sons sailed back to Australia in 1924. They arrived at Sydney, where some of their descendants still live, on Christmas Day. Although the family have always kept in touch with the Bowdens in England, their links with the Greenings had understandably been broken. Len, the eldest, was twenty having been born in Bristol in August 1904. He had left school at the age of thirteen and worked in a munitions factory during the final year of the war, but was then lucky to be able to study Art at the West of England Academy. Within a couple of years of arriving in Australia he found employment as a commercial artist with WD and HO Wills (his grandfather's old Bristol employers), where he stayed until his retirement in 1962. Len had a fine bass-baritone voice and was a member of the Sydney Male Voice Choir for twenty-five years. He and his brother Ernest were also in 'Ye Idlers' singing group and a number of church choirs. Len was a keen sportsman and, as a member of amateur dramatic groups, had a special interest in the theatre. In the Second World War he served with the Australian Field Service Corps in the Pacific. As Len was a skilled draftsman he was involved in mapping remote islands, like New Britain and Bougainville to the east of New Guinea.

On retirement, Len visited the United Kingdom for eighteen months. He studied Fine Art at the

Hatherley School of Art in London, before touring Britain and Europe making sketches for later paintings. It seems sad that he didn't know of the existence of his cousin. I am sure my father, one year older than Len, would have been so pleased if they could have met.

Len married Jessie Leix and they had two daughters, Leone and Elizabeth. Ernest married Yvonne Gooden, who now in her mid-nineties is still enjoying life at the time I write this. They had two daughters, Margaret and Helen, and one son – Garth Richard Greening. Frank married Doreen (I do not have her surname) and this couple had one daughter, Jane, and one son – another Harry Greening. Although the three brothers are no longer with us, there are now three further generations of their descendents either living – or who were born – in Australia. Although most have different surnames, a few of them still respond to Greening.

Samuel Owen Greening (1847)
Great-grandson of Old Ben
Industrialist in Canada

Edward Owen Greening (1836)
Great-grandson of Old Ben
Freethinker and social reformer, one of the founders of the Co-Operative and Labour Movement

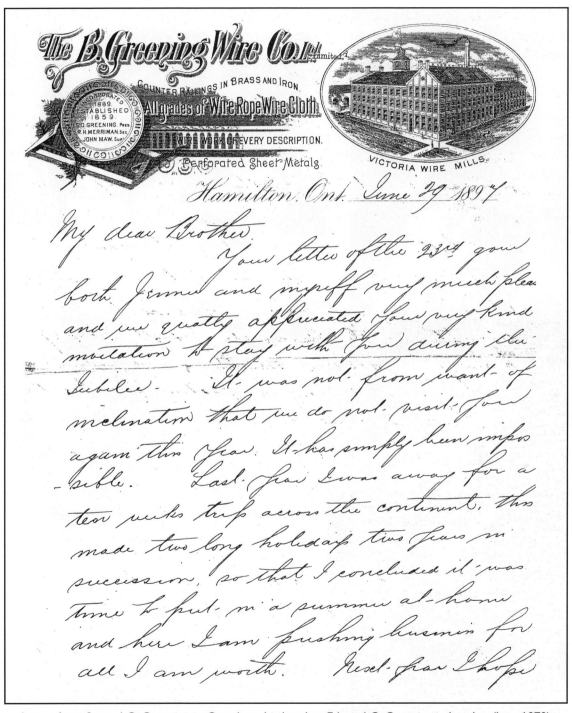

Letter from Samuel O. Greening in Canada to his brother, Edward O. Greening in London (June 1879)

Linnaeus Greening
Son of Noah, grandson of Nathaniel (1780), and great-grandson of Old Ben

and

Postcards from Lin to George
All communications were covered in cut-out illustrations, feathers and jokes

LINNAEUS GREENING.

~~TERRA:~~
~~DE GE EXPRESS CE.~~

~~RATA FEASED~~
~~ELECTRONIC FUNDS~~

33, Wilson Patten Street,
~~FAIRLIGHT,~~

~~GRAPPENHALL~~

~~NR.~~ WARRINGTON.
12-6-1924.

George Ellison, Esq.,
    C/o. Mrs. Imes,
        Eirianallt,
            Berwyn,Nr. Llangollen.

Dear George,

        Many thanks for your interesting list
of birds from a place in Wales, which my typing
machine refuses to write, also letter with
cutting enclosed.   With reference to the
pheasant that you record, do you remember
whether it was a phasianus colchicus or
phasianus torquatus ?   The latter bird has
ousted our old English form of pheasant, which
is supposed to have been introduced by the
Romans, that is my experience, and I shall be
glad to know which of the two you saw.   The
cutting about the Puffins is an extremely
interesting one, and the fact is that ✗ is not
the only bird that returns to the same nest
every year as you say.   The question of
orientation is about the most remarkable
phenomenon that I know of in animal life.
Batrachians, fish, reptiles and birds all
possessing this remarkable faculty in a high
degree not only in the above groups, but it is
also a faculty possessed by many of the
molluscs.   The absence of the skylarks in
your district is very curious for round about
Warrington it is one of the commonest birds of
the country side, perhaps they are migrating
from your district to a better land near
Warrington.
        The question of the Terns leaving
their nests and young for migrating purposes is

        ✗ the Swallow

A Typical letter from Linnaeus to his friend George
Most cards and letters were hand written, but by 1924, Lin's eyesight was failing
and he used a typewriter

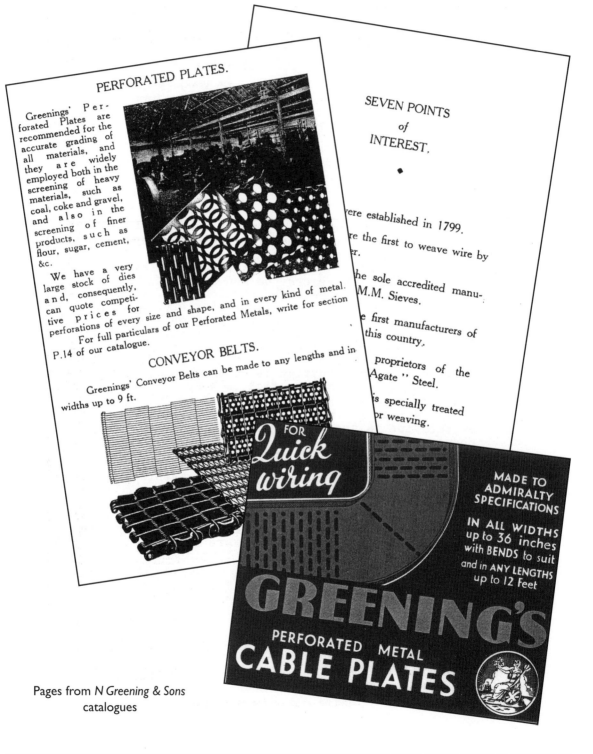

PERFORATED PLATES.

Greenings' Per-forated Plates are recommended for the accurate grading of all materials, and they are widely employed both in the screening of heavy materials, such as coal, coke and gravel, and also in the screening of finer products, such as flour, sugar, cement, &c.

We have a very large stock of dies and, consequently, can quote competi-tive prices for perforations of every size and shape, and in every kind of metal.

For full particulars of our Perforated Metals, write for section P.14 of our catalogue.

CONVEYOR BELTS.

Greenings' Conveyor Belts can be made to any lengths and in widths up to 9 ft.

SEVEN POINTS of INTEREST.

were established in 1799.

re the first to weave wire by er.

he sole accredited manu- M.M. Sieves.

e first manufacturers of this country.

proprietors of the Agate " Steel.

s specially treated or weaving.

FOR Quick wiring

GREENING'S PERFORATED METAL CABLE PLATES

MADE TO ADMIRALTY SPECIFICATIONS

IN ALL WIDTHS up to 36 inches with BENDS to suit and in ANY LENGTHS up to 12 Feet

Pages from *N Greening & Sons* catalogues

A.D. 1877, 25th APRIL. N° 1622.

SPECIFICATION

OF

NOAH GREENING AND JOHN GREENING.

SCREENING LIME FOR BLEACHING POWDER.

LONDON:
PRINTED BY GEORGE E. EYRE AND WILLIAM SPOTTISWOODE,
PRINTERS TO THE QUEEN'S MOST EXCELLENT MAJESTY:
PUBLISHED AT THE GREAT SEAL PATENT OFFICE,
25, SOUTHAMPTON BUILDINGS, HOLBORN.

Price 6d.   1877.

1877 patent application (Noah and John)

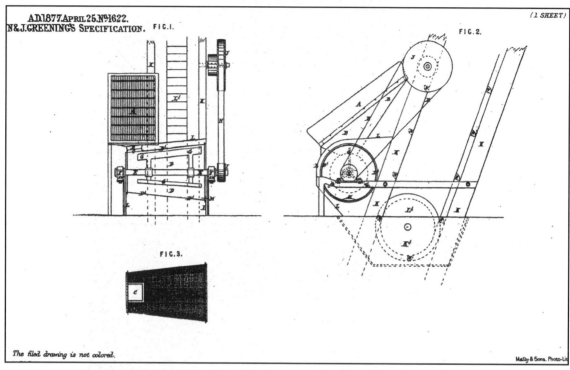

Drawing with the patent filed by the brothers Noah and John Greening in 1877
Machinery for screening Lime in the manufacture of Bleaching Powder

Nathaniel Greening 'the second' (b. 1855)
Son of John, grandson of Nathaniel (1780)
and great-grandson of Old Ben

Harry Richard Greening
with his wife Elizabeth and their four sons
Harry died from wounds received at the Battle of the Somme in 1916

CHAPTER FOURTEEN

✛

It was a clear and peaceful morning when the population of Tokyo woke up on the eighteenth of April 1942. Japan had been at war with the United States for just over four months and, following Pearl Harbour; their armed forces had achieved unrivalled military success in the Pacific. Radio Tokyo had repeatedly assured the citizens of Japan's capital city that they were safe. They were far too far away from their enemies to be threatened by a sea or air attack. It had been nearly seven hundred years since the country's last threat of invasion. On that occasion, back in 1281, the Mongol fleet of the Kublai Khan had been destroyed by a violent storm that the Japanese had named "Kamikaze" or the Divine Wind. The people thought themselves invincible.

Just after noon the serenity of the city was suddenly shattered. Some very low-flying dark green aeroplanes suddenly appeared from nowhere and commenced to drop their bombs. History would later call this the 'Tokyo Raid' or the 'Doolittle Raid', after its legendary leader Lieutenant Colonel Doolitle.

Like the terrorist attack on the eleventh of September 2001, the attack on Pearl Harbour had deeply shocked America. A rapid military advance by Japanese troops had followed this. They had taken Hong Kong from the British and invaded the Dutch East Indies. Guam and Wake, two Pacific islands that belonged to America, had been captured and the Philippines were about to fall. The United States feared that Hawaii would be next on the Japanese agenda and that it was likely that this would be followed by an attack on the American Pacific coast. Day following day the news was bad and the morale of the American people and its armed forces was low.

President Roosevelt decided that it was imperative that some action be taken that would revitalize the American spirit and gave the go-ahead for what at first seemed a hare-brained proposal, from a US Air force commander, to mount a raid that might be regarded as the dramatic retribution the population desired. The raid, still recognised today as one of the most illustrious actions ever undertaken by the USAF, was to be led by America's top flying ace, Lt Col James Doolitle, a stunt flyer and test pilot and a larger than life character who was also the holder of aviation speed records. The raid would attack Japan's four main cities, Tokyo, Yokohama, Osaka-Kobe and Nagoya, and would be carried out by sixteen medium sized B 25 bombers.

This plane was chosen, as it was small enough to take off from aircraft carriers providing they could get near enough to the Japanese coast without being seen. However, at ten tons, they were far too large to re-land on the carriers and, in any event, could only carry enough fuel for a one-way trip, even after large additional tanks had been fitted. Each twin-engine bomber had a five-man crew and would be loaded with four 500 lb bombs. They would fly to their targets at 150 miles per hour to conserve fuel, hugging the sea to avoid detection. After they had unloaded their cargo they would make for the Chinese coastline with whatever fuel they had left. Doolittle, a supreme optimist, rated the chances that the mission would succeed at 50/50. All crewmembers, the pilot, co-pilot, navigator, bombardier and flight engineer were volunteers as their chances of returning home were slim.

Luck was with the Americans. The Navy carriers arrived at a point within seven hundred miles of the Japanese coast without being spotted and all the planes managed to take off without hitch. The B 25's were normally fitted with highly classified 'Norden' bombsights but as these were unsuitable for low-level raids and as the Air Force did not want to risk them falling into Japanese hands, they were removed and replaced by a two-piece 'aimer' which cost twenty cents. The mission's second-in-command, who was the bombing and gunnery officer, had designed this. As the planes could not afford to carry the weight of additional guns, this officer also had two broomsticks, painted black, mounted to look like guns in each bomber's tail. He trusted this might discourage enemy fighter planes.

The first plane to take off was piloted by Doolitle and his second in command, the bombing officer, was the pilot of the eleventh plane. He was Captain Charles Ross Greening, named after his father and grandfather, Charley the farm boy, soldier, tinsmith and banker.

The nearest 'friendly' airfield, which might be reached by the Doolittle bombers, was Vladivostock in Russia. However Stalin, under great pressure in his war against Hitler, did not want to risk a conflict with the Japanese and refused the American request for permission to land. One of the pilots, believing that he was too short of fuel to reach China and wishing to save the lives of his crew, disregarded that instruction and landed in Russia. Although officially America's allies, the

Russians were not pleased so these fliers were interned and treated little better than prisoners of war. This crew, who managed to escape a year later through Iran and were able to return home, were the only ones who had been able to land in the conventional way.

The other fifteen planes made for the Chinese coastline and, although they were lucky enough to have the wind blowing in the right direction (it usually blew from China to Japan), their fuel gauges were at zero and their engines spluttering as the Asian mainland came in sight. As some Chinese coastal areas were already under Japanese control and the nearest friendly airfields someway inland, their plan was to keep in the air as long as possible and then bail out.

Two of the crews did ditch in enemy territory, one on the shore where two crewmembers were drowned and a third was very badly injured. The eight survivors were severely tortured during much of their incarceration and three were later executed by firing squad. A fourth died of malnutrition and illness in custody but the other four survived the war and were able to bring those responsible for the murder of their comrades to Justice.

The remaining thirteen crews, including Doolittle's and Greening's, did reach areas controlled by Generalissimo Chiang Kai-shek, the Chinese Nationalist leader, who had given his rather unwilling permission to the Americans to fly there – although one airman was killed after bailing out. The Chinese leader's misgivings were well founded. Months later many hundreds of his people who had helped the Americans, most of them poor peasants, were most brutally tortured to death and their villages raised to the ground in a wave of inhuman reprisals.

Although only sixteen aircraft took part in the raid, the Americans wanted to create the impression that they were part of a much larger force than was actually the case. So the attack was spread over a fifty-mile band. Not including Doolitle, the raiders were grouped into five flights of three planes and the group led by Captain Greening was successful in its mission to hit the docks, oil-refineries, warehouses and industrial areas of Yokahama – which they bombed from only six hundred feet. All pilots had been instructed to avoid targets, which were not military or industrial. Although the Doolittle raid destroyed about ninety buildings in and around Tokyo this, of course, made very little impact on Japan's war machine. The success of the raid was entirely psychological. For the Japanese it was a shattering blow to their pride, they were no longer solely dictating the course of the war and their military had failed to protect their homeland. For the Americans the effect was even more important. Their pride had been restored; they had successfully raided the heart of the Japanese empire.

Charles Ross (usually called Ross) and his crew all successfully parachuted to safety and within a few weeks were back in America. Ross was later promoted to Lieutenant Colonel and, stationed in North Africa, flew 27 missions over Italy before being shot down near Naples in July 1943. Here he had a very lucky escape, as he just managed to avoid landing his parachute inside the active volcanic crater of Mount Vesuvius. The Germans captured him but, while being transferred by train from one prison camp to another, he escaped and evaded re-capture for nearly eight months. The last four of these were spent in a cave on the Italian-Yugoslav border with two New Zealanders, where local villagers provided them with food and clothing. Here Ross spent his time sketching and making model planes for the village children. When re-captured he was incarcerated in the infamous Stalag Luft I, at Barth on the German Baltic coast. Here he became Senior Officer in one of the compounds. In civilian life Charles Ross had been a commercial artist and in the prison camp he started Art and Craft classes, to help his fellow prisoners fight boredom and retain their sanity. One of his fellow inmates had said to him, "Nothing is the hardest thing in the world to do".

Speaking about that time after the war, Ross said:

> I realised that the best thing I could do would be in the field of art so I started art classes. We had little or no materials but organized classes anyway. Any scrap of paper became drawing paper; human hair became paintbrushes; twigs from trees were baked and made into charcoal for drawing materials; coffee was used for dye; can labels were boiled to extract colour for paints.

> We needed knives and hammers with which we could do some wood carving and sculpture, The German stoves were pulled apart; heavy iron bars were removed and kept hidden from the German search parties. These were heated and pounded into various forms of cutting tools, then sharpened to a fine edge on rocks and bricks found in the camp. The International YMCA provided phonograph records that were played until they were worn out. They were then broken into workable bits and heated; the plastic that resulted was used to make sculptures, model airplanes and holders for paintbrushes.

After the camp was liberated in May 1945, Ross thought that many of the items that had been made by his fellow prisoners should be preserved and shown to the American public. He sent a message to the commander of the US 8th Air Force in England – General Doolittle – asking him to send an aircraft to pick up boxes weighing 5,000 pounds, that he had labelled as classified intelligence materials! The General immediately arranged for three B-17s to be flown to Germany, while Ross commandeered fifteen lorries to take his top-secret load to the airport. Unfortunately

Doolittle had been transferred back to the States before Ross arrived in England, where he found that intelligence officers were about to consign his cargo to the scrap yard. He assured them that his exhibits had General Doolittle's blessing and they were shipped to the Pentagon, marked to be only opened by specially cleared intelligence personnel.

Arriving back in America, Ross persuaded the Air Force command to co-sponsor a travelling exhibition of POW life with the YMCA and the Red Cross and he was authorised to pick former American POWs to design, build and man the displays. These included a typical POW hut, a German guard-tower and a large model of an escape tunnel.

The show started in New York in October 1945. Mayor La Guardia performed the opening by cutting the barbed-wire 'ribbon' with a pair of cutters, that had been made by a POW from ice-skating blades. Ross took his exhibition to 15 more cities throughout the United States and it drew large crowds wherever it went. Its last stop was at Washington DC in September 1946. Many of the exhibits were then transferred to the National Air Force Museum, where they can still be seen today.

Charles Ross Greening was born in November 1914, the middle child of three of Charlie Greening – who was the middle son of the Charley born in Worcester, England. Charlie, who was born in 1882, became a banker like his father but did not join Elgar and Elmore – his elder and younger brothers – in the Exchange State Bank. He lived and worked in Montana and then Tacoma, Washington State. He died in the late 1930s.

Elgar, Charlie and Elmore's two sisters, mentioned in the chapter about their father, were Nana and Josie. Nana, the eldest of the five children was born in 1871. She married Will Lockwood when she was quite young and lived a hard life as her husband suffered from ill health and was frequently out of work. She bore two sons and three daughters and is remembered as a small, quiet woman, gentle and uncomplaining. Josie, the other sister who was born after Elgar, is described by her nephew as having a taste for the exotic. She played the harp and took up painting, which she worked at all her life. Apparently her father's favourite, he paid for her to attend an art college in London, England. She married Samuel Croft, a civil servant at the Library of Congress.

Elgar married Jessie Rowell. They had three children but the first died as a baby. Their son and second child, Rollin, followed his father into banking. His only son, Bill Greening, lives with his wife and family in Long Beach, California. Elgar's youngest child, retired teacher Dorothy, also lives in the LA area and – although now in her nineties – until very recently drove herself to Church and the shops.

Charlie's son Charles Ross graduated in Art from Washington State University in 1936 and, on leaving the Air Force, resumed his career in commercial art in 1946. In 1947 he published a limited edition of his wartime watercolours, sketches and cartoons in a book titled "Not As Briefed". Ross died in 1957. He was only 42 but had lived a very eventful life.

Elmore had two children; Phyllis – now in her late eighties – lives in California with her husband of 65 years, Allan Scholl. She had a talent for music from a very early age and met her husband when they were both trying to earn extra money after their day jobs, playing with a local dance band. Phyllis, later a church organist for over thirty years, and Allan have two sons both of whom have had successful careers.

Charles (Chuck) Greening, Elmore's son, has supplied me with much of the information on the American Greenings in this book. He has also given me encouragement in putting some of the stories together. When he was a boy, his family lived through hard times after the failure of the Exchange State Bank – and there were no funds to send him to college. However, by studying hard and working at any job to earn a little money (he once worked in a grocery store for 25 cents an hour), he managed to obtain one of only ten annual scholarships to the Carnegie Technical College in Pittsburgh. Chuck obtained a degree in Physics and, together with many other young scientists, found himself drafted to work on the Manhattan Project – to produce the World's first Atomic Bomb. After the war Chuck returned to University. This time to Berkeley where he earned an MA and PhD in Psychology. This was followed by work as a university lecturer and teaching technical courses in the aerospace industry. At this point in time a new discipline was emerging, in which Chuck was able to combine his two fields of knowledge. He became an Ergonomics advisor – a Human Factors Engineer in more descriptive American terminology. This new career in Engineering Psychology, in the North American aviation industry, took up the major portion of his working life.

In retirement Chuck became an environmental campaigner. He has been very active in the preservation of Wildlife Sanctuaries, such as the one in Upper Newport Bay – where we went bird watching together in 2004. Chuck also played the euphonium in a trad jazz band for many years. Now a widower in his early eighties he is still very busy with many activities, including writing a bi-weekly column for his local newspaper. Chuck's son, Eric Greening, is another member of the family deeply involved in the preservation of the past, especially music. He is a member of the New World Baroque Orchestra in Paso Robles, which specializes in the recovery of the music of the 18th century – that was brought to California from Mexico.

During his time in the aviation industry Chuck made a number of business trips to England, to the

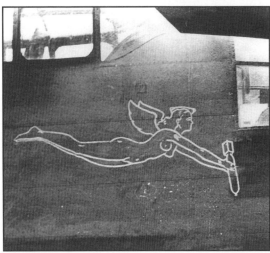

Nose of the B-25B bomber, mission plane no. 11 (nicknamed "Hari Carrier" and decorated accordingly by the pilot Capt. C. Ross Greening), tied down on the flight deck of USS *Hornet* – en route to the take-off point before the raid on Japan

Royal Air Force at Farnborough and to British Aerospace at Bristol. When in Bristol Chuck decided to take the opportunity to visit one of Britain's most famous bird-watching locations, the Severn Wildfowl Trust at Slimbridge. This is a wildlife sanctuary, by the mudflats of the Severn Estuary that was created in the late 1940s by Peter Scott – the wild bird artist and son of the legendary British hero, the polar explorer Robert Falcon Scott. As a boy, keen on bird watching, I also visited this wild bird Mecca on a number of occasions. At Slimbridge you can sit in the hides and look over the salt marshes and mudflats, to view the enormous flocks of wild geese, ducks and waders that rest and feed here – when breaking their Autumn and Spring migration flights. If you turn your head to the right, the mudflats narrow to where the river turns west into the lower loop of its 'S' bend and you can see the tower of St Andrew's church. Neither Chuck nor I realised, when we were there, that what we were looking at was the village where the surname ancestors of both of us once lived – where this story begins.

CHAPTER FIFTEEN

✛

In the early part of the eighteenth century, records of The Old Bailey – London's famous criminal court, include the sad stories of two Greening females who found themselves on the wrong side of the law. On the sixth of September 1716, Elizabeth Greening appeared before the Court for shoplifting. The original text reads:

> Elizabeth Greening, of the Parish of St. Bennet Gracechurch, was indicted for privately stealing 1 pair of Gold Ear-rings, value 4 shillings, out of the shop of Henry Harfield, on the 6th Instant. This was sworn upon her, and the story appear'd likely, upon which she was found Guilty to the Value of 10d (ten old pence).

As a deterrent to thieves and a support for shopkeepers, shoplifting at this time was regarded as a much more serious crime than stealing from a private house. By today's standards, the penalties for both crimes were severe in the extreme. If a defendant was convicted of shoplifting goods worth five shillings or more the death sentence had to be imposed, whereas for stealing from a private dwelling house the same sentence did not apply until the items taken were eight times that value – forty shillings or above. In practice, Juries were likely to be less harsh with first offenders and borderline cases. In such trials they would often agree a partial verdict, where the defendant was found guilty of the theft of goods to a lower value than on the charge sheet – and so avoid the death penalty.

The sentence for shoplifting goods between the value of one shilling and five shillings was usually branding. We see that in Elizabeth's case, she was found guilty of stealing goods to the value of less than one shilling and so avoided that fate. Ten pence (4p Sterling or about 7 US cents) in 1716 had perhaps the equivalent value of ten pounds or eighteen dollars today.

Elizabeth was not that lucky. She received the standard sentence given to women for shoplifting items worth less than a shilling. This was a whipping. In 1716 this punishment was carried out in public to humiliate the wrongdoer. The offender would be stripped to the waist and flogged *at a cart's tail*, along the length of a public street near the scene of the crime, *until her back be bloody*. Although little used after the 1770's, the public whipping of women was not abolished until 1817.

There were eighty-seven trials at the Old Bailey on the same day as Elizabeth's. Many of them had multiple defendants. Seven of the cases were of women charged with shoplifting and all were found guilty. Elizabeth Greening received the lightest sentence. Mary Sutton and Elizabeth Wallbank were sentenced to branding and the other five, Margaret Thurland, Mary Williams, Frances Williams, Elizabeth Nicholls and Mary Harding all received the death penalty – although some of them *'pleaded their bellies'*. This was a common practice and was proven or not after an examination by a jury of matrons, chosen from women present in the courtroom. If the defendant was found to be *quick with child*, her sentence was deferred until the child was born. This usually resulted in a pardon, provided the baby lived, as a mother was needed to take care of the infant. There must have been some women who, expecting to be convicted, did their best to delay their trials and made attempts to become pregnant while in custody awaiting their time in court.

Eighteen months after Elizabeth's trial a change in sentence was introduced for petty larceny. In April 1718 a servant girl, Elizabeth Saunders, was the first person to be tried at the Old Bailey under the new law. She was also found guilty of stealing goods to the value of ten pence. In her case this was a set of chinaware, which she was accused of taking from her employer Robert Saunders (the records do not mention if they were related or not). In her defence this Elizabeth told the Judge that Mr Saunders had given her the china after offering *to lie with her several times*. She was not believed and was sentenced to seven years transportation to America.

Elizabeth Greening lived in St Bennet Gracechurch. This was a small parish in East Central London near The Monument, north of where London Bridge crosses the Thames. St Bennet was a derivation of St Benedict's and Gracechurch had originally been called Grass Church Street, as it had been the location of a 'grass' or herb market. The architect of St Paul's Cathedral, Sir Christopher Wren, designed the Monument – still the tallest isolated stone column in the world. It was constructed in the 1670s to commemorate the Great Fire of London and is sited at the end of Gracechurch Street, not far from Pudding Lane where the fire started in 1666.

Unlike today, when the age of a person is invariably the first item of information we are given about them in any news item or document, ages were not recorded in the Old Bailey trial reports of the 1700s. With no national birth registration, some people would have only had an approximate idea of their own age. It is therefore not usually possible to accurately tie together scraps of historical data with parish records. We do have an Elizabeth however, living in central London, who was most probably the same person. Not at St Benedict's, but at the next-door parish of St James, Clerkenwell, an Elizabeth Greening was baptised on 11 April 1694. Her birth would have been a few days earlier so she would have been twenty-two at the time of her trial and conviction. She was the daughter and eldest child of John Greening and Sarah Mayes, who were married at St James, Duke's Place – a couple of streets away from Gracechurch, in May 1693. We also know she had a younger brother, Thomas, who was baptised at the same church in May 1702. With her father having John as his Christian name, it would be pure speculation to pick out his antecedents. Yet it must be possible that his father or grandfather may have been baptised in some small village church in Dorset or Gloucestershire.

September 1716 was not a good month for Elizabeth but twelve months later a much happier occurrence happened in her life. On the third of September 1717 – at the age of twenty-three – Elizabeth Greening was married to John Davies at London's premier parish church, St Martin's-in-the-fields.

Deborah Greening, who only lived about fifteen miles from Elizabeth and who appeared at the Old Bailey eight and a half years later, may have lived a very different life to her surname namesake in the city. Deborah was a country girl. She lived at South Mimms, today better known as a motorway service area where the A1(M), originally the Great North Road, joins the M25 – London's circular highway. In Deborah's day South Mimms was just a small village on a hill, half a day's ride north of the capital. It was a place where travellers, then on horseback or in coaches, might break their journey before visiting the metropolis – much as they do today.

Deborah was a farm servant. The part of her life that is preserved for posterity, like that of many other people who stood before a jury, is a tragic episode. On 24 February 1725 she appeared at the Old Bailey charged with infanticide. The original text of her trial reads as follows.

> Deborah Greening, of South Mims, was indicted for the Murder of her Female Infant Bastard, by wilfully strangling the said Infant, on the 13th of Jan. last. She was a second time indicted on the Coroner's Inquisition for the said Murder.
>
> James Wallis despos'd, that going to fetch up a Bullock, he saw a Hog on a Dunghill with part of a Child in his Mouth, the Head and Arms of it being eaten off. William Shorrard, Farmer, deposed, that the Prisoner was his Servant, had been sick two or three

days, and was gone to her Father's about a mile off, when Wallis call'd him out to see the Child that the Hog had partly devour'd. This gave him a Suspicion that the Prisoner was the Mother of the Child; upon which he caused her to be apprehended, and carry'd before the Justice, to whom she confess'd that she was deliver'd of a Child in her Master's House; that it was still-born; that she bury'd both it and the After-birth in the Dunghill, then went home again, and turned the Bed to prevent a Discovery, and afterwards went to her Father's.

The Midwife desposed, that to the best of her Judgement, the Prisoner did not go her full time, for the Toe Nails of the Infant were not perfect. Justice Smith deposed, that when the Prisoner was first brought before him, she produced some Child bed Linnen, which she said was as much as she had time to make in her Service. The Jury acquitted her.

Before more recent times, very few Greening females were baptised with the Christian name Deborah and there is only one noted in easily accessible archives during the half century in question. This is Deborah, the daughter of John and Susan, who was baptised at St Peter's, Winchcombe, on 13 September 1708. As that Deborah would have been sixteen at the time of the birth of the illegitimate stillborn child, a most likely age for a servant girl to find herself in that predicament, it seems probable that she was that girl. John Greening had married Susan Trowton at Winchcombe, a small historic Gloucestershire town, on 13 January 1705. If this was the same family I have no idea why they moved from Winchcombe to South Mimms but both places were on a frequent stagecoach route, from Gloucester to London, so it is possible that John worked for a landed family with estates in both places. We are unable to find out what happened to Deborah or know if she survived this traumatic period in her young life. We can only hope she found some happiness. By some strange coincidence, thirteen seems to have haunted her. Her parent's marriage, her christening and the stillbirth all occurred on that unlucky date.

Although Elizabeth was lucky that her trial predated the eighteenth century transportation era by eighteen months, there were other Greenings who suffered that fate. One was James Greening, from Gloucestershire, who appeared before the Lent Transportation Board at Sudeley Castle in April 1757. His sentence for stealing was to be sent to the Americas. Transportation was usually for seven years and many of those convicted stayed on after that time had expired. We do not know if James ever returned to his homeland. As Sudeley is very near Winchcombe, James, like Deborah, is likely to have come from one of the Greening families there.

There had been 'transportation' in the previous century, but this was supposedly with the consent of those transported. These were usually very young men and women who, believing promises of employment and good wages, had left these shores to work for masters in the new settlements of America. Some of the promises were honest and legitimate; many were not. The practice of abduction, inveigling and bribing youngsters onto ships bound for the labour hungry colonies was common. The state itself had connived in the rounding up of vagrant children in London and their forcible shipment to Virginia. Because numerous complaints of kidnapping had been made by a number of influential members of society, a new act was passed by Parliament in 1654. *To prevent such mischief* it was ordained that *all boys, maids and other persons, which for the future shall be transported beyond the seas as servants shall, before their going a shipboard, have the indentures of their service inrolled.* All this meant was that a documentary record had to be kept of all people leaving by boat to work abroad, which had to show the length and terms of their employment.

Although this was designed to stop the practice of taking young people away against their will, it did not remove many of the abuses of the system. Many indentured servants were no better off than the African slaves, who were also being taken across the Atlantic at the same time. The slaves were worth money as they could be auctioned – and would then work for their owners for nothing. Indentured workers could not readily be sold and they had to be paid a small wage! Two hundred years later, Irish immigrants to America suffered even less well. Because they had already paid some unscrupulous shipping agent for their passage, a quarter of those who left Irish or British mainland ports never arrived. They either succumbed to sickness and disease on the voyage or drowned – when their overcrowded, rotten and un-seaworthy sailing boats sank beneath the North Atlantic waves.

One member of a Gloucestershire family who went overseas for employment was Jabez Greening, as an indentured servant to William Davis. He left Bristol for Maryland aboard the sailing ship 'Expectation' on 11th September 1679. A dozen years earlier, in April 1667, Jane *Grining* had left the same port for Barbados to work for Foulke Adams. The name of her ship is not recorded.

There were also Greenings on the other side of the fence. On the 26th January 1675/6 (the years were still ending in March at this time) two men, Charles Mines and John Gardner, are recorded as due to leave Bristol on the sailing ship 'Baltimore' – bound for Virginia. They were indentured servants for four years to Daniel Greening. This is almost certainly the same Daniel Greening, for whom a marriage licence bond was issued in Bristol eight days previously. His wife to be was Sarah Clare and the wedding was to take place at St Stephen's church. The prospective bride and groom's ages are not given but Daniel is described as a mariner. The bondsman, a friend or associate of the groom – who would have made a sworn statement that he knew of no impediment to the marriage – was William Cox, gentleman. Reading between the lines, it is possible that Cox was a plantation owner and may have also owned the 'Baltimore'. Daniel was probably going to Virginia as his agent or plantation overseer. One other piece of information is given about Daniel – he was from Wheatenhurst, Gloucestershire. He was therefore more than likely a member of the Greening branch featured in this book. I have not been able to find a record of his baptism, but this would have been during the Civil War period from which few records survive. It is possible that he was a cousin – if not a brother – of Nathaniel (1647).

Marriages usually followed a few days after the application for a licence, but I have not found any record of one at St Stephen's. Perhaps the couple planned to marry on the Baltimore, after it sailed, or even in Virginia? I strongly suspect that a Daniel Greening, who appears in Bristol seven years later, is the same man. This Daniel, described as a sailor of St Stephen's parish, registered a marriage licence bond on the sixth of February 1682/3. His bride was to be Mary Hunter of St Mary's, Redcliffe, and this time the bondsman was Thomas Evans – sailor. The marriage was to take place at either Redcliffe or the Temple church.

A wedding did take place, seven days later on the thirteenth of February, at St Mary's, Redcliffe – Bristol's most famous medieval church – between Daniel and Mary Haytor. It would seem that the marriage licence clerk had misheard Mary's surname. Mary, the daughter of William Haytor, had been baptised in Bristol in January 1667/8 so would have been only fifteen years old. At that time fifteen was not an unusual age for marriage. The then Queen of England, Mary the Second – joint sovereign with her husband, William of Orange – had only been fifteen when she married in 1677. If this was Daniel's second marriage, Sarah Clare must have died. A more likely possibility is that Sarah got cold feet and the earlier licence had not been used.

I originally thought that this Daniel might have retired back to his birth area of Gloucestershire. Although I had no proof, I thought it possible that a Daniel Greening who died in 1731 and was buried at Standish – a parish adjoining Moreton Valence and Wheatenhurst – might have been the mariner. He was a rich man and freehold landowner with ready cash assets. As he left no livestock or agricultural impedimenta, I thought he was unlikely to have been a farmer so must have been a trader. I thought this man might have accumulated his wealth from voyages to Virginia, so could have returned to the Moreton Valence district when his sailing days were over, this now seems unlikely. Although he didn't appear to have had any surviving children the Standish Daniel left numerous sums of money to family members.

The first bequest was *to my dear and loving wife Mary Greening* who was given *my best Bed and* bedstead with all manner of appurtenances therto belonging and also my Clock one Silver Tankard & four Silver Spoones. Daniel did not leave his wife any money or property, but presumably he had already made arrangements for her before making the will. He left ten pounds each to ten separate relatives. His sister Mary (ye wife of Richard Andrews), their children William, Sarah and Katherine. The same was left to the three daughters of his deceased brother Joseph – Katherine, Jane and Mary, and also to Elizabeth (Greening) the wife of John Eagles (relationship not given), kinsman Antors (Anthony) Greening and grandson George Pach. His grandson and some of his nieces were to receive their ten pounds when they attain to ye age of one and twenty. He gave his brother Samuel two annuities during ye terme of his natural life. One was six pounds a year out of Hill Mead (probably the estate where Daniel and Mary were living), to be paid halfe yearly without any deduction or abatement whatsoever. The other was the same amount, three pounds every halfe yeare during his life was to come from his other freehold estate lands, premises and Hereditaments which he left to his nephew John Andrews (a gravestone shows he was a lawyer) – who was also his executor. Daniel left five pounds to ye poor Inhabitants of ye parish of Standish … to be distributed upon ye feast of St Thomas ye Apostle next after my decease and forty pounds to his sister Ursula Greening (no doubt a spinster sister more in need of funds than the others). He also gave a Guinea to both of the overseers of the will. Daniel was however a vain man as he also left forty pounds (a vast sum then) to erect a Tombe over my grave. Although it is not possible to exactly equate the sums in the will to today's money, it must be in the region of many tens of thousands of pounds.

I visited the Church of St Nicholas at Standish to try and find Daniel's tomb. If he had been the mariner I thought a sailing boat might have been carved on it, which would strengthen my suggestion that he was the man who married in Bristol. This church with a rather foreboding interior has an interesting history. It was in here that the body of King Edward the Second was laid, on the night after his murder, before being carried on to Gloucester Cathedral. The churchyard contains a number of large and very ornate early eighteenth century tombs. However, after 275 years, the names of all the people they commemorated have now weathered away. I then discovered that some years ago the writing had been visible and the engravings had been recorded. One of the Tombs had given details of this Greening family. A Daniel senior – who had died in 1718 at the age of 86 – is shown with Daniel (who must have been his son), yeoman of this Parish, who died 4th of May 1731, aged 64. This makes the one who made the will too young to have been the mariner. I am not certain how these Daniels fit into the main family tree in this book but, with first names like Samuel, Joseph and Daniel, it seems quite probable that this family were related to the Nathaniels we met at the start of Chapter One.

Although most of the Greenings I have picked up in criminal records were charged with minor offences, there was one capital case over ninety years ago.

A year before the outbreak of the First World War, on the 13th August 1913, Frank Greening was hanged for murder at Winston Green Prison in Birmingham. Frank is described as a 34 year-old house painter but he was in essence a small time crook, part of the underworld in Britain's second city and had been in and out of prison for much of his life. Frank had been found guilty of the murder of his girlfriend, Elizabeth Ellen Hearne, who had previously lived with him and – probably in a fit of jealous rage- he had shot her after she decided to leave him. This happened on Sunday 6th April. Some unusual features of this case, soon forgotten and buried by the events of 1914, held the public's interest in that last summer of peace. Elizabeth Ellen was not killed outright and as she lay dying of her wounds in hospital Frank, who was being hunted by the police as the obvious suspect, disguised himself as a relative and visited her bedside to try and persuade her not to press charges against him. Whether he was full of remorse and asked her forgiveness or what her reply was is not recorded. Elizabeth died the day after the shooting, Frank was arrested, found guilty of her murder on 14th July and had lost his life on the scaffold within a month. Justice a century ago moved at a far more rapid pace than today.

For some reason Frank's recorded age was not correct. He was born in February 1881 so was 32 at the time of his death. His father, Thomas Greening, was an Irish bricklayer and Frank – his youngest son – had been born in a Birmingham tenement block amongst a large Irish community of building workers. In April 1881, Thomas had told the census enumerator that Frank's mother Ann came from County Mayo and that he had been born in Leinster, the Dublin area of Ireland, in 1837. This was before Civil Registration had been introduced and, as many Irish records were destroyed in a fire when that country achieved free rule, it is unlikely that we will ever be able to discover the name of Frank's Greening grandfather. However as the Greening name does not crop up much in Ireland, it is quite possible that Thomas's father came from Gloucestershire.

Elizabeth Hearne was shot with a handgun, which was and still is relatively rare for a domestic murder in England. This suggests that Frank had possibly been involved in armed robbery. All that we know of his disastrous life had been lived out within a tiny perimeter of central Birmingham. He was born at the back of Livery Street. Lived with his girlfriend and then murdered her only two streets away, at the back of Bissell Street. Then, just over a mile from those locations, he was finally hung in the same prison where he had been incarcerated at least once previously.

The April 1881 census shows that Frank had at least two siblings, a seven year-old brother John and a seventeen year-old sister Mary Ann. By the time of the next census, ten years later, the family appears to have broken up and the only member I can find in the records is father Thomas – still a bricklayer but living on his own in lodgings in Birmingham. Mary Ann had probably married and Ann may have returned to Ireland with her sons. By 1901 Frank was back in Birmingham again. The census gives his age as twenty-four but he was only twenty. He was a prisoner at Winston Green. I have found no evidence of Frank fathering any children, but it is possible that his sister had a family and there may be Greenings around today descended from his brother John.

I accept that the contents of this chapter are not exactly related to the main stories in this book. However – I include them in the hope that they may give some extra dimension to our understanding of the way in which some lives were lived, during the periods in which other events that I describe took place. Many readers may have little compassion with excusing the course of circumstances that ended Frank's unhappy life, but I would like to end this chapter with the story of a Greening 'criminal' – with whom I think we can all feel sympathy. What strikes me most about this story is how recent it is; the central character was only a decade older than my grandfather. How our attitudes to crime, punishment and children have changed in the last one hundred and thirty years!

In the early 1870s the Richmond police had been issued with a new piece of equipment to help them fight crime, one of mankind's greatest inventions – a camera. This enabled them to take 'mug-shots' of convicted felons, for their records and possible reference in future investigations. This was an age when the use of aliases by law-breakers was standard practice. One of their earliest subjects, whose portrait I have reproduced in this book, was – at four feet, four and a quarter inches – quite a small criminal. His description, filled in next to his photograph, tells us that he had a fresh complexion, light brown hair and a scar on his forehead. His trade or occupation is given as *none*, and he is recorded as *single* rather than married. However, as this was his third offence, the court had to deal severely with him. He was sentenced to Hard Labour for one calendar month, to be followed by five years in a reformatory.

This serial criminal was John Greening and his age, on completion of the hard labour, was eleven. His heinous crime was stealing a quart of growing gooseberries! John had first been convicted twenty-eight months earlier, a couple of weeks after his ninth birthday. This was for stealing coal and, although a first offence, he was given ten days hard labour (or ten shillings fine – more than a weeks wages for his father). As his second crime – two years later – was also for stealing coal, the court was obliged to award a higher penalty. This time in February 1873, on his actual eleventh birthday, he was sentenced to be first whipped and then suffer two calendar month's hard labour. John may have wanted the gooseberries for himself but the theft of coal, by a boy between the ages of eight and ten, could only have been on behalf of his impoverished family. The winters of 1871 and 1873 were cold ones.

Most English football (soccer) fans would agree, that their most memorable match of all time was when the home country beat West Germany in the 1966 final of the World Cup. The English Captain, Bobby Moore, and the two players who scored the four English goals – Martin Peters (1) and Geoff Hurst (3) – all played for the same club in East London, the Hammers or West Ham United. There is now a statue, depicting these three soccer stars, at the club's Boleyn Ground at Upton Park. The club's supporters main public house, just outside the ground, also bears the name 'The Boleyn'. In 1873 this popular football stadium was the site of a large Victorian mansion, Boleyn Castle, which in 1870 had been turned into an institution for wayward boys – and was later to be called St Edward's Reformatory for Roman Catholic Boys. This was to be John's address until he reached the age of sixteen.

A poor dwelling in Garrets Alley in Mortlake, then a small town on the south bank of the River Thames – just west of London, was the birthplace of John on 15th February 1862. He was the son of William and Margaret Greening. William was a labouring gardener and Margaret an Irishwoman who had been born in Cork. Records inform us that John had an elder brother James and two younger sisters, Ellen and Margaret. After the age of eleven John does not appear in any criminal archives again but I have found it interesting to follow his progress in life, over the three decades following his last appearance in court.

Within a year or so of leaving reform school, where discipline would have been very harsh, John had joined the army. By the time of the 1881 census we find him as an Infantry Private in the East Surrey Regiment, stationed at Grand Shaft Barracks, Dover. This was the home base of the East Surrey's at this time, but John was probably awaiting shipping overseas. He appears to have served with the First Battalion (31st Regiment of Foot) so may have been in Gibraltar in 1882 and in India from 1884. If in the Second Battalion, he would have fought in the Sudan War (1884) – following the assassination of General Gordon. A few years later, on New Year's Day 1887, John married twenty year-old Rose Collins at St Mary Magdalene's Roman Catholic chapel in Mortlake. John had left the army and was working as a maltsman at Randall's Malting. Rose's father William was also a maltsman, so would have been a work colleague. He was also one of the two witnesses at the wedding. The initial of the other witness – a Greening – is a little difficult to read, but it is probably 'E'. So this would have been John's sister Ellen. John's father is shown on the certificate as deceased. At the time of the 1891 census John was still a civilian and still living in Mortlake. He and Rose had been joined by two small sons, William aged three and Edward five months. John's two sisters can be found in the census. They were both 'in service', working as living in servants in Richmond. Ellen was a parlour maid and Margaret a nursemaid.

By 1901 John was back in his regiment again, living in army quarters at Kingston-on-Thames. His eldest son William was now fourteen and employed as a railway messenger. Edward does not feature so may have died, but Rose had added three daughters to the family – Margaret 9, Rose 6 and Lillian 3. Brother James, who was a bricklayer, was living with them and, as I cannot find Ellen and Margaret in the records, it seems likely that John's sisters had both acquired new surnames on marriage. At this point we leave John and his family – and this chapter on Greening 'criminals'. It seems highly likely that John has grandchildren or great-grandchildren living today. I would be delighted to hear from any who, by chance, may come across this book.

Police record of John Greening (b. 1862)

The River Severn at Awre (2005)

Handley Cottage (2004)

Joseph Greening's tombstone
in Claines Churchyard

'Chuck' Greening with the author in California in 2004

Long-case clock made by 'Old Ben' Greening in about 1797 with Averil Ambrose (on a visit to England from Canada in 2002) and the author.

'Old Ben' was each of our Great-Grandfather's Great-Grandfather, so we are 5th cousins

Jane and Michael Woodall with the author (on a visit to England from Australia in 2005) with Claire and Kath

The River Severn from Newnham Churchyard (2005)

Bullo Pill (2004)

Tombstone of a William Greening – Royal Marine (see Chapter 10)

A new slab incorporated in the pavement at High Street, Chepstow, in 2005

Memorial Plaque on the site of Oak Lodge, Belmont Grove
(The London home of Edward O. Greening at the time of his death in 1923)

Justine Greening MP

River Severn from Minsterworth (looking South)

River Severn from Minsterworth Church (looking North towards Elmore Back)

Laura Greening

CHAPTER SIXTEEN

✠

The nineteenth century saw a large rise in the population of England and Wales. In very round numbers this was from nine million at the time of the 1801 census (no names were included at this date) to thirty-two and a half million in 1901. The number of people carrying the Greening surname will have also expanded by similar percentages. There were 647 Greening males listed in 1901 and, although there were now a few living in all areas of the land, the county of Gloucestershire – with Bristol – still held the largest concentration at 144. If we add to this the number living in the adjoining districts of South Wales (most of them will have been descended from Gloucester families) we reach a figure of nearly 200. There were 85 males of the surname in Dorset – the other main Greening 'homeland' and 170, the majority of the remainder, in London and the South East counties of Middlesex, Essex, Kent and Surrey. Most of these, or their ancestors, will have migrated from Gloucestershire or Dorset during the nineteenth century. As well as numbers, the tally of Greening occupations had also multiplied by 1901. There was still a fair sprinkling of men involved in agriculture, especially back in the original two counties, but the name could now be found in a wide variety of trades and professions.

In the Eighteen-eighties the daughter of a titled Hungarian composer came to London to study at the Hatherly School of Art (she became a successful artist who exhibited some of her paintings at the Royal Academy). She was also interested in writing and initially helped in the translation of some Hungarian fairy stories and folk tales into English, a language of which she knew nothing until the age of fifteen. This lady then wrote a play that, because it was initially not very successful, she re-wrote as a novel. Amazingly this is only said to have taken her five weeks. Finding a publisher for a new fictional story, by an unknown author, was no easier in the London of 1904 than it is today. Twelve publishing houses rejected it. For her thirteenth attempt she submitted her manuscript to a small recently established firm, who agreed terms with her and the first edition was in the booksellers in January 1905. It was an immediate best seller. By May 1908 forty-six

Impressions had been printed, twenty-six in the illustrated Standard Edition and twenty of the cheaper 'Popular Series'. Many more reprints were made in the months and years that followed. With *A Tale of Two Cities* by Charles Dickens, it is still today one of the two most well known English novels using the French Revolution as its backdrop. The book was *The Scarlet Pimpernel* and the writer Baroness Orczy. Possibly because the Baroness had seven Christian names she didn't usually use any of them – but she was occasionally known by the first one, Emma or Emmuska in Hungarian.

The thirteenth publisher, who went on to produce the detective stories, historical novels and many of the sixteen Pimpernel sequels that the Baroness wrote during the next eight years, was Greening & Co Ltd. I have a copy of *The Scarlet Pimpernel*, 1908 twentieth impression in the 'Popular Edition', worth just a few pounds (there are still many thousands around). I would need to spend about £2,000 to obtain a first edition. Although Greening & Co were very prolific publishers for a decade from 1902, they seem to have vanished before the onset of the First World War. I have been unable to ascertain whether they were taken over by a larger firm or just ceased trading. Their old catalogues show that they concentrated mostly on fiction, but they also produced a number of more serious factual titles and had a go at a monthly magazine.

The magazine was called *The Imp* and the first issue of thirty-two pages was available for sale at one penny in June 1907. Although this started as a 'Literary Digest', with articles as well as stories, it soon became fiction only with a running serial to encourage readers to buy the following month's edition. The Imp survived for fifty-four issues, the final one coming out in November 1911. In America, the *Argosy* 'pulp-fiction' magazine was to run for over a hundred years. Perhaps The Imp was ahead of its time for England. The Baroness was – of course – the most well know of the magazine's contributors, another was Gerald Biss an early writer of 'supernatural fiction' or horror stories. In 1909 Greening & Co published his most well known novel *The House of Terror*. The editor of *The Imp* and, I assume, the principle director of Greening & Co was Arthur Greening.

With the real life horrors of the Great War now history, London in 1919 was experiencing the dawn of a new era. In October, at the Queen's Hall, Sir Edward Elgar conducted the first performance of one of his greatest works, his *'Cello Concerto*, while at another venue in the capital a completely new type of music had arrived. This came from America and was played by *The Original Dixieland Jazz Band*, which had made the first ever record of Jazz music in New York only two years earlier. Also in 1919 the *Diaghilev Ballet* from St Petersburg were performing a season at the Empire Theatre in Leicester Square. The leading 'cello, under orchestra conductor (later Sir) Adrian Boult, was a talented musician who had won medals at the Royal Academy of Music after winning a scholarship there at the age of thirteen and a half. In addition to the 'cello he had also studied piano and composition at the Academy. Then, as now, the working life of a classical musician was not easy. There was a shortage of good orchestra appointments and the pay was not particularly attractive. The temptation to move over to the new popular music world with its emerging record industry was a large one.

Stan Greening had just turned thirty and, at this crossroads in his life, decided that it was in his best interests to traverse the floor and swap his 'cello for a banjo and guitar. He would join the Jazz Age and become a bandleader and band 'provider' to the new gramophone record companies. Although he did play Solo Guitar and Banjo for Sir Thomas Beecham at the Royal Opera House in Covent Garden, during the 1920s he made his principal living as a band director and arranger for most – if not all – of the major recording studios. Among his regular session players was young trombonist Ted Heath, who a couple of decades later became Britain's biggest name in the world of dance band music. Stan had an office just off Shaftsbury Avenue and his letterhead for that period is styled *The W. S. Greening Orchestras – as Supplied to The Leading Gramophone Companies*. It goes on to list *"Columbia"*, *"Duophone"*, *"H.M.V."*, *"Imperial"*, *"Mimosa"*, *"Oliver"*, *"Parlophone"*, *"Regal"* and *"Winner"* as the labels for which they recorded. I have a compilation CD of some of Stan's recordings. Although a little scratchy, the 'Greening's Dance Orchestra' rendering of numbers like *Who takes care of the Caretaker's Daughter, Miss Annabelle Lee* and *On the Midnight Special* still have their original bounce with strong banjo lead from Stan.

By the early 1930s popular music tastes were changing. Stan's visits to the studios and having one of his orchestras booked for the annual dinner-dance, at venues like the Essex Yacht Club, were starting to come to an end. He became a theatre musician (he played the Banjo and Guitar for the whole of the three and a half year run of Oklahoma at the Theatre Royal, Drury Lane) and did occasional stints with the new BBC broadcasting bands – like Jack Hylton's for the next twenty or more years. Stan was in his eighties when he died in 1971.

I have included Arthur, the publisher, and Stan, the musician, in this book as examples of Greenings who had interesting careers and were in the public eye in the early years of the last century. As, almost certainly, the surname ancestors of both men had come from either Dorset or Gloucestershire it was my intention to try and trace them back to those roots. I hoped that I might even find a connection between one of them and someone in an earlier chapter. As well as some intuitive interpretation of any records, I knew my quest would require a fair modicum of luck. This commodity has unfortunately not been available.

I have found nothing about the Greening & Co Ltd publishing firm, except for many thousands of books in second-hand bookshops and old libraries. Arthur's name is recorded as the editor of *The Imp* and he is recorded in the 1901 census as a *publisher of books*. As there were no other Greening publishers at that time, any other directors of his company must have had other surnames. On the 31st of March that year Arthur was living at 12 Albert Mansions in Lambeth, with his wife Martha, daughter Minnie and son Douglas. Although many census records can be most informative, Arthur's family entry is a highly frustrating one.

Today most householders fill in their own census returns, which are then posted to a central registry. However, during the years we are considering, the country was divided up into small 'enumeration districts' and it was the responsibility of a local enumerator to distribute forms to each household and also to collect them. If, due to illiteracy or any other reason, the householder had not completed the form the enumerator would complete it himself. He would then transcribe these schedules by hand into the book for that particular district. There were therefore many areas where mistakes and errors were almost certain to occur. Some enumerators were better and more diligent than others, some have difficult handwriting to decipher and sometimes names are not easy to read because checking clerks have superimposed crosses and ticks over the writing. Quite frequently the information given by the householder was either incorrect or is recorded incorrectly. For instance the enumerator quite often either misread or, if completing the schedule himself, misheard initials. A spoken 'C', especially with an accent, might be written down as an'E'. One of the biggest areas of misinformation – as I have mentioned earlier – was the place of birth. Many people did not know or remember where they had been born and – one gets the impression – some enumerators, who would have always been in a hurry, may have just guessed or filled this information in later.

In the 1901 record Arthur is shown as 35 with wife Martha the same age, a daughter Minnie 11 and son Douglas 9. With this information, especially as Arthur is a much less common name than Thomas, William or John, it should be possible to find the same family in the census taken ten years earlier – as a couple around the age of 25 with a daughter of one. One entry can be found but it only partially corresponds. At 6 South View, Swindon, Wiltshire on the night of the 5th April 1891 we have recorded an Arthur Greening –aged 26 with a wife Martha – aged 27 and a one year-old daughter. This Arthur's occupation was *Coachfinisher*, which meant he was a carpenter and no doubt working at the Swindon Railway Works. In ten years this man might have become a publisher and his wife has the correct name, but the other information differs. The coach finisher's daughter is recorded as Hilda with her birthplace Swindon, not Minnie born in Brixton. This Arthur is shown as having been born in Cirencester, Gloucestershire, and his wife in Marlborough.

In 1901 the publisher Arthur's place of birth is listed as Clapham and that of his wife Loughborough. These are not the same people. This was confirmed to me by Alan Greening, one of my correspondents who is a retired local government officer living in Buckinghamshire. Alan writes that the Swindon 'Arthur' was an enumerator's error, His grandfather, who this entry refers to, was actually named Ashley! As Alan believes his great-grandfather came from Minsterworth (near Elmore) it is likely that his line is related to the family tree in this book.

One way to discover more information would be to obtain one of the Lambeth children's birth certificates. If Douglas was nine in March 1901, he should have been born in the year 1891/92 and Minnie two years earlier. With a birth certificate, we would be able to find out the maiden name of the child's mother and that would lead us to the marriage certificate of Arthur and Martha. This, in turn, would give us the name of the publisher's father. However neither child appears in the birth registration list for those periods or later. Unless the family omitted to register the children's birth (an unlikely possibility), this can only mean that both children were using different names when they were nine and eleven to the ones they had been originally registered with. This was not an uncommon occurrence and there are a number of reasons why it might have happened. Most commonly, boys and girls were often registered with the same first name as their respective parent. They would have then been known by a second or third Christian name (not recorded) to avoid confusion!

Edward Owen did have a son called Arthur who is the right age but, as I have written in a previous chapter, his wife's name was Sybilla and in 1901 he was a shipbroker's secretary. There were a number of other Arthur Greenings but they were all too young or too old. I can therefore only assume that, like his children, Arthur was not the name the publisher was registered with at birth! I'm sure that someone who may be interested and more persevering than myself will find his ancestors. As he is not a major player in this story I will leave that to them. I would be interested to know where his family came from; although his publishing house was short lived it did produce the best seller of 1905.

Tracing the ancestry of Stan, the bandleader, has only proved a little more profitable. Stanley was his second name. His first was William, like his father, and he was born in Kensington on 1st March 1888. William Thatcher Greening was a successful 'master tailor' and Stan was his youngest child. William Thatcher Greening was born in Newington, Surrey, in June 1852. He was the illegitimate son of Martha Greening and Charles Thatcher, who provided his son's second name. Charles was a 'clicker', which is the job title of either a person who worked in the shoe trade – cutting out the uppers and making the shoelace holes – or a person in the print business. This was the man who was in charge of the final type layout before printing. Martha and Charles did not subsequently marry and I have been unable to find their son in the 1861 census, when he would have been eight years old. There is a Martha in that census, who is probably his mother. She was then a living-in cook, aged 36, in the household of a Reverend gentleman in Kensington. Ten years later William can be found in the census. At the age of eighteen he was an apprentice to a tailor in Shoreditch, London. The '61 census records Martha the cook's birth county as Dorset. So, if she was the tailor's mother, Stan's Greening ancestry stems from that 'other' county.

We are now in the opening years of another century and, although the last hundred years did not match the dramatic population rise of the nineteenth century, the number of people in Britain doubled. The number of Greenings will have multiplied by at least two as well. Today, as in their other areas of domicile – The United States, Canada, Australia and New Zealand, Greenings will now be found in all sections of society and in most of the walks of life. There may be no Yeomen any more but there are Farmers and Shopkeepers, University Professors and Plumbers, Doctors and Architects, Lawyers and Television Producers, Businessmen, Scientists, Soldiers and Clergymen – and everything else.

A few Greenings have become well known names, but most of these I know little about. In Britain we have Jonathan – the Premiership Footballer who played for the England under-18 team, Phil – the England and Wasps Rugby Hooker who certainly came from Gloucester so his ancestors are likely to be in this book, Leon – the much admired Jazz Pianist, Professor Andrew – the expert on lung diseases, David – the Yacht Designer and Professor J R (I don't know his name) Fellow of the Royal Society of Edinburgh. Kevin, the London DJ – formerly on BBC Radio One and now with 'Smooth/Jazz FM' – did write to me. He believes his ancestors were immigrants from Italy and that may be so. I have also corresponded with John Greening, the prize-winning poet. John's poem Awre is published for the first time at the front of this book. John has traced his Greening family tree back to his 3x Great-Grandfather also called John, who was married to Elizabeth Twaites at Newington, Surrey, in about 1800. I have not been able to help him extend these roots.

In 1978, shortly after I first started to take an interest in Family History, I enjoyed a correspondence with Sarah Grayson. Sarah possessed far more knowledge than myself and helped to point me in the right direction. This was during the early days of Family History Societies, when few records were indexed, and – of course – long before the Internet or emails. My enthusiasm for the subject, I suspect like most people who research their ancestors, came in bursts and there were very many fallow years when I did no research at all. So, apart from the occasional Christmas card, Sarah and I lost touch. I knew that one of her ancestors was a Benjamin Greening and that she thought there might be a connection with the Chepstow clockmakers. Very recently I decided I would try and discover, for this book, if her Greening forebears came from Gloucestershire.

Sarah (now Lady Sarah) comes from a branch of the surname that has reached the high echelons of British 'Society'. Her cousin, who wrote me a nice letter about my first book, is Rear Admiral Sir Paul Greening GCVO, Naval Equerry to Queen Elizabeth. Between 1986 and 1993 he was the 'Master of the Queen's Household' and had previously been the Captain of the Royal Yacht Britannia. He held that post during the honeymoon cruise of Prince Charles and Lady Diana. Sarah and Paul's grandfather was Benjamin Charles Greening who lived in Hove, Sussex. Benjamin had married in September 1902, when he was 35, and his marriage certificate records that his father was James Berry Greening (deceased) with the profession of Publisher. When I saw this I thought there might be a connection with Arthur and *The Scarlet Pimpernel* but this was not so. James Berry had died thirty years before, when his son was only five. He was also a printer rather than a publisher. They were obviously a 'well healed' family; on Benjamin's birth certificate of 1867 his father's occupation is given as 'Stock Holder' and, when he was a boy, he was an early border at Cranleigh Public School in Surrey (then known as Surrey County School).

Benjamin and his sister were the children of James Berry's second marriage. In August 1863 James, printer by profession, married Fanny Cousins who was the daughter of a printer (possibly a business partner of James?). It was from this man, his maternal grandfather – Benjamin Davy Cousins, that Sarah's grandfather obtained his name. James Berry's first marriage took place at Holy Trinity Church, Newington, Surrey in October 1836. His bride was Elizabeth Jefferys. Two of their daughters are shown in the 1861 census living with their widower father, who at that time was a printer employing thirty men and fifteen boys. The eldest child, Emily Eliza (born February 1838), was a schoolteacher and the youngest, Agnes (then 11), was at school. It is likely that there would have been other children, in between their ages, who had left home. James Berry was born on 7th February 1812 and baptised on the 30th of the following month at St George the Martyr's Church in Southwark, London. His parents were Joseph Moore and Ann Greening. According to James Berry's second marriage certificate, Joseph Moore was a 'Decorator'. Joseph was the son of an earlier Joseph who married Elizabeth Moore at St Marylebone, London on 28th November 1781. This first Joseph was probably born in the 1750s but, without more information (possibly in a will), we are unable to know who his parents were or where he came from. There was a Joseph baptised at Frampton-on-Severn, Gloucestershire, on 28th December 1751. He was the son of Old Ben's uncle and aunt, Thomas and Hester (see chapter 3). Whether or not that Joseph moved to London is pure speculation.

Berry is an unusual middle name. I find it interesting that one of John the poet's ancestors not only had the same second name but also passed it on to all his children, both boys and girls. This was William Berry Greening (born 1843), who was a chartered accountant and lived in the same area of South London as James Berry. I can find no link between the two families.

As I was completing this final chapter another Greening became news, both on television and in the press. This member of the surname family is directly descended from the main lines in this book.

One of the sons of Zachariah (Elgar's great-grandfather's brother) and Jane (see Chapter Four) was William, who was baptised at St John the Baptist Church at Elmore on 21 November 1779. William, a thatcher by trade, married Ann (usually known as Nancy) Phelps at her home parish church of St Peter's at Minsterworth, in April 1808. Nancy was a seamstress and she and her husband lived most of their lives at Elmore Back, a hamlet in Elmore parish. This is situated on the east bank of the Severn, directly overlooked by the tower of the church where their wedding took place on the opposite side of the river. They named their eldest son Thomas, and he was baptised at the same church as his father in 1809.

Like his parents Thomas, who was a carpenter, also lived most of his life in Elmore Back. He lived in a cottage a couple of doors away from the Salmon Inn, which for many years was kept by his younger brother Henry. Elmore Back is well worth a visit today. The little Ale House closed in the early 1940s but the building now a private dwelling and others, in this backwater hamlet, have changed little over the years. It is still possible to walk along the riverbank and project a picture in your mind of what life might have been like here in the nineteenth century. Part of the enjoyment of researching family history is trying to resolve the anomalies and mysteries the records frequently throw up. There is one recording of a man who may be this Thomas, which needs some interpretation. My suggested explanation of the documents may not be the truth.

Although households are marked separately in the first census of June 1841, relationships between the people listed are not explained and the ages of adults are not exact. However we can conclude that the carpenter, Thomas Greening (Age 30), living at Elmore Back with Mary (Age 35) and two boys – James (9) and Edwin (7) was William, the thatcher's son, with his wife and sons. Ten years later, in the March 1851 census when adult's ages were given more accurately, Thomas is recorded as being 41. James, now 19, is identified as his son and both men are described as 'Journeymen Carpenters'. Mary is listed as the head of the household's wife, but her age is recorded as only 34 and there is a new son – 'young' Thomas aged three. This is not an enumerator's error. There would not have been such a large gap between children and, although she had the same name, this

Mary is obviously a second wife. Some further investigation confirms this. I have not been able to find a record of the marriage of Thomas to the first Mary so do not know her maiden name. It seems likely that she died in 1842 and was the Mary Greening, aged 36, whose burial took place at Elmore in December 1842. I do have a copy of the certificate recording the wedding of Thomas to his second wife, which took place at Elmore Parish Church on 20th October 1845. This states that Thomas was a widower as well as a carpenter. His new wife was Mary Drinkwater and the document confirms that the father of the groom was William the thatcher. In 1851 Edwin was not at his father's house. He is recorded as an agricultural labourer aged 16 and was living with his grandparents, William and Nancy.

If you take a boat journey north, up the River Severn from Elmore Back, after about eighteen miles you will reach Tewkesbury and pass out of the county of Gloucestershire into Worcestershire. Then, after travelling another five miles north, you will reach the small town of Upton-upon-Severn. This is only fifteen miles from Elmore if you are a flying crow. Here in 1841, at a riverside inn kept by Thomas Bundy, there lived a young servant named Thomas Greening. On October 20th the following year this Thomas married Ann Smith at St Clements Parish Church in Worcester. The ages of the couple are not given but Ann is described as a widow and the daughter of Isaac Jones – a waterman. Thomas is recorded as the son of Thomas Greening, carpenter, with the occupation of servant. In the 1851 census, nearly nine years later, Thomas is shown as being 31 and Ann 41. They were then living in Court Street, Upton-upon-Severn, with Gloucestershire given as the place of birth of Thomas. There were five children in their household, Elizabeth Smith (Ann's child from her first marriage) plus Clara, William, Mary and Thomas Greening – in age order. Young Thomas, aged two in 1851 (and his father) are the Greening ancestors of Jane Woodall, who lives in Australia and appears in the narrative about Elgar in Chapter Seven.

We are unable to know for certain who might have been the father of Ann's husband. However because of what is written on the Worcester marriage certificate, it is 'just' possible that he was the first son of Thomas the carpenter and the first Mary from Elmore Back. As far as I am able to discover this was the only carpenter, named Thomas Greening, in Gloucestershire at that time. If the Upton Tom had been born about 1820, as he affirmed, this would be impossible. The carpenter can have hardly fathered a child when he was eleven. However, it seems quite probable that the man who married Ann made out that he was a few years older than he actually was. Ann was a widow, possibly with a small inheritance, and he was a servant with few prospects. He would not have wished the already large discrepancy in their ages to look too out of line. A 'just possible' scenario, if we accept that the age given by the Upton Tom was not correct, is that he was a very early child of carpenter Thomas and probably the first Mary born before their marriage. This could have been when the carpenter was only fourteen (Mary was about four years older). The illegitimate baby boy might possibly have then been 'adopted' by boat people – and taken up river to Upton? If this is what happened, Elmore Thomas must have believed that this early child had died as he also gave the name Thomas to his first child by the second Mary when that boy was baptised in 1848! Upton Thomas was born before the arrival of Birth Registration so, unless a baptism entry can be found, we may never know the truth.

Upton Thomas did die at a fairly early age. By the time of the 1861 census Ann is recorded as being a widow again. She was still living in Worcestershire but had moved with the children to Pershore where, rather curiously, she is described as an 'Industrious School Governess' with her daughter Clara as her 'Assistant'. Ann lived a long life. In her eighties she was residing in Birmingham with her married daughter Mary, the wife of Boot Shop Manager – John Moss.

We can follow James and Edwin, the 'certain' sons of the first Mary, through the Public Record files. In 1857 James married a local girl, Elizabeth Dangerfield, at her home village of Westbury-on-Severn. Although he was a carpenter like his father he had married into a 'sailing' family, who were involved in the transportation of goods by water between Gloucester and Cardiff. By 1861 James had set up home in Cardiff, where Elizabeth ran a greengrocery (assisted by her sister) while he was away engaged in the river trade. The 1871 census shows that while Elizabeth (now with five children) and her sister were minding the shop in South Wales, James was in Gloucestershire. He is described as a mariner, aged 39, and was in charge of *"The Kate of Gloucester"* at Haresfield. Also aboard were his brother-in-law, Joseph Dangerfield, and a 'Henery' Greening. At first glance I found this census entry puzzling. The adjoining entries were all agricultural properties and Haresfield is some way from the Severn. I then realised that *The Kate* must have been moored on the Gloucester-Berkley Canal (now the Sharpness Canal), which cuts through this parish. When it opened in 1827 this waterway, which runs in parallel to the Severn, was the widest and deepest canal in the World. By 1881, now with two more children, James was back on land in Cardiff. He was a carpenter again, assisted by his eldest son William. This was still his occupation in 1891. By the time of the 1901 census James had become a widower and was living in the home of his married youngest daughter Florence (Mrs Orchard). His occupation is not given as carpenter or mariner; He is listed as a retired greengrocer. Today there are a number of Greening families in Cardiff and South Wales; some of them will be descended from James.

In 1858, a year after his brother, Edwin also married a local girl. She was Eliza Browning and came from Longney, a village adjoining Elmore. However the couple were not married there but many miles away in Wakefield, Yorkshire. Edwin had moved to the North of England, in the opposite direction to his brother and in the 1861 census we find him living in Normanton, a town northeast of Wakefield. He was employed as a 'Railway Horse Driver' and was with his wife, two sons (Arthur and Walter) and Eliza's unmarried sister with her son. In 1871 Edwin was still in Yorkshire but now a farmer, living with Eliza, three sons and a 21 year-old lodger George Stiles. Edwin must have died within a year or so of that census as by 1881 we find Eliza with the three boys and also two daughters. However the daughters, aged 8 and 2, have a different surname. Eliza is now Mrs Stiles and her new husband, twelve years her junior, is shown to be a Railway Guard. There is a further twist to this story. George did not last long and, by 1891, Eliza was a widow for the second time. Her eldest son Arthur was the head of his own household and had set up in business as a Carter's Agent. Ten years later his business had prospered and he had a number of employees plus, rather strangely, two domestic servants who were his stepsisters. In the census column, where the relationship to the householder was entered, in each case the word 'stepsister' has been crossed out and amended with the word 'servant'. On reflection I don't think this was a family feud in an odd Victorian household, it was an enumerator's error. The girls lived in their stepbrother's house but must have worked as domestic servants somewhere else.

Reverting to 1861 and back in Elmore Back, 'young' Thomas – the eldest son of the second Mary and now thirteen – was already an apprentice carpenter to his father. He still described himself as a carpenter when he married Melina Burnett, five years older than himself, at the St Mary de Crypt church in Gloucester on 8th August 1867. Melina was an unmarried mother who already had a three year-old son Alfred. As this boy kept his mother's surname we must presume that Thomas was not his father. Although living in the city of Gloucester at the time of her wedding, Melina had been born in Elmore like her husband. Her parents were not married when she was baptised but she had taken her father's surname. George Burnett was a fisherman and his son in law must have joined him, as this Thomas – for the rest of his life – calls himself a fisherman rather than a carpenter.

Thomas and Melina set up home in Minsterworth, the village were the grandparents of Thomas had married. Here Melina gave birth to a large family of three daughters and six sons in addition to her earlier son. The six Greening boys were William, Edwin, Tom, Henry, Albert and Arthur. By 1901 all the sons, except one, were still in Minsterworth. They lived in the same row of houses and must have been a very well known family in the village. William the eldest, who was a general agricultural labourer, already had a wife and six children of his own. Tom was a pig butcher, working for himself, and had a wife and one child. Henry, Albert and Arthur were still at home with their parents. Henry had learnt his father's original trade and become a carpenter, Albert was a fisherman with his father and Arthur worked for a wagon company. The 1881 census shows us that one year-old Albert had a second name with the initial 'Z'. Confirmation that this name was in honour of his great-grandfather can be found on his tombstone in Minsterworth churchyard; Albert Zachariah Greening – died 13 March 1944 age 64.

Second son, Edwin, had left Minsterworth some years before. In 1891 he was living in Lancaster, with his wife Frances who came from Derbyshire. Here Edwin was employed as an 'Iron Turner'. At the time of this census he was aged 22, Frances was 24 and they had no children. However later that same year their eldest son Edwin Gregory was born. By 1901 Edwin and his family – now with four children (Olivia, Charlotte and Henry as well as Edwin G) – were living in Rotherham on the other side of the Pennines. By an odd coincidence Edwin had moved to the same county, Yorkshire, where his same name uncle had migrated over forty years before. One wonders if he was in contact with his first cousins or even aware of their existence? They lived little more than twenty miles away from him. At Rotherham Edwin had become a foreman in a railway wheel works.

The Greening in the news, as I finish this book, is Edwin Gregory's granddaughter. In the first hour of the morning of Friday 6th May 2005, Justine Greening was pronounced the elected Member of Parliament for Putney in London. Her victory was the first declared for the Conservative Party that night and also the first Tory win of a seat previously held by a supporter of Tony Blair. Justine is the first Greening to reach the House of Commons.

I would like to conclude this chapter with a personal story. A few years before my widowed mother's death, I drove her down to the Somerset city of Wells to attend the funeral of my Aunt Doris. Doris had been in her late eighties and was the widow of my father's only brother, but I had met her on only half a dozen or so occasions in over sixty years. After the very sparsely attended service – my mother and I were the only family members and most of Doris's acquaintances had pre-deceased her – we took tea with a lady called Joan, who had lived as companion to my aunt for many years. As we rose to leave Joan handed me a small brown envelope, "these are your uncle's papers Michael, I have kept them for you as I thought you should have them". The rather sad brown envelope now resides in a drawer in my desk. All it contains are the two official letters from the bishop, appointing William Harry Greening deacon and then priest. I had hoped the envelope might have contained photographs or a personal letter but all that was left of my uncle's life are these two official scraps of paper.

Although both my father and his brother were Church of England clergymen and they had both started out as Methodist ministers before becoming ordained Anglicans, they were as different as chalk and cheese and they rarely met. My father was a very gregarious and popular man; he had become an army chaplain for the duration of World War Two and mixed easily with all types and conditions of men. He also, of course, had children. Uncle Will and Doris never had a family and never seemed to settle anywhere, moving from one obscure parish to another every few years. For many of these the household had a third member who ruled the roost, the formidable Mrs Wadsworth, Doris's invalid mother.

The only time I called to see them during my adult life was when they had a parish in the holiday county of Cornwall. I had motored down there for a vacation with my wife Laura and our two eldest children (the younger ones had not yet been born) and drove up to their rambling vicarage to pay my respects and introduce my Belgian wife and young family. My uncle came to the door but had no idea who I was. He did accept my explanation that I was his brother's son and tea and cake were produced. However I'm sure Doris was glad when we left, young children might break the china.

I think the only other time I ever met them on their home ground was when I was about ten and living near Cheltenham in Gloucestershire, where my father had taken a parish after the war. My uncle and aunt had moved to a parish in the same diocese and county. They had already been there about two years and as father said 'should have settled in' but as they had not been to see us, it was decided that we should drive over in my father's ramshackle old Austin car to visit them. It was only about 35 miles, which today would be less than an hour's drive in the car. In the 1940's it was certainly a little more of an expedition. We arrived at my uncle's Rectory, a large rather gaunt house, to discover that he and my aunt had not yet unpacked. All their possessions were still in packing cases and cardboard boxes, in the situation where the moving contractors had dropped them. They were cluttering the hall, the passageways, the rooms and the stairways. My uncle apologised that they had not yet found their kettle, so hot water was boiled in a saucepan to make tea. I don't think we stayed there long, sitting on assorted bits of furniture amongst my uncle's books and unpacked tea chests. My father told me years later that my uncle and aunt had stayed there another three or four years, about five or six years in all – their usual sojourn in any one parish – but that they had never unpacked. Mrs Wadsworth and my aunt had found the house damp and draughty and had not wanted to make a home there.

My uncle was an academic but rather humourless man. He had been a very clever student, as a number of cuttings about her eldest son's achievements in my paternal grandmother's scrapbook confirm. However, as I have explained, I never really knew him. As the episode of the brown envelope depressed and saddened me, I have decided to include his photograph in this book for posterity. The large damp house he was living in when I was ten is, after all, a part of this book. It was Awre Rectory. Although I'm fairly sure my uncle did not realise his surname connection with his parish, from 1944 to 1950 he was the Rector of Awre.

Stan Greening
Bandleader

Rev William Greening
Rector of Awre 1944–1950

APPENDIX 1
WILL & TESTAMENT OF NATHANIEL GREENING, MORETON VALENCE (16TH APRIL 1722)

In the name of God Amen, I Nathll. Greening of ye
P(ar)ish of Mourton Vall: in ye County of Glouc: being sick
& weak in body but of sound & perfect mind &
memory doe make this my last Will & Testam(ent) in
manner & forme following – (viz) first I will that
my Debts & funerll: expences be p(ai)d & discharg(e)d

*Imp(rim)is: I doe give & bequeath unto **my three brothers Sam(ue)ll, Tho(ma)s***
***and William** all my Freehold Estate lying in ye p(ar)ishes of Mourton Vall.*
& Saule for ye term of five yeares after my decease w(i)th ye rents
Issues & profits thereof to be equally employ(e)d by them (for & towards
ye maintenance & education of my Children) as they in their discre-
tion shall think fitt and after ye Expiracon of ye s(ai)d term of five yeares
I doe give and bequeath my s(ai)d Freehold lands [prmises] tenem(en)ts &
*Hereditam(en)ts unto **all my five sons** to be equally divided only **my Eldest son Natll.***
***Greening** to have ye first Choice.*

It(em). All ye rest of my personll: Estate Goods & Chattell w(ha)tsoever I doe give
to my s(ai)d three brothers whome I doe make full & sole Exec(utor)s in
trust willing them to pay all my Debts & funeral expences &
ye overplus to be & remaine to & for ye use & benefit of all my
s(ai)d Childr(e)n & to be equally divided amongst them as they shall
respectively attaine to ye age of one & twenty yeares. In witness
whereof I have hereunto sett my hand & seale the Sixteenth day
of Aprll: Anno Dom. 1722.

Natl: Greening

Sealed & delivered
In ye p(re)sence of
John Werne
Samuell Walkly
Matt: Fryer   (Record Office Ref: 1723/88)

Note
Letters / words (in brackets) have been put in to simplify reading, bold type to emphasise
names.

EXTRACT FROM THE WILL & TESTAMENT OF NATHANIEL'S YOUNGER BROTHER

William Greening – Clothier of Saul (13th December 1724)

*In the name of God Amen, I **William Greening** of Saul in the County of Gloucester, Clothier, being sick and weak in body but of sound and well disposing mind and memory ... bequeath unto my cousin Mary Morris the full sum of twenty pounds of good and lawfull money of Great Britain ... All the rest of my Goods and Chattells and personal estate whatsoever (my debts and funeral Expenses being first paid and satisfied) I give and bequeath to ... my brother **Samuel Greening** my Sister **Mary Probert** and my Sister **Elizabeth Blanth** to be equally divided between them share and share alike*

APPENDIX 1A

A True and perfect Inventory of all & singular ye Goods Cattles & Chattells of Nathaniel Greening of Epney in ye Parish of Moreton Valence in ye Countey of Gloucester taken & appraised By us Whose Names are herunto subscribed this Twenty Seventh Day of April Anno Dom: 1722.

		£	s	d
Imp's	His wearing apparel & Money in purse	3	00	00
It.	In the parlour Chamber 1 Bed & furniture & 1 Chest	1	10	00
It.	In the parlor 1 tabell Board 6 Chiers 1 Jine Stole	00	10	00
It.	In the Chichin Chamber 1 Bed & furniture	00	15	00
It.	In the Hall 2 Bedes & furniture and the Rest of the Goods	2	00	00
It.	In the Citchen 1 tabell Bord 6 Chaiers 2 fliches of Bakon Bras and puter	3	10	00
It.	Corne in the House	1	05	00
It.	19 Coues and A Bool	70	05	00
It.	19 sheepe & 13 Lames	8	00	00
It.	6 peges	3	00	00
It.	5 horses and harness	21	00	00
It.	8 Working Boolockes	29	00	00
It.	34 Acers of Corne on ye Ground	64	00	00
It.	7 Erlings	9	00	00
It.	A wagon & dungwain yokes and Strenges & plows	9	10	00
It.	2 Rickes of Hay	12	00	00
It.	In Apolls	2	00	00
It.	Bages fir the musmell & Cabell	1	05	00
It.	In Cheese	1	00	00
It.	In Hogshets pailes Coules Cloths & all Rest of ye Lumber	6	10	00
	The totall	249	00	00

Simon Meade   }
James Birt   }   Appraisers
Samell humfries   }
Christopher Baldwin his mark   }
            CB

APPENDIX 2

WILL & TESTAMENT OF HENRY GREENING, AWRE (26TH APRIL 1552)

In the name of god Amen the xxvi th daye of Aprille in the yere of o(u)r lorde god mcccclii And in the yere of the regyne of o(u)r Soveraynge lorde Edwarde the vi th by the g(ra)ce of god of England Fraunce and Irland Kynge defend(er) of the faythe and in ...of the .....of England and Irland ....the first, I **Henry Grynynge of Awre** *in the Countie and diosc(es)e of Gloc* **husbandman** *Sike in bodye and hole of mynde do macke my testament and last wyll in manere and forme folowynge; first I bequethe my sowlle to god the father and to his sonne Jhesus (crossing out) Christ my Saviour the .g be the merits of whose passion my death by faythe trust to be savid.And my body to be buyryed within the church yard of Awre aforesaid. It(em). I geve and bequeathe to my eldest daugh(te)r Margerye an oxe which commonly I calle store and a fole w(hi)ch commonly I calle burnett and a heyf w(hi)ch commonly I calle Silke and two sheppe and aq flock bedde w(i)th therpptinences yt ys to saye a coverlydd a blanket a payer of shites and a bolst(er). It(em). I do ordeyne and apoynt* **my wyfe Als** *and* **my daugh(ter) Marian** *my executres jointly to whome I geve charge that they truly and Justly filfill my testament and laste wylle to whome also I geve and bequethe the residue of my movable goods unbequethyd I doo desire also and put in trust my well lovid frynde and neyghburg Edmund barowe gent, John Shere John Baylye and John Dymmock to ov(er)see for this my testament and truste wylle by truly and justly fullfillidd And then* **my mother Christian grynnynge** *maye have an honest ..... at the cost and charge of my executors to this being witness phillipp hulinge John Shere John bayle Thomas of Awre John Dymmocke (John Kedicke – crossed out) Thomas Trippett Williasm Kedicke and otherse On the daye and yere above written.*

Dettes owing to me (whch I doo owe – crossed out)
(I doo owe Xpofer hopkynes xxd – crossed out)

dettes owynne to me
morishe Rydden owysh me ixd

dettes which I doo owel doo owe
to Christopher hopkynes a xxd

be me henry grynnynge

On reverse
Henrico Greenynges/ nuper de awre pbat (proved)/...glouc coram/John Williams/ ....28 June 1552

TREE 1: GREENING showing only the names included in the text of this (or the earlier) book

KEY

B:	BORN
b:	BAPTISED
[m]:	MARRIED
MV:	MORTON VALLANCE
<W>:	WILL
- - - :	POSSIBLE LINK
c:	CIRCA

JOHN - [m]
Christian (Awre?) - B-15th Cent. *(Husbandman Awre)*

HENRY
(Churchwarden) - <W-1552>

JOHN
B-c1510
(Yeoman-MV) - <W-1565>

THOMAS
<W-1613>

GUY (MV)
B-c1595

GUY (MV)

GUY - [m] Elizabeth
B-c1560 *(Yeoman)*

THOMAS
(Yeoman)

(Rev) THOMAS
B1620
(BA Cambs)

JANE
b.1606

RICHARD - [m] Alice March

NATHANIEL (i)
b.1614 (died as infant)

NATHANIEL (ii) - [m] (i) Mary Humphries,
b.1618   (ii) Judith Linck
(Yeoman MV)
<W - 1680>

NATHANIEL - [m]
Elizabeth Collins
B c1655 *(Yeoman)*

DAUGHTER? - [m]
William Hammon

DAUGHTER? - [m]
Richard Nayle

ABIGAIL - [m]
Richard Godfrey

SAMUEL
b.1677
(Tombstone in MV Churchyard)

NATHANIEL - [m] Martha
b.1679 *(Yeoman)*
<W - 1722>

THOMAS

WILLIAM
b.1684
(Clothier of Saul) <W - 1724>

MARY
b.1687 - [m]?
Probert

ELIZABETH - [m]
John Blanch

NATHANIEL (i)
b.1702
[m] Mary Moss
(see Tree 2)

WILLIAM
b.1703

BENJAMIN
b.1706

JOSEPH
b.1708
[m] Mary Bodnam
(see Tree 3)

DANIEL
b.1711

TREE 2

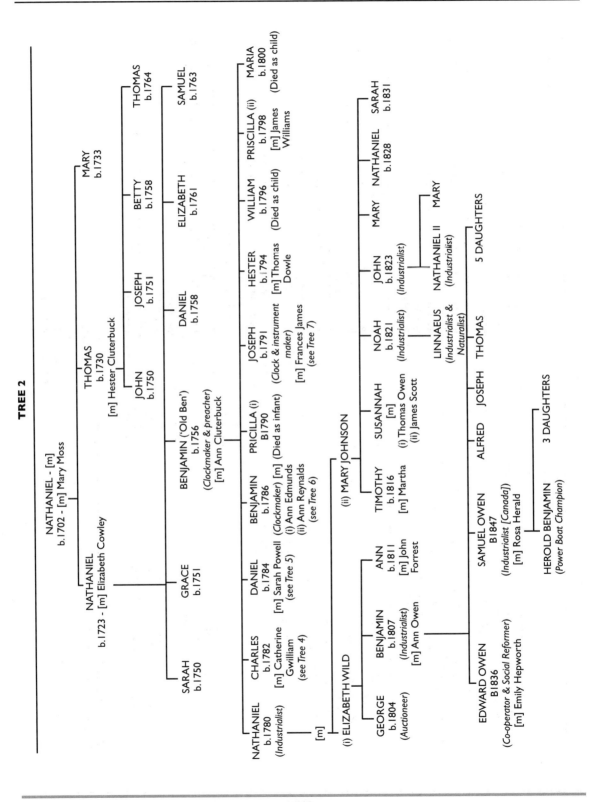

TREE 3

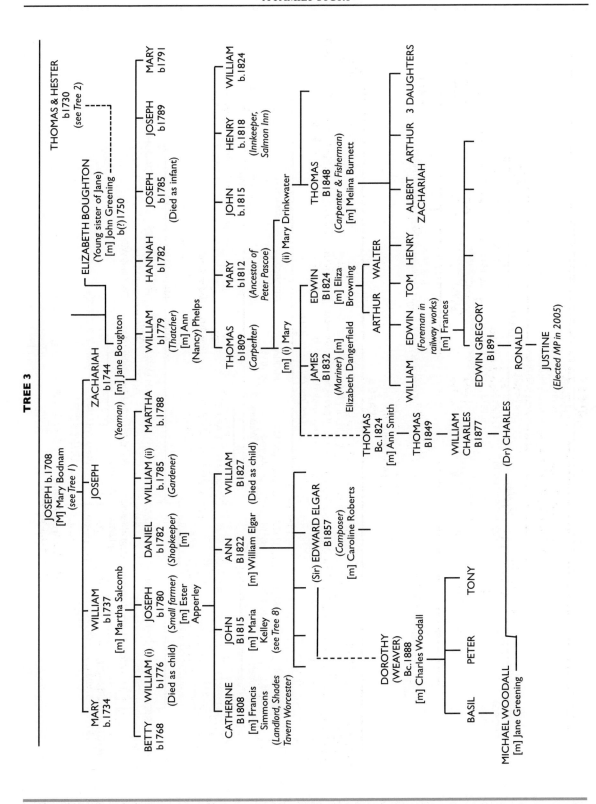

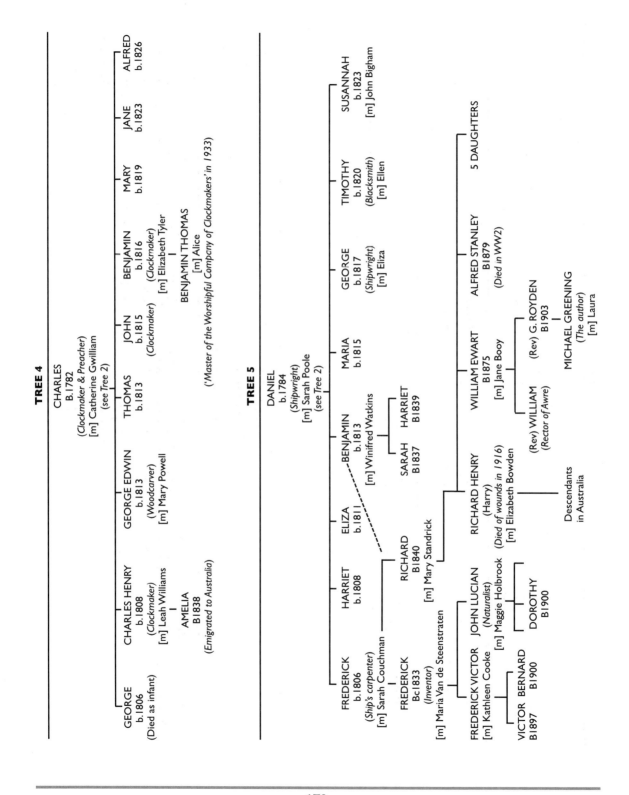

TREE 4

CHARLES
B.1782
(Clockmaker & Preacher)
[m] Catherine Gwilliam
(see Tree 2)

GEORGE
b.1806
(Died as infant)

CHARLES HENRY
b.1808
(Clockmaker)
[m] Leah Williams

AMELIA
B1838
(Emigrated to Australia)

GEORGE EDWIN
b.1813
(Woodcarver)
[m] Mary Powell

THOMAS
b.1813

JOHN
b.1815
(Clockmaker)

BENJAMIN
b.1816
(Clockmaker)
[m] Elizabeth Tyler

BENJAMIN THOMAS
[m] Alice
('Master of the Worshipful Company of Clockmakers' in 1933)

MARY
b.1819

JANE
b.1823

ALFRED
b.1826

TREE 5

DANIEL
b.1784
(Shipwright)
[m] Sarah Poole
(see Tree 2)

FREDERICK
b.1806
(Ship's carpenter)
[m] Sarah Couchman

HARRIET
b.1808

ELIZA
b.1811

BENJAMIN
b.1813
[m] Winifred Watkins

MARIA
b.1815

GEORGE
b.1817
(Shipwright)
[m] Eliza

TIMOTHY
b.1820
(Blacksmith)
[m] Ellen

SUSANNAH
b.1823
[m] John Bigham

FREDERICK
Bc1833
(Inventor)
[m] Maria Van de Steenstraten

RICHARD
B1840
[m] Mary Standrick

SARAH
B1837

HARRIET
B1839

RICHARD HENRY
(Harry)
(Died of wounds in 1916)
[m] Elizabeth Bowden

WILLIAM EWART
B1875
[m] Jane Booy

ALFRED STANLEY
B1879
(Died in WW2)

5 DAUGHTERS

FREDERICK VICTOR
[m] Kathleen Cooke

JOHN LUCIAN
(Naturalist)
[m] Maggie Holbrook

DOROTHY
B1900

(Rev) WILLIAM
(Rector of Awre)

(Rev) G. ROYDEN
B1903

MICHAEL GREENING
(The author)
[m] Laura

Descendants
in Australia

VICTOR
B1897

BERNARD
B1900

170

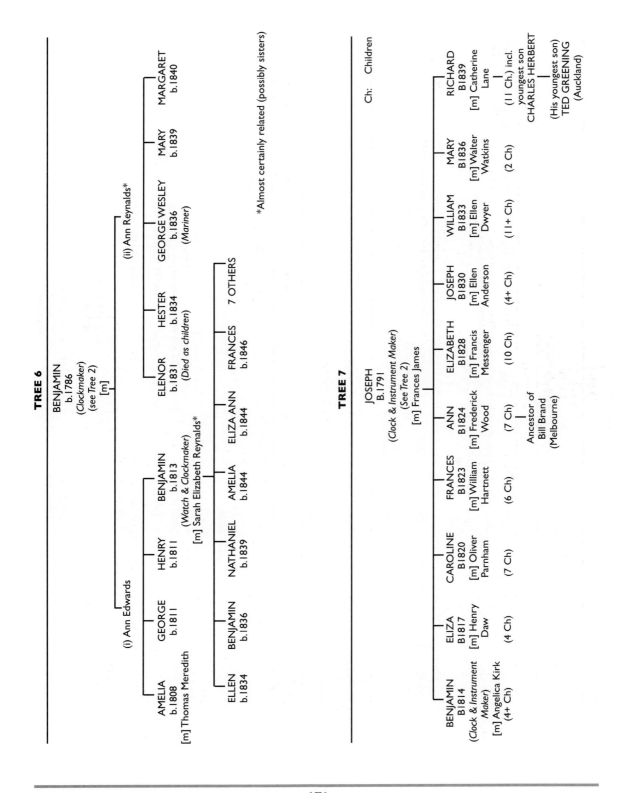

TREE 6

BENJAMIN
b.1786
(Clockmaker)
(see Tree 2)
[m]

(i) Ann Edwards

(ii) Ann Reynalds*

AMELIA
b.1808
[m] Thomas Meredith

GEORGE
b.1811

HENRY
b.1811

BENJAMIN
b.1813
(Watch & Clockmaker)
[m] Sarah Elizabeth Reynalds*

ELENOR
b.1831
(Died as children)

HESTER
b.1834

7 OTHERS

GEORGE WESLEY
b.1836
(Mariner)

MARY
b.1839

MARGARET
b.1840

ELLEN
b.1834

BENJAMIN
b.1836

NATHANIEL
b.1839

AMELIA
b.1844

ELIZA ANN
b.1844

FRANCES
b.1846

*Almost certainly related (possibly sisters)

TREE 7

Ch: Children

JOSEPH
B.1791
(Clock & Instrument Maker)
(See Tree 2)
[m] Frances James

BENJAMIN
B1814
(Clock & Instrument Maker)
[m] Angelica Kirk
(4+ Ch)

ELIZA
B1817
[m] Henry Daw
(4 Ch)

CAROLINE
B1820
[m] Oliver Parnham
(7 Ch)

FRANCES
B1823
[m] William Hartnett
(6 Ch)

ANN
B1824
[m] Frederick Wood
(7 Ch)
Ancestor of Bill Brand
(Melbourne)

ELIZABETH
B1828
[m] Francis Messenger
(10 Ch)

JOSEPH
B1830
[m] Ellen Anderson
(4+ Ch)

WILLIAM
B1833
[m] Ellen Dwyer
(11+ Ch)

MARY
B1836
[m] Walter Watkins
(2 Ch)

RICHARD
B1839
[m] Catherine Lane
(11 Ch.) incl. youngest son CHARLES HERBERT
(His youngest son TED GREENING (Auckland)

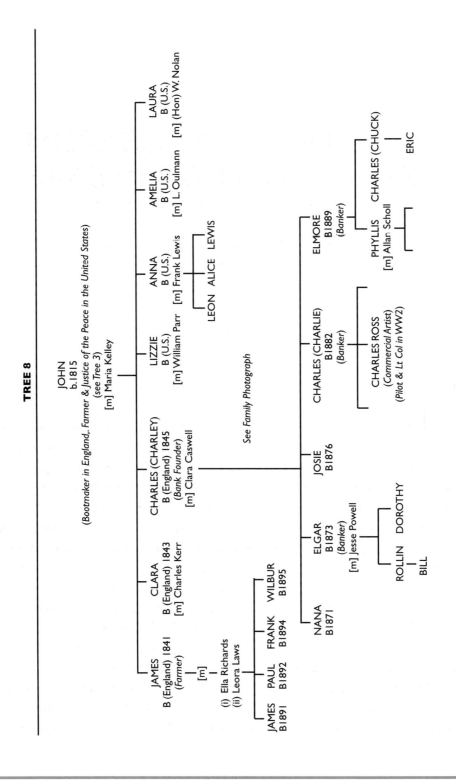

TREE 8

JOHN
b.1815
(Bootmaker in England., Farmer & Justice of the Peace in the United States)
(see Tree 3)
[m] Maria Kelley

JAMES
B (England) 1841
(Farmer)
[m]
(i) Ella Richards
(ii) Leora Laws

JAMES B1891   PAUL B1892   FRANK B1894   WILBUR B1895

CLARA
B (England) 1843
[m] Charles Kerr

CHARLES (CHARLEY)
B (England) 1845
(Bank Founder)
[m] Clara Caswell

See Family Photograph

NANA
B1871

ELGAR
B1873
(Banker)
[m] Jesse Powell

ROLLIN   DOROTHY
BILL

JOSIE
B1876

CHARLES (CHARLIE)
B1882
(Banker)

CHARLES ROSS
(Commercial Artist)
(Pilot & Lt Col in WW2)

ELMORE
B1889
(Banker)

PHYLLIS
[m] Allan Scholl

CHARLES (CHUCK)

ERIC

LIZZIE
B (U.S.)
[m] William Parr

ANNA
B (U.S.)
[m] Frank Lewis

LEON   ALICE   LEWIS

AMELIA
B (U.S.)
[m] L. Oulmann

LAURA
B (U.S.)
[m] (Hon) W. Nolan

JOURNAL OF A VOYAGE FROM LIVERPOOL TO NEW ORLEANS

on the Sailing Ship *RADIUS*, 1150 tons burthen, 500 tons register.

(Written by John Greening as an open letter to his parents, sisters and close friends back in England)

Captain: Mr Johnson
First Mate: Mr Pike
Second Mate: Mr Allen

Sailed from Liverpool April 2nd 1847 (Good Friday)

Hauled out of Waterloo Docks at 11 o'clock am. Two hours earlier than the specified time, in consequence of the dishonest practice of booking more passengers than the ship dare carry which is three adults for every five tons register. In this case there were 36 more paid their passage than could possibly go, hence the early start to make them lose their money. I got my family on board the day before, and so made sure, but I deeply regret not speaking to my Sister Elizabeth (who had accompanied us to Liverpool and done all in her power to make us comfortable during several days we had to wait for a ship) who I saw was pacing the quay, so long as I could discern any object; and then all was over, the die was fairly cast. Oh, it was a trial --- we had to wait and took three turns around in the river, steam tug and all, to take on board our Steward who had gone to the Post Office. The cook was left behind; we did not wait for him fearing more of the passengers would arrive. A man from Liverpool came out till they were all sick and then selected some 10 or 12, that were too many, to go back. The scene was distressing. The sea ran so high that the steamer refused to come alongside, for 20 pounds, to take them out. Our Captain said he would throw them overboard as he dare not take them, so the poor wretches were dragged from their berths and lowered to a boat from the steamer, the sea breaking over them. Some luggage that was put over after them was all lost. Some took the remainder with us to New Orleans, including their

173

provisions. I sent two letters by the officer who came to perform this horrible business.

April 3

We passed Tasker Lighthouse off the Cove of Cork. Kept company with the ship *Scotland* bound for Quebec, Canada, and she sticks to the Irish coast too close to please our Captain who keeps a wider range to seaward. Bye the bye, this same *Scotland* nearly ran into us yesterday coming out of Liverpool. She got her jib entangled in the rigging of the *Radius* and grazed our side. One foot more and she would have driven us in.

April 4

The first thing today was to look about us and see the effect of a change in the wind that took place this morning early. We see the *Scotland* beating to the wind with close-reefed royals and topsails and she cannot keep off that ugly coast. We are carrying every stitch of canvas, studding sails and flying jibs, and can afford to edge in a little before the wind. Our Captain intends to steer straight for Cuba and Jamaica, not south for Tenerife and the trade winds or the western isles, and steer the Atlantic in as straight a line as possible, trusting in his own judgement and as tight a ship as ever 'walked the waters'.

April 5

All put on half allowance of water already and all sick for three days past. Tis very windy, we take observations daily at 12 o'clock and find ourselves 400 miles from Liverpool today and abominably crowded.

April 6

A fine plain sailing day. We had two ships in sight; we out sailed one and lost the other.

April 7

Getting over seasickness a little and begin to look about us. We find two first cabin passengers, 'Gentlemen' who keep aloof from all others and get drunk daily. The passengers are all Irish and German except about 14 or 16 English who are fortunately all respectable. Mrs Greening is become quite acquainted with a Doctor McDonnell and lady. He is a Scotsman, his wife was born in Barbados. We have a Mr Tattersall in the second cabin who is an old sailor. He has been 25 years the mate of a vessel in the navy and, through a reduction in the officers, is now thrown out of employ and emigrating to just above St Louis, and a Mr Wilson, a Yorkshire farmer's son, is going to the same place. Tattersall is the very nicest man that ever lived and we call him our guardian angel, for he watched over us during seasickness with a father's care and made us gruel when we could not help ourselves. God bless him for it. I feel very unhappy; for this is as miserable a hole as ever man existed in. Maria spends all her time on deck, she is become a special favourite with some of our companions in misery.

April 8
A light wind all day, the ship rolls sluggishly on the ocean and don't get on much. The weather gets sensibly warmer but tis only 60 in the shade.

April 9
Almost a calm; we don't get on at all, but the ship rolls horribly. Tis an impossibility to write legibly. The two mates and I have become the best of friends. Mr Allen gives Clara American walnuts by the handful but the Captain has not spoken to us yet. We found two men and a woman stowed away in the hold. Got them out and put them the dirtiest work to do.

I think a good deal of home, or rather my native land; for Mr Pike says I must call it <u>home</u> no longer. 'Ri' (*pet name for Maria*) is walking the deck with Tattersall and Wilson; I have counted her pass 59 times by the hatchway. Goodbye for today, the eighth of horrors, in a crowded ship 900 miles from land.

3 o'clock: We have just spoken to a brig; the *Eugene* of Ostend homeward bound from Portugal, has been out 17 days. Ought to have done it in four owing to having no wind. It seems strange to meet a fellow traveller on this vast and trackless ocean, to exchange compliments and tell them to report us to the first British subject they may meet. As tis <u>possible</u> twill be the last England will ever hear of us. Once more, farewell for today.

April 10
We have no wind to do us any good. The Captain has scarcely spoken to any of us yet, but he took CHARLEY on the quarterdeck today for a long time. CLARA is Mr   Allen's favourite while Mr Pike says he will take JIM home and keep him. Saw no ship today at all, nothing but sea and sky, always aye always, and tonight we are 1100 miles from Liverpool. The first cabin passengers don't speak to anyone, except one gentleman, who is like Mr Colville, spoke to 'Ri' last night.

April 11
Light winds today, no sail in sight all day. I have been studying navigation. Mr Pike is my tutor, and I shall be able to tell you scientifically all about it as we go on. I find we are 1412 miles W by SW of Liverpool at noon today, and that is what we call a good run. Mr Pike gave us a quarter of a

peck of hickory nuts just now and an arm full of American Newspapers to amuse ourselves with. We had a little music and singing on deck this evening. – Jim's oranges are all rotten already and the beer I brought has been seasick and ferments. It was not old enough.

The children are all in good health and excellent spirits and we manage to get along much better than at first. We have had one serving of biscuit from the ship, they are very brown but sweet good wholesome food. Henry and I have lived on them for three days past, but now I have a cold and hoarseness and can 'hardly speak out'. Maria lives on gruel and keeps Mr Wilson employed in making it.

April 12

A very fine morning with a light east wind. I get up at five o'clock and go on deck to see the sun rise every morning and to reflect on what a little world a ship is. 220 souls are here and all bustle, hum and stir all day, each one following his or her own pursuits. I firmly believe not ten persons in the whole ship ever gives a thought that we are alone on this vastly deep ocean, 1500 miles from any possible communication with our fellow men. Mr Tattersall and I are inseparable companions, and he is a man of great knowledge and experience besides great affability of manners. I have engaged the cook (or steward, for he is both) to cook for my family, or we should not get a drop of tea once a week. As it is, we get it done very expeditiously. I had to pay one pound for it.
Goodbye Father, Mother and Sisters for this time.

April 13

We have a good wind today and are 'walking the waters' in fine style. We saw three Dolphins today, playing about the ship but have no tackle to catch them with. Also I saw some Nautilus fish, like an eggshell with an air bag, they can inflate or depress at pleasure.

Verily we are alone, though not lonely for we tried to raise a dance on deck last night. old Mr Watkins 'tried his hand' at dancing. We kept it up till we danced one man through the hatchway; it was the greatest wonder he did not kill himself. He is a young man, his name is Strong. Maria says he deserves a mention in my letter. He is a great fool and makes fun for all our end of the ship, although he is a gentleman. But, poor fellow, he can't help being a gentleman or a fool. We may as well dance and try to make the best of it now we are here. But tis horrible in the extreme to be crowded together like so many slaves and not a quarter water enough on board for the voyage. The poor wretches beg for it, then steal and are confined and punished for it. What can they do?

April 14

A fair wind still and no sail in sight. We saw lots of porpoises jumping about the ship; I suppose

100. They <u>look</u> the size of Salmon, of 15 to 20 pounds weight, and our Sailors harpooned two this evening but they both broke loose and got away. I thought it was a great cry and fuss over a fish that size. Such a pulling of ropes, and when the hold broke cut, to see a dozen men fall backwards on the deck sprawling. But about six o'clock this evening, Mr Pike harpooned one of middle size. It took 15 or 20 men to haul it out of the water. It was so strong and when it was on deck I measured it. It was 7 feet 7 inches long and three feet nine inches around and weighs 400 lbs or thereabouts. Joshua Smith has its tail and is drying it. I had a dinner of this flesh given me for tomorrow.

We had a strange sail in sight today. After trying to get near enough to speak for four hours she went away, but we found she was the *Nanchez* of Boston bound for some place in America. We could not find out where or what cargo. Our Captain has turned out an unfeeling brute. We have been put on a short allowance of water ever since the third day and bread only once a week. I have not touched my barrel of water yet for fear of worse times. Some of the passengers have been tied up to the capstan a whole night for stealing water from the ship's barrels. I get seven quarts daily for my family and Mr Watkins, the old gentleman, is kind in the extreme and will suffer any privatation rather than see Maria or the children deprived of comforts.

April 15
The Boston ship has out sailed us this morning at daylight by 10 miles. I generally get up at daylight and go on deck to think for an hour or two while the busy lot below sleep. We breakfast about half past seven, Mr Watkins and us together. The old man's heart is in the right place and I am sincerely glad we have him with us. We had a heavy shower of rain at three o'clock this morning, the first since we sailed, and I got up wishing to see the garden refreshed after so long. Twas all sky, sea and sky. Oh when will this end? At 11 o'clock we had a monstrous shark come along side of us, playing about the ship, and we don't like him a bit. You know the superstitions of sailors about sharks following ships for dead bodies, but at present we only have one seaman unwell.
Farewell, dear Father and Mother.

April 16
Hottish, 72 to 78 during the day, Lots of flying fish.

April 17
We were within 60 miles of Madeira last night. The heat in between decks is 78 today, still it is comfortable. Saw lots of flying fish today and lost sight of the shark. Can still see the Boston ship about 20 miles off. We have a fine wind all day and are just one third of our way, oh that it were all!

The ship rolls horribly today as the wind is right behind us and we sail most steady with a side wind. Good night.

April 18 Sunday

Still a rolling ship. We had the beef boiled today that we brought with us and were just sat down to dinner when it was pitched all about. Rather pleasant you'll say. Goodbye.

April 19

A little more steady today. Mr Tattersall has been fishing up seaweed and got some fine specimens. It beats Ilfracombe hollow. We had lots of sacred music and singing yesterday, being Sunday. I played the flute. It has a singular effect on the mind to see 40 or 50 Germans dancing and singing songs at the fore part of the ship, 100 or more Irish celebrating Mass amidships and a small knot of about 14 English aft (as they call it) singing some of the old favourite Psalms and Hymns to the old tunes, accompanied by my flute. And near 1000 miles from land with the ship rolling and tossing in immense waves, and sheets of white foam flying from our bows, as wide as a moderate garden. Now elevated on the crest of a wave and now in a valley with the wind whistling and hooting through the rigging. All of us are in as much glee and security as in a permanent house. The grinding and creaking at night banishes sleep for a while, until at last we sink off and forget all around us. Then it is that home becomes most vivid to the mind. We tell our dreams of home and kind friends we have left <u>forever</u>. But I am growing gloomy and that won't suit my own health or those about me.

We just got a glimpse of the Boston ship this morning, by climbing to the masthead. Once more, dear friends, Farewell.

April 20

We are, thank God, more than halfway now. Greenwich being in longitude 1 and New Orleans in 90 west, it follows of course that when we gain 45 degrees of west longitude we must be halfway. Now the altitude of the sun being 53 at 12 o'clock, that gives us west longitude of 46 or 29 miles and one half more than half our ocean journey. But, as a set off to that, we have two people ill in the steerage with, we fear, fever. Water runs so short and not a drop of rain falling, still we are all well and in decent spirits. The children were never better in their lives, JIM is as mad as ever and a bit madder.

April 21

Rather warm this morning, 80 in the shade and 78 between decks, the sun is two feet neared the zenith and consequently our shadow is shorter than ever it was in England. The heat is quite bearable so long as we keep so splendid a sea breeze. We had singing (songs) on deck till a late hour last night. You have no idea how large and bright the stars are in this southern latitude and the sun rises like fire and sets the same. We have an awning put up over the after deck this morning. That's comfortable but we are obliged to stay below, one at a time, or we should lose our supply of water and that would be a severe loss. I tapped our barrel yesterday; we have got along pretty well as yet but tis hard to see some of the improvident ones. The water is served out at 7 in the morning and some will wash and rinse away for an hour or more, and then thirst or steal.

April 22

Still a fair wind and no sail in sight, we are alone on the ocean but still progressing favourably. Mr Wilson and Mr Tattersall are still as kind as ever and make the voyage quite pleasant under the circumstances. 'Ri' is mending a shirt for Mr Pike today. The Captain has been telling her that every friend he has lives in Wisconsin and speaks very highly of the country. Mr Tattersall plays the accordion and the flute most nights on the deck after dark, sometimes until a late hour, and he smokes too. Heat was 83 in the shade at two o'clock today; still it is not uncomfortably hot although the sun is nearly over our heads. We had a little shower of rain last night. I caught a quart of water and had a good wash in it.

April 23

We had a good deal of lightning last night from the north and west, but no thunder. Mr Allen says there will be some every day or night till we land now. I saw the sun rise this morning; it was grand because there were no clouds. We had a sad robbery last night in the steerage, a poor lad had his box broken open and lost every rag he had. The Captain won't do anything or interfere, and we have all found out that he cares no more for the comfort of his passengers than if it was a slave ship. The ship is his own, he just complies with the act and that is all.

We have no water closet convenience, it being out of order. Shame, shame.

April 24

Still fair winds but no sails in sight; the heat is 83 in the shade and 100 in the sun. The days get shorter than yours and shorter to us every day till we have done southing. When we ascend the Mississippi, within one fortnight we shall have them lengthen from 12 hours to 16 and a half hours and get cooler every day. Oh, that Orleans was passed; the heat was 135 in the shade there last summer. Good-bye.

April 25 – if I have not missed my reckoning

We went to dinner with Mr Watkins today on boiled ham and gooseberry pudding; what do you think of that after being at sea 23 days, and we had half a pint of Worcester ale between five of us after dinner, with a pipe. Master CHARLEY is a good boy and gives no trouble. He is quite a favourite while JIM scrapes acquaintances with all the sailors and all the rough and ready ones in the ship. Tell Elizabeth I have not beat him yet. Goodbye dear Father, Mother, Sisters and all. It seems hard to say <u>forever</u>. I hear they are singing 'Come Let us Join' so I must join them.

Well let us be talking to you a bit more. I shall have something else to do sometime I suppose. You can never conceive how thick the stars are here at night when the moon has gone, tis the clear sky that makes so many visible. The moon is not full for four days, yet tis lighter at night than ever you saw it in your lives. What it will be at full I cannot guess, I suppose it will be so light we shall not see.

Our cases of fever in the steerage get worse, we quite expect death daily. The Captain, the most unfeeling man I ever saw, never inquires about anybody. When anyone complains he will put them in irons. There were six caught stealing water last night, I have had enough of the dirty Irish to last me a lifetime. We hope to make New Orleans in two weeks.

April 26

Saw a seagull this morning at 7 o'clock. Got a fair wind so we are going to the south of Cuba, if the wind holds out, and then up the Gulf. Oh, that we were there. Tis nothing here but sea and sky always. The ship has never been still one minute since we sailed. It is the most uncomfortable thing you can imagine to be always rolling. You can do nothing still but lie down and that is not easy. We have been out 25 days.

April 27

Still a fair wind. The fever case is better but we have had an accident today. One of the sailors dropped a heavy bar aloft on a poor boy's head and cut it open, but it is not very serious although the blood flowed copiously. We had a number of birds around us today, the size of a Thrush. They are called Mother Carey's chickens and are a species of Stormy Petrel. I had some conversation with the Captain today and we expect to see St Domingo or Cuba in a few days. We shall run between them, they are only 60 miles apart so we will see land on both sides once more. Mr Tattersall told me his history last night, tis strange how some people of the same mind become acquainted. I can't write more, it is so blessed hot.

April 28

Saw some stormy petrels and porpoises and flying fish in shoals. Caught a shark and ate him too.

April 29
We have been in the West Indies three days past. We passed the Island of St Thomas last night, but out of sight. The Captain is now looking anxiously to the larboard for St Domingo but the weather is hazy. The Stormy Petrels left us yesterday and numerous seagulls took their place. We are now sailing back north, we crossed the Tropical Line on Monday last and shall re-cross it again in a few days. Now I am anxious to see the end of it as we are beset with islands on every side. While others are secure in their ignorance, I find it unpleasant to know too much. The 'fever' is better and the 'accident' can sit up.

April 30
Looked for land at the masthead last night at sunset, saw none but at 2 o'clock this morning made the island of St Thomas, or Hayti or Hispaniola, the same place bears all three names. At daylight we had a fine long coast of 100 miles on our side, very hilly and within 20 miles of us. It grows coffee. I got a peep through the Captain's glass at it.

May 1
Saw an island called Tortuga 20 miles long and 7 broad, in shape just like a barn, 6000 feet high and desolate. Light winds and hot.

May 2
Lost sight of St Domingo, caught a glimpse of Cuba. Light winds and fair.

May 3
Becalmed all day with a vertical sun and no shadow at all. Very hot, 88 between decks, 84 on deck in the shade and 109 in the sun. Not going one mile an hour, verily this is awful.

May 4
No wind, melted, roasted, broiled.

May 5
Last night we had signs of a storm. It began to lighten at dusk and about 8 o'clock it was brilliant in the extreme. The fact is we must go to the Indies to see tempest. We often got 11 flashes in a minute, before the moon got up and partly extinguished it. The ship seemed in one awful blaze. At last 'Ri' went to bed but I sat up all night, the children being poorly. At half past six in the morning it came to rain and burst upon us in all its fury. I can safely say that until then I never saw it rain, for it came down in spouts as it only can in tropical latitudes.

May 6

Squally all day. Dead calm one minute and roaring wind the next with rain and thunder, and <u>such</u> lightning. We have only gone 125 miles in four days and our usual speed is nearly 200 miles in the day and night.

May 7

Squally, windy, calm, thunder, sunshine, drowning and roasting all in an hour or two. All our party, 12 or 14 <u>respectables,</u> sleep on deck in the open air all night. Maria has been sleeping there last night. I am watching her and the lightning flashing from 7 points of heaven, and thunder rolling around, at the rate of 8 or 10 flashes a minute. We think no more of it than seeing a lamp lit perhaps. Tattersall and I smoking our pipes at 12 or 1 o'clock discussing some scientific point or other, while the elements are clashing, bashing and foaming all around us until driven in by the rain. What singular beings we are thus to accommodate ourselves to circumstances. There is one thing we can never fall in with and that is the abominable filthy Irish passengers. The vermin are so thick we are literally swarmed with them. Tis horrible, if you ever wish anybody ill send them across the Atlantic in a crowded emigrant ship. That will punish them for all the sins they ever did or ever can commit. Goodbye once more.

May 8

Becalmed the last 28 hours and almost dissolved into air by the heat, 123 in the sun. The water has got so bad we cannot use it until compelled to do so. It stinks the moment they begin to serve it out. You would be surprised to see me sitting on the head of a barrel to write this, with as much noise and bustle about me as in the tap room of the "Shades" on a Saturday night. Clara has had a severe rash on her skin but it is better now.

May 9

Sunday again and we got a good breeze last night which kept up till 12 today. Now tis died away we are within 600 miles of Orleans. We passed an island named St Cayman yesterday. Today two pelicans came on board and the swallows migrating from South America alighted on our ship on their way to Europe. Oh what would I have given to send a little line by one of them to assure the many dear friends in Worcester of our safety, who I well know would have welcomed both bird and billet, but such could not be. Farewell till after tea and such a tea as twill be when it comes. God help us but my spirits don't fail me one bit, only when the wind won't blow. Maria is still the favourite here.

May 10

Had an excellent wind last night and we expect to see the last of Cuba tonight or in the morning, tis 700 miles long and has some very high mountains. We are looking out for the Isle of Pines, formerly a great rendezvous for pirates but not now. Tobacco has risen 300 per cent and not one pound on board, and 150 smokers. I have a good stock yet, having been careful at the outset but the Irish bear out their character for improvidence. Tis quite a joke to think of working in such a crowded ship, Mrs G has done a little but not as much as you or she expected she would. We are almost the colour of parchment and quite thin. Henry is quite poorly, the water I think, putrid.

May 11

Got no wind, tacking off and on Cuba and <u>doing nothing</u>. I sleep on deck every night and have not undressed or gone to bed since I left Liverpool. This is a horrible place for women and children to be in, still we are all well. Master JIM has got acquainted with all the sailors and knows them all far better than I do. He tells them and the passengers that his Aunt was proud of his legs and that she spoiled him. He says something about her every day, but tis short and soon over, then goes off to some other random freak. Goodbye.

May 12

A little more breeze today, <u>going it</u> a little again. We hope to lose sight of Cuba tomorrow but the wind is so spiteful. I am studying maps and charts of the Atlantic daily, and find that it don't add to ones happiness one bit to be acquainted with all the reefs and shoals within 200 miles of us. What is most singular is that the trade winds were never known <u>not</u> to blow in this latitude in the history of the place and we have a dead calm. We can see ships in the same position and can do nothing. We are getting very irritable. I have my fear of it being the stillness preceding an earthquake, especially as we are close to Cape Hayti that was shook all to smithereens but four years ago. We have seen some of the river hills in the distance. Dr McDonnell caught a swallow on the ship this morning, quite exhausted on its way to Europe. I gave it some water and it drank freely in my hand. I breathed a little prayer for the little voyager, hoping it will twitter sweetly in the land of my birth. I let it go its way that I shall never travel again.

May 13

A dead headwind and much to do to keep our position. At 6 this morning we spoke to the *Success* of London, from Calcutta homeward bound via Jamaica, and requested her to report us. Three days we had her in sight, at last she headed up and spoke. Until then we could not make her out as she showed no bunting (as they call signals). Then however up flew the British flag, which was returned by the Stars and Stripes from us.

That well known English flag drew tears from my eyes, with the remembrance that it waves over and protects so many dear friends that I will never see again. We have verified the old saying about the sharks following ships for corpses. We have been pretty well followed and at about 6 o'clock this evening our sick sailor died, unattended, uncared for, unknown. He was ill all the voyage and gradually grew worse, till about two weeks ago he appeared consumptive. Then inflammation of the bowels came on and lastly black vomit. He has been insane and raving frightfully some days past but the brutal Captain never saw him but twice. He said he was skulking from work, even when the poor wretch was dying, and when dead ordered him to be heaved overboard in one hour after death. He refused to read the burial service over him, but Dr McDonnell did the duty and then during this time, the Captain ordered the Star Spangled Banner to be thrown over him pall fashion. Vile mockery after neglecting and ill-treating him, aye to death. I stood close to the side and saw the water close over him like a stone.

May 14

The wind is still dead ahead and very hot. We have been at sea six weeks today. Henry is better and putting new knees to his trousers. Tobacco more scarce than ever, I have a little yet but Mr Watkins' foolish plan of making free while it lasts has cost him and me pretty well.

May 15

Still tacking, we've been 14 days making 11 degrees of longitude (40 miles to a degree). A calm again, oh horrid, but at last we have got into the Gulf of Mexico after knocking about in the West Indies under a vertical sun for 14 days. We are 600 miles off New Orleans, including the river. We have cleaned the ship thoroughly three times with chloride of lime to kill diseases but the filthy, lazy, lousy Irish baffle all our attempts to reclaim them. The very name 'Irishman' will make me feel ill, seven years hence. God help them, for it is past the power of man.

May 16

Got a fair wind at last. This is our seventh Sunday at sea, I am heartily tired of it.

May 17

A cool breeze and now the folks are busy eating all up, poor unthinking mortals.

May 18

A good breeze again from twelve last night till 12 this day and now calm again, we are within 150 miles of port. There is a young man just about dying in our apartment today. He has been ill all of the voyage – of decline. We saw Campeachy, South America, yesterday in the distance, tis high land. I have been to the main top today to look about me a little. I got a glimpse of a ship through the Captain's glass yesterday and we see ships two or three times a day here in the gulf. The days are 12 hours long in the latitudes all the year around. Our longitude is 89. I have been reckoning it up today at 12 o'clock and there is 5 hours and 50 minutes difference between this and English time. Vis, tis now striking one PM and that answers to 7, all but 10 minutes, with you. So you are going to bed when we are taking tea. I begin to want to know all the news and how the garden goes on. I hope you will all write and make a long letter to send, when you get a proper address. At present I am a wanderer on the face of the <u>sea</u>.

May 19

The young man died of decline at four o'clock today and at 7 we buried him. It was a solemn sight, and all the friends he had was an uncle in England and a cousin in America. He came from County Derry, he had no money and very few clothes, and with nobody to own that. He was ill when he sailed but the Irish were very kind to him. Is it not singular that the sharks were round the ship so long. When we buried the sailor it did not stop them, so now they have got another.

We have sailed since noon yesterday near 100 miles, and today at noon we find we have gained but 20 miles. We have sailed in all nearly 10,000 miles while the real distance is but 5,000 miles.

May 20

Took the longitude today at noon and find tis only 31 miles to the mouth of the river and very light winds. We expect to get a steamer tomorrow morning and get in on Saturday. I am writing as though I am sure of landing and forget that we have not seen the land yet, although we have been meeting huge logs of wood all day that have drifted down the Mississippi river. Some are as large as any I ever saw in England, whole shoals of them. Mr Watkins has lost overboard a cap and a handkerchief and sixpence, and Smith a straw hat.

May 21

Got no sight of land yet but a steamer and pilot arrived at 2 pm. Thank God this day, seven weeks after leaving Liverpool or 49 days out we are no longer the sport of the wind and the waves. We are under the all-powerful steam. Our next danger consists of 'Busting the boiler'.

It was amusing to see two newspapers hurled aboard at us, almost before we spoke, which told us of grand doings in Mexico that you don't know yet, also news of <u>England</u> up to April 19 being 17 days after we sailed. Oh, I hope that some mail brought me a letter. Our Pilot tells us we are 50 miles out of our way, although we were sounding and measuring all night and believed ourselves to be within ten miles of the bar at the mouth of the river. The current drifts us imperceptibly 40 miles a day in all manner of directions, even with no wind.

May 22

Got up to the bar at the entrance of the river last night and dropped anchor till daylight, while the towboat went up for wood. At 5 o'clock we got underway and entered the stream. When we got into fresh water we began to rejoice. There is grass on the banks 7 feet high and the land is low and swampy. I heard a bird sing like a lark at 6 o'clock, I could hardly restrain my joy. The land for 90 or 100 miles each side is one grass bog, formed by millions of large timber trees drifted down and lodged at the mouth. Then the land settles on it and rank grass grows 7 to 10 feet high.

Thus the land is formed, the whole 120 miles up to Orleans. I find every ten miles or so it shows a difference and gets more solid. About 25 miles up I saw a log house and a garden close to the riverside. Here are no breaks at all, and nothing is more pleasing than to observe than how the vegetation increases in size as we progress.

The next dwelling was 40 miles up and we saw a man just come out of his boat and going up to his door took up one of his children and kissed it. Soon after, we passed some crocodiles basking in the sun, close to us. Tell Jim Neal that some mosquitoes have come on board but I'm not stung yet. In the evening we passed Fort Jackson and Fort Phillips, two batteries on opposite sides of the river.

May 23

Whitsunday, seven weeks and two days out. We shall get in, in a few hours now. Oh that my wanderings were over, tis a long way and near 2000 miles to go yet. We can see horses, mules, carriages, carts and slaves in abundance, as now the land had become firm enough for a road by the riverside. There is one darkie I see, carrying a parasol over his master, and five teams at work among the sugar canes. WE have just passed one small field of sugar quite two miles across. Tis planted in rows near two yards apart and looks like Indian corn. Tis about 18 inches high now and ripens at Christmas. They are quite busy ploughing between it. For all tis Sunday, I shall be in Orleans presently.

May 24

We got in about 2 o'clock. I went ashore and found Suter and Wm. Smith. I took some dinner and they came back with me to the ship and made Maria go to tea. They behaved with the greatest possible kindness. We got back at ten at night but got no sleep at all for the mosquitoes.

Mr Watkins hands are bit and swollen quite frightful, but he got tipsy and heated his blood while we kept cool and our bites soon died away.

We had to go to the Custom House to get a permit to land the luggage, and then get a steamboat.

Clara was taken ill, so I got some quinine powders for which I paid dreadfully dear. This is one of the dearest places in America. I believe that every one who has written back has grossly misled us regards the inconvenience of the journey. I have reason to thank Suter for everything like comfort or information that I got. He is a very nice, calm, sedate thinking man with three of the best behaved children I ever saw. And that speaks well for the parents. The moment Mrs Suter saw Maria, she burst into tears and kissed her. They are very respectable, not so with Smith. His is a vagabondizing kind of life (travelling with quack medicine and perfumed soap). The contrast between the two shows me plainly that a man energetic, persevering and <u>sober</u> improves by coming to Orleans. They rise early, eat quickly, work hard and get extravagant wages.

Suter is getting 9 shillings and 4 pence ($2.25) per day and living near. He is saving money very fast, while the brothers Tearn (of Hallow) were extravagant and rather idle and so poorer than when in England. Ultimately when they found that I and my party were coming this way, rather than meet us, they packed up and went to Cincinnati three weeks ago. Mr Lower is lately dead in Cincinnati, with dropsy.

May 25
Rained in torrents all day. It cost me almost as much to get my things on the *Eclipse* as it will to go to St Louis, besides having more than five pounds worth of damage done. I paid six shillings for taking the beds and the children <u>dry</u> for a quarter of a mile. The fact is, it never rains in England as it does here and thunders terrifically. The fluid shivered a main topmast to atoms, thirty yards from our ship and the *Radius* herself quivered from stem to stern under us. The torrents of water pouring down make a man bend like a reed. We were out in all of it shifting luggage, or lose a passage. I kept Maria dry somehow, I don't know how for umbrellas are useless in such a rain.

There is not a stone as big as a man's fist in 200 miles of Orleans and the mighty river runs on the highest ground of the two, having cast up its mud on the sides and the town rather lower. If you stick a spade in the street (you don't need a pick axe), the hole runs full of water in one minute. There is but one cellar in the city. That is cemented and cost more to build than twenty houses. Yet strange as it may seem, the houses stand secure and firm. Everything like a garden is raised artificially two feet high but they get the greatest abundance of green stuff from up the river. They cannot plow the ground for the furrow runs full, so they sow rice on the top twice a year. There are no drains for there is no place to drain to, so the mud is ankle deep in the streets and stinks like a charnel house. All the dead bodies are bricked up in holes in the walls.

May 26

Got up and shook myself, for I slept among our packages to take care of them. I have got a few things today, but the damage done by the wet is more than I can reckon until I get home. The inconvenience and expense in getting up the country is very great. A man may shift and do very well, but with a woman and children tis heartaching to think upon. I don't know what I shall find when I get there, but I would not go through what I have with a family for fifty pounds. I would rather shoot them all and then myself, but when I can look in their faces and see all in health (such as it is) my courage don't fail me a bit.

May 27

The Mississippi water is muddy and it causes my legs to swell. I am giving CLARA quinine daily for a weakness in her back, caused by irregular living and bad water.

May 28

Half way to St Louis, our boat is the *Eclipse*, 350 horse power, 900 tons burthen, much larger than the ship *Radius* with 7 boilers and two engines, and paddles as large as the Shades Inn or nearly so. It burns 250 pounds worth of wood in five days, purchased on the bank for $3.00 per cord, of 8 ft long, 4 feet high and 3ft 6ins wide. We took in 44 cords last night and this morning it is all gone. Our speed is 220 miles per day, against a current of from 4 to 6 miles an hour.

May 29

Nine weeks yesterday since leaving you all. We have three slaves on board, the servants of the officers. They seem quite happy and fat but they don't work like free men. The fact is they don't belong to themselves and they feel it. Everything is much dearer in Orleans and at all stations up the river than in England, costing us an immensity of money, in consequence of the Mexican war and European demands. It will not be quite so bad in Wisconsin, if ever we get there. I shall fill this up before I get home, I dare say, and post it. I am never tired of conversing with those dear friends who are now separated from me by one third of this vast globe, or nearly so. I hope you will not think me tedious but no letter, that I have seen, has yet done justice to the subject. Mine is but a poor attempt. I have not seen a copper coin yet, nothing but silver and no change out. The smallest is half a dime or five cents, next a dime or bit then quarter dollar and so on. I must henceforth tell you in dollars and cents for I forget the English.

May 30

An English sovereign is worth $5.00 all but seven pence half penny, all over the States. So you may call a dollar 4/- (*four shillings*) without further trouble and they are no less at that.

June 2

I took the fever suddenly and in about three hours was quite incapable of anything. I got a powerful fever dose prepared from Actons powders (Corn Market) and took a dose oil, bathed my head in vinegar and got quite sensible again in about 12 hours. Before I got so bad I spoke to a man to shave my head and bleed me if necessary but, when I got the pulse down a little, I began to have confidence in my treatment. People die here in a very few hours. We got to St Louis on 31 May, 6 days in the *Eclipse*. I went on shore but could not find Pritchard. I believe he is not in St Louis. I left my friend Tattersall with deep regret.

I got another boat to Galena, the *Lynx*, on the same night and did not let one of my family set foot on land. I crawled about the wharf more dead than alive. At night all lay down in our clothes and in the morning found we had not got a fast boat. We expect to be a week going to Galena, 450 miles, but fast boats do not run now for the water is low and we have to ascend two rapids, one 14 and the other 20 miles long.

We hope to get to our journey's end about the 20th of June.

Continuation by Maria

> Dear friends, we got to Galena on Sunday, June 6th, at half past one in the morning and had to take our luggage off by torchlight. With John so ill, he was not able to help at all. He got a little better in the course of the day and engaged the wagons to take us to Gorstville. The next day he was so much worse that we were afraid we should have to leave him behind and made arrangements accordingly. The people of the house where we were staying were very kind and promised to pay him every attention. The next morning he found himself a little better and thought he would try and go, for we were obliged to pay for the wagons whether we went or not and I should be obliged to go with them to take care of the children. You may question what my feelings were. We all set off on Tuesday at 12 o'clock and got about 25 miles that day. The next was very wet and John got wet through. He was obliged to dry his clothes on his back. We got to Mineral Point at midday and accidentally met Mr Cotterell. He had been working there about two months and had left his family in Gorstville (*the Greenings had met the Cotterells in England*). He set out with us at once, and that night we slept at Dodgeville. The next day at about 4 o'clock we got to the Cotterell's home. John was so ill he could scarcely get out of the wagon, with cramp in the stomach and a violent cough. We are still at the Cotterells and I am not well myself. The children are quite well and I hope soon to have better news to send you.   —   M.G.

This is the end of John (and Maria's) letter/journal of their journey from Liverpool to Wisconsin.

AN EXTRACT FROM ONE OF JOHN'S LETTERS TO HIS SISTER ANN IN ENGLAND

April 8, 1849

Thank heaven I have not lost any other of those I held so dear and so near my heart. A letter from you gladdens the cabin all around but that horrid black seal imparts a gloom over all. At the same time you don't know, you can never know my feelings. I would not wish you to feel one-tenth part of my anguish. Oh my Father, my Father, I shall never see any part of him again, never. In the dark and silent woods, in the open fields and travelling on the roads, sometimes miles from human habitation, I have my Father there, consulting with me how to manage the cattle and crops, but I question and Answer myself now for he don't speak to me as he used to when I knew he was alive. I envy you, you have a Mother. So have I but then she is there and I am here and cannot speak even to her.

At present I am lonely, for my dear wife is on a visit to the Cotterells at Mineral Point. The first time she has left me for a day since we both left you. May she enjoy herself poor girl, she has little but hard work at home, but God be praised we have plenty of right good food and no rent to pay, little taxes, plenty of fuel and any quantity of livestock. I had a young heifer bring me a calf three weeks ago, and a gentleman sent me a fine bull calf yesterday, a week old. I thought him dear at a little onion seed .. …. Just love the big boy for me and thank you for giving him my unworthy name. Tis a comfort to know that you are happy and doing well.

(Ann Elgar named her firstborn Henry John. He died at the age of sixteen when his younger brother Edward was seven)

SURNAME INDEX

Surnames of Greenings' Wives in the book (Husband & Chapter in brackets)

SURNAME INDEX B (HUSBANDS)

Surnames of Greening daughters' Husbands in the book (Wife and Chap' in brackets)

BLANCH, John	(Elizabeth – 1)	MOSS, John	(Mary – 16)
BROWNE, Christopher	(Mariana – 2)	NOLAN, Hon. W A	(Laura – 6)
CROFT, Samuel	(Josie – 14)	ORCHARD, -	(Florence –16)
DAVIES, John	(Elizabeth – 15)	OULMAN, L C	(Amelia – 6)
DAW, Henry	(Eliza – 11)	PARNHAM, Oliver	(Caroline – 11)
DOWLE, Thomas	(Hester – 5)	PARR, William	(Lizzie – 6)
EAGLES, John	(Elizabeth – 15)	SCHOLL, Alan	(Phyllis – 14)
ELGAR, William	(Ann – 7)	SIMMONS, Francis	(Elizabeth – 4)
GODFREY, Richard	(Abigail – 1)	WARNER, Frank	(Anna – 6)
HARTNETT, William	(Frances – 11)	WATKINS, Walter	(Mary – 11)
KERR, Charles	(Clara – 6)	WILLIAMS, James	(Priscilla – 5)
LOCKWOOD, Will	(Nana – 14)	WOOD, Frederick	(Ann – 11)
MEREDITH, Thomas	(Amelia – 5)	WOODALL, Michael	(Jane – 7)
MESSENGER, Francis	(Elizabeth – 11)	WOOLES, John	(Mary Ann – 10)